The Responsibility to Protect in Darfur

This book analyzes the Responsibility to Protect (R2P) in the context of the conflict in Darfur, using detailed empirical evidence.

The volume traces Darfur's evolution from forgotten conflict to a major global cause and back to obscurity. The emergence of a far-reaching international response to the war in Darfur began in 2004 and included the most influential international advocacy movement since the anti-apartheid campaign and one of the world's largest peacekeeping missions. The book analyzes how Darfur slid back into international obscurity after 2011, despite ongoing violence against civilians and the continued risk of conflict escalation following Omar al-Bashir's ousting in April 2019. Based on an analysis of more than 100 interviews and over 1,000 media reports, the book examines one of the most pressing questions related to the R2P: why do some situations of mass atrocities cause an international outcry, while others are met with complacency and silence? It argues that the presence or absence of a compelling narrative, which frames a situation in moral terms and unambiguously conveys who is responsible, who suffers, and what should be done, facilitates whether or not sufficient traction will be gained to beget a robust R2P response.

This book will be of much interest to students of the Responsibility to Protect, human rights, peacekeeping, conflict resolution, African politics and International Relations in general.

David Lanz is currently co-head of the swisspeace Mediation Program and lecturer at the University of Basel, Switzerland.

Global Politics and the Responsibility to Protect

Series Editors: Alex J. Bellamy *University of Queensland*, Sara E. Davies, *Griffith University* and Monica Serrano *The City University of New York*.

The aim of this book series is to gather the best new thinking about the Responsibility to Protect into a core set of volumes that provides a definitive account of the principle, its implementation, and its role in crises, that reflects a plurality of views and regional perspectives.

Evaluating the Responsibility to Protect
Mass atrocity prevention as a consolidating norm in international society
Noële Crossley

International Organizations and the Rise of ISIL
Global responses to human security threats
Edited by Daniel Silander, Don Wallace and John Janzekovic

Reviewing the Responsibility to Protect
Origins, Implementation and Controversies
Ramesh Thakur

Ethics, Obligation, and the Responsibility to Protect
Contesting the Global Power Relations of Accountability
Mark Busser

Implementing the Responsibility to Protect
A Future Agenda
Edited by Cecilia Jacob and Martin Mennecke

The Responsibility to Protect in Darfur
From Forgotten Conflict to Global Cause and Back
David Lanz

For more information about this series, please visit: www.routledge.com/Global-Politics-and-the-Responsibility-to-Protect/book-series/GPRP

The Responsibility to Protect in Darfur

From Forgotten Conflict to Global Cause and Back

David Lanz

LONDON AND NEW YORK

First published 2020
by Routledge
4 Park Square, Milton Park, Abingdon, Oxon OX14 4RN
605 Third Avenue, New York, NY 10017

First issued in paperback 2023

Routledge is an imprint of the Taylor & Francis Group, an informa business

British Library Cataloguing-in-Publication Data
A catalogue record for this book is available from the British Library

Library of Congress Cataloging-in-Publication Data
Names: Lanz, David, author.
Title: The responsibility to protect in Darfur : from forgotten conflict to
global cause and back / David Lanz.
Other titles: Global politics and the responsibility to protect.
Description: Abingdon, Oxon ; New York, NY : Routledge, 2020 |
Series: Global politics and the responsibility to protect | Includes
bibliographical references and index. |
Identifiers: LCCN 2019028929 (print) | LCCN 2019028930 (ebook) |
ISBN 9780367183707 (hardback) | ISBN 9780429061172 (ebook)
Subjects: LCSH: Sudan–History–Darfur Conflict, 2003–Law and
legislation. | Responsibility to protect (International
law)–Sudan–Darfur. | United Nations–Peacekeeping
forces–Sudan–Darfur. | Civil war–Protection of
civilians–Sudan–Darfur.
Classification: LCC KZ6795.S73 L36 2019 (print) |
LCC KZ6795.S73 (ebook) | DDC 341.584–dc23
LC record available at https://lccn.loc.gov/2019028929
LC ebook record available at https://lccn.loc.gov/2019028930

ISBN: 978-1-03-257068-6 (pbk)
ISBN: 978-0-367-18370-7 (hbk)
ISBN: 978-0-429-06117-2 (ebk)

DOI: 10.4324/9780429061172

Typeset in Times New Roman
by Wearset Ltd, Boldon, Tyne and Wear

Publisher's Note
The publisher has gone to great lengths to ensure the quality of this reprint but
points out that some imperfections in the original copies may be apparent.

For my parents, Dorothee and Christoph

Contents

Acknowledgments

If raising a child requires a village, then surely the same is true for writing a book. The long journey towards completing this project was enriched and made possible by the help of my teachers, mentors, colleagues, friends, family, and my supportive employer. I am grateful to swisspeace for giving me the time and space to pursue this project and to my team within the Mediation Program for their patience, support, and feedback on drafts. I was fortunate to spend a short sabbatical as a visiting scholar at the Kroc Institute for International Peace Studies at Notre Dame University. Kroc provided the ideal environment for writing this book, despite—or maybe because of—the cold Indiana winter. I am thankful to Asher Kaufman and Erin Corcoran for welcoming me at Kroc, and especially to Laurie Nathan for his guidance—both intellectual and physical, on South Bend's running trails. My apologies for the moment of panic caused to Notre Dame's security staff, when the posters for my talk led them to believe that George Clooney was coming to campus without the proper security measures in place.

The earlier part of the research for this book was conducted for my PhD dissertation. I am indebted to the members of my PhD committee, in particular my main advisor, Laurent Goetschel, for giving me the space to try out different ideas, for providing guidance when it was needed, and for creating an environment at swisspeace that allows projects like mine to thrive. I also immensely benefited from the advice of Séverine Autesserre, who makes her research resonate well beyond academic circles. She is a role model for anyone who takes an immersed, field-based approach to research. And I am grateful to Didier Péclard, for introducing me to the ins and outs of African politics and for his excellent company on frequent train rides between Bern and Geneva. My PhD research was generously supported by the Swiss National Science Foundation in the framework of the Doctoral Programme on Global Change, Innovation and Sustainable Development associated with the NCCR North-South and later the International Graduate School (IGS) North-South.

I am extremely grateful to all the people who agreed to be interviewed, for giving me their time and sharing their insights. While in Sudan, I enjoyed the hospitality of the University of Khartoum Peace Research Institute and its director, Mohamed Majoub Haroun. I am grateful to Musa Abdulgalil, Atta al-Battahani, Omer Awadalla, Guma Kunda Komey, and many others Sudanese who will have to remain unnamed, for helping me better understand the intricacies of their country. My research has been enriched by discussions with international Sudan experts, who we hosted at swisspeace, including Julie Flint, Douglas Johnson, Annette Weber, Peter Schuman, Daniel Large, and Zach Vertin. On the difficulties of peacekeeping in Sudan, I have benefitted from the insights of Roberta Cohen, Ian Johnstone, Richard Gowan, Courtney Fung, Romain Esmenjaud, Garth Schofield, Omar Dia, and Philipp Lustenberger. I am indebted to Joachim Savelsberg, Jens Meierhenrich, and John Hagan for inviting me to debate Darfur in beautiful Bellagio, Italy.

As a PhD student, I benefitted from a stimulating environment at the University of Basel and at swisspeace, with its growing community of peace researchers. Discussions with colleagues, including Matthias Siegfried, Martina Santschi, Sandra Rubli, Stefan Bächtold, Sara Hellmüller, Andreas Graf, Jamie Pring, Julia Palmiano Federer and Dana Landau all improved this book, as did Alexandre Raffoul's superb research assistance. The same is true for comments I received from research mentors and peers, often on the margins of academic conferences. They include Susanna Campbell, Tobias Hagmann, Jonas Hagmann, Enzo Nussio, Maria Gabrielsen Jumbert, Jacob Høigilt, Carmen Wunderlich, Jeff Gifkins, and Allard Duursma.

For permissions to reuse previously published material, I thank Cambridge University Press for material from "Globalised rebellion: the Darfur insurgents and the world" (co-authored with Maria Gabrielsen Jumbert and published in 2013 in the *Journal of Modern African Studies*); Taylor & Francis for the chapter "The Perils of Peacekeeping as a Tool of RtoP: the case of Darfur" (published in 2014 in *Peacekeeping in Africa: The Evolving Security Architecture* edited by Thierry Tardy and Marco Wyss); and Oxford University Press for the chapter "African Union-United Nations Hybrid Operation in Darfur (UNAMID)" (published in 2015 in *The Oxford Handbook of United Nations Peacekeeping Operations* edited by Joachim Koops, Norrie MacQueen, Thierry Tardy, and Paul Williams).

I am grateful to the series editors, Alex Bellamy, Sara Davies, and Monica Serrano, for their interest in this project, and to the efficient team at Routledge, in particular Andrew Humphrys and Bethany Lund-Yates, for their support during the publication process. The manuscript has been much improved thanks to the superb editing of Heather Cantin. It goes without saying that any remaining mistakes and the opinions expressed are my own.

A last note of gratitude goes to the people closest to me: my wife Medina, for tolerating the toll this book took on my time and for debating many of the ideas contained within its pages. I am also grateful to my brothers: Matthias, for enlightening me on matters related to international law, and Simon, for his frequent political science reality checks. Finally, I thank my parents, Dorothee and Christoph, for teaching me, among so many other things, to be curious about the world. It is to them that this book is dedicated.

Geneva, June 2019

Abbreviations

ACLED	Armed Conflict Location & Event Data Project
ADT	Atrocities Documentation Team
AMIS	African Union Mission in Sudan
AU	African Union
AUPSC	African Union Peace and Security Council
BBC	British Broadcasting Corporation
CAR	Central African Republic
CIA	Central Intelligence Agency
CNN	Cable News Network
CPA	Comprehensive Peace Agreement (Sudan)
CRED	Centre for Research on the Epidemiology of Disasters
DDPD	Doha Document for Peace in Darfur
DPA	Darfur Peace Agreement
DRC	Democratic Republic of Congo
EU	European Union
EUFOR	European Union Force (Chad/CAR)
GI-Net	Genocide Intervention Network
ICC	International Criminal Court
ICG	International Crisis Group
ICISS	International Commission of Intervention and State Sovereignty
ICRC	International Committee of the Red Cross
IDP	Internally displaced person
IRIN	Integrated Regional Information Networks
JEM	Justice and Equality Movement
LJM	Liberation and Justice Movement
MSF	Médecins sans frontières
NASA	National Aeronautics and Space Administration
NATO	North Atlantic Treaty Organization
NGO	Non-governmental organization
NCP	National Congress Party (Sudan)
NIF	National Islamic Front (Sudan)
R2P	Responsibility to Protect
RwP	Responsibility while Protecting

RSF	Rapid Support Forces (Sudan)
OLS	Operation Lifeline Sudan
P5	Permanent members of the UN Security Council
PCP	Popular Congress Party (Sudan)
SAF	Sudanese Armed Forces
SDC	Save Darfur Coalition
SLM/A	Sudan Liberation Movement/Army
SMC	Sudanese Media Centre
SPLM	Sudan People's Liberation Movement
SRF	Sudan Revolutionary Front
STAND	Students Take Action Now: Darfur
SUDO	Sudan Social Development Organization
SUNA	Sudan News Agency
TMC	Transitional Military Council (Sudan)
UK	United Kingdom
UN	United Nations
UNDPKO	United Nations Department of Peacekeeping Operations
UNOCHA	United Nations Office for the Coordination of Humanitarian Affairs
UNSG	United Nations Secretary-General
UNSC	United Nations Security Council
UNAMID	United Nations-African Union Hybrid Operation in Darfur
UNMIS	United Nations Mission in Sudan
US	United States
USAID	United States Agency for International Development

Introduction

Darfur and the responsibility to protect

A personal journey

After my graduate studies at the Fletcher School, I spent the summer of 2007 working in the United Nations Mission in Sudan. One morning in August, I sat in the backseat of a white Nissan Pathfinder en route from the capital of South Darfur, Nyala, to the nearby Kalma displaced persons camp. As we drove along the defunct rail tracks of the Nyala-Babanousa line, passing several police checkpoints on the way, a colleague gave a briefing about on the latest developments in Kalma. Our task there was to prepare a meeting that Jan Eliasson, the Special Envoy of the UN Secretary-General, was going to hold with the camp sheikhs in the afternoon. As we were inspecting the meeting place, a boy of around eight approached me and handed me a stack of children's drawings that depicted scenes of violence. In flawless English, the boy explained that the drawings showed the destruction of his village by the *janjawid* and the Sudanese army, which had forced his family to flee four years earlier. He urged me to take the drawings and show them to people in my country.

A few hours later, Eliasson arrived in a convoy with soldiers from the African Union peacekeeping force in Darfur. The peacekeepers were armed, and several of their vehicles were mounted with heavy machine guns. About 100 camp leaders had gathered. The atmosphere was tense as they came forward to make their speeches. They spoke about the suffering of their people but mostly focused on the international community. They wanted an international force to protect them and for justice to be delivered by the International Criminal Court. Some pledged their allegiance to one of the rebel movements, and many expressed reservations about the relaunched Darfur peace talks that Eliasson had come to promote. Several people said that no peace was possible without justice. At one point, the meeting almost broke down because speakers from rival rebel factions began hurling accusations at each other. Even though Eliasson managed to calm the situation, the African Union peacekeepers became nervous. Outside the meeting hall, camp residents had gathered to demonstrate. When the meeting concluded we were told to leave quickly. Driving out of the camp, the convoy took a wrong turn and we got stuck in a dirt alley. The locals gave us bewildering looks, and the peacekeepers became increasingly edgy. In the end, we managed to depart without incident.

Back in Nyala, I reflected on this experience. I remembered the Darfur rallies I had witnessed as a graduate student in Boston. The protesters, many of them college students, were chanting: "Save Darfur! Stop genocide! Never again Holocaust, never again Rwanda! Justice for the victims!" To protect Darfuri civilians from the evil *janjawid*, they were demanding the deployment of a robust UN peacekeeping force to replace the existing African Union mission. I remembered the pictures from a September 2006 Darfur rally in New York's Central Park that had been attended by thousands: Protesters wore light blue berets—the UN's characteristic color—to emphasize their demands. When the UN Security Council debated the matter, the Save Darfur Coalition plastered New York City with advertisements calling for peacekeeping—a level of public attention that is highly unusual for UN debates.

But safe in my guesthouse in Nyala, I felt uneasy. International peacekeepers were supposed to protect civilians in Darfur—an area the size of Spain that was experiencing major armed violence and had seen one third of its population uprooted. Yet the peacekeepers had difficulties in handling the visit of a foreign dignitary. These were African Union peacekeepers, but would the UN be any different? I was also surprised that the sheikhs had concentrated so many of their demands on the international community and that many of them opposed relaunching peace talks. I also thought back to the encounter I had had with the boy. I was moved by the drawings, which provided a glimpse into the unimaginable horrors the children of Kalma had experienced during the war. At the same time, the encounter felt staged. It surely was no coincidence that I—a *khawaja*, as many Sudanese call white Europeans and North Americans—had been approached by the boy.

Fast-forward to 11 years later. It was July 2018 when my work brought me to New York for meetings with UN officials and diplomats from permanent missions. A few days before my visit, the UN Security Council had met to decide the future of the joint UN-AU peacekeeping mission in Darfur. The mission had been deployed in 2008 after protracted negotiations, first among Security Council members and then between the UN and the Sudanese government. But now the Council was deciding to reduce the mission's troop strength by half and to prepare it for withdrawal within two years, provided the security situation in Darfur did not drastically change. The decision did not come as a surprise. The drawdown and eventual exit had been recommended in a joint UN-AU report, confirming an earlier decision by the AU Peace and Security Council.

The problem, though, was that conditions were not really different from when the mission was deployed in 2008. The security situation had somewhat improved after 2017, but a third of Darfur's population lived in displaced persons camps, and an even higher percentage were dependent on humanitarian aid. Violence against civilians was still common. Darfur was no longer in the headlines but, given the attention that Darfur and UN peacekeeping had garnered just a few years before, I thought there would surely be a reaction to the decision to withdraw peacekeepers from Darfur. Sitting in my hotel room in Midtown New York, I scoured the Internet. A few news agencies did report on the decision, but major newspaper ignored it. As far as I could see, there was no significant reaction from civil society. How could this be? Where were the celebrities, activists, and blue-beret clad protesters? Where were the campaigners who had raised their voices for Darfur when it was famous? I wondered what had changed and what these changes would mean for the people of Darfur.

The purpose of this book

This book aims to answer these questions and, by drawing on the Darfur case, to generate broader insights about the international push to prevent mass atrocities through R2P—the Responsibility to Protect. The R2P concept goes back to a 2001 report by an expert commission, which had been initiated by Canada in the aftermath of NATO's controversial intervention in Kosovo. The commission's primary aim was to galvanize international action to prevent mass atrocities, if necessary through military force (Evans 2008). This idea had been well known, but framing it through an R2P lens made it harder for critics to dismiss. R2P defined sovereignty as a responsibility of the state towards its citizens. Under this logic, international intervention to prevent mass atrocities would safeguard sovereignty, rather than subvert it. Four years later, in 2005, UN member states unanimously endorsed R2P at the World Summit. At the same time, they narrowed its scope and raised the bar for international intervention, clarifying that R2P only applies when a government is "manifestly failing" to protect its population in cases of mass violence involving war crimes, crimes against humanity, ethnic cleansing, or genocide (United Nations 2005, paras 138–139). The UN subsequently translated the concept into a broad-based policy agenda to prevent conflict and protect vulnerable populations, appointing a senior adviser to the UN Secretary-General on the topic. R2P proved influential. Within a few years, it became one of the most important reference points in international debates about peace and security. In other words, R2P became an international norm. It is not a legally binding principle, but a social norm that defines expectations about appropriate behavior. This does not mean that international R2P responses are always adequate to prevent mass violence. On the contrary, they are often inadequate, as the situation in Syria and Yemen painfully demonstrates. It also does not mean that R2P is universally embraced or that action taken under the R2P banner is unproblematic or uncontroversial. The 2011 intervention in Libya is a case in point. However, argument and contestation do not invalidate R2P as a norm. Instead they show its relevance, as states promote the interpretation that best suits their interests and justify their actions relative to R2P. In that sense, Glanville (2016) correctly pointed out that R2P "matters." This book aims to explore the ways in which R2P matters.

It does so by looking at Darfur, a region on the western periphery of the Sudanese state that borders Egypt, Libya, Chad, the Central African Republic, and South Sudan. In the early 2000s, an anti-government insurgency led by two rebel groups formed in Darfur. The government attempted to quell the rebellion, sending in militias from Arab tribes in North Darfur that committed mass atrocities of horrific proportions. The victims and the displaced were mostly Darfur's non-Arab tribes. The world ignored the conflict at first. But in 2004, around the tenth anniversary of the Rwanda genocide, attention skyrocketed. Darfur became a prominent global issue, described by observers as a "test case" for R2P.[1] This gave rise to a far-reaching international response that included the largest humanitarian operation in the world, the deployment of several large peacekeeping forces, and various diplomatic initiatives. It also included the first declaration by the US government that an ongoing conflict constitutes genocide, the first referral by the UN Security Council of a situation to the ICC, and harsh sanctions against the Sudanese government. Violence has diminished over the years, but the conflict remains unresolved and Darfuri civilians are still at risk. Despite this, public attention has waned and international engagement has shifted, as evidenced by the partial lifting of US sanctions against the Sudanese government in 2017 and the UN Security Council decision to withdraw peace-keepers by 2020. Darfur is again a forgotten conflict—a status that international reactions to the ousting of Omar al-Bashir and to the turbulent events that fol-lowed only seem to reinforce.

Against this background, this book examines 16 years of armed conflict in Darfur, from the onset of violence in 2003 through to 2019, analyzing a series of international responses that have vacillated between obsession and indifference. This analysis adds to the literature on R2P by shedding light on two under-explored questions. First, based on Paris' (2014) verdict that existing research has not paid enough attention to the practical application of R2P, it conducts an in-depth empirical analysis that examines how R2P developed in a specific context and how actors in countries experiencing mass atrocities engaged with the norm. Picking up a common theme in peacebuilding research, it treats the agency of local actors as a key factor—an issue that has been insufficiently addressed by R2P researchers. Second, the book examines R2P's inconsistent application, using fluctuations in international engagement on Darfur to under-stand why R2P forms the dominant framework in some crises but not in others. This key challenge for R2P implementation has been treated superficially in existing literature.

This leads to the following questions that guided the research: How is R2P translated into practice in countries where mass atrocities take place? And how can we understand inconsistencies in implementing R2P? The book answers these questions empirically, based on 110 interviews conducted with activists, policymakers, opposition figures, and government representatives in Sudan, and by examining over 1,000 newspaper articles published in Sudan and across the world.

The analysis is based on a constructivist approach, treating R2P as a norm that defines how international actors ought to behave and that provides a common vocabulary for those committed to atrocity prevention. Recent con-structivist research has treated R2P as a bundle of norms, prescribing—on the one hand—the way states ought to treat populations under their care and—on the other—how the international community ought to behave when mass atrocities are imminent or occurring. In a broader sense, the bundle of R2P norms is understood as a modification of sovereignty, with the responsibility for mass atrocity protection introduced as one of its core features.

Diverting from this, this book argues that sovereignty norms are more constant than is often believed and that the R2P doctrine, as articulated by states at the 2005 World Summit, confirms rather than challenges deeply entrenched beliefs about sovereignty. Instead, the normative essence of R2P is about delegitimizing mass atrocities and indifference to them based on a vision of shared humanity. Therefore, the core R2P norm centers on the idea of saving strangers and comprises three interrelated beliefs: first, that mass atrocities are morally wrong, regardless of where or by whom they are committed; second, that action should be taken to protect victims of mass atrocities, regardless of their nationality, religion, ethnicity, or social group; and third, that there is no acceptable pretext to eschew such action, based on considerations of national interests, stability, or sovereignty.

To conceptualize how R2P as a norm affects change in the world, the book draws on the "spiral model" developed by Risse and Sikkink (1999) to distinguish the three levels on which R2P is translated into practice: R2P inspires activists to galvanize international action to protect civilians from atrocity crimes; it prompts governments and international organizations to take action in response to mass atrocities; and it provokes a reaction from the government and opposition forces in countries where mass atrocities occur. However, what classic norm-diffusion theories, such as the spiral model, insufficiently capture is how norms are redefined and renegotiated during their implementation. This also applies to R2P (Acharya 2013). The book, therefore, draws on concepts of localization and translation, acknowledging that as norms are transferred from one context to another, they are rearticulated and reinterpreted in their new locales.

What Darfur means for R2P, and vice versa

What key findings about R2P does the Darfur case bring to the fore? One relates to the mobilizing potential of R2P. Darfur showed that R2P is a powerful tool to attract attention about far-away situations of mass atrocities. Given associations with past cases of genocide, especially the Holocaust and Rwanda, R2P has a strong framing effect, with the potential to catapult previously unknown situations of violence into the international spotlight. Indeed, Darfur was transformed from a forgotten conflict into a global cause after a senior UN official compared it to the Rwanda genocide. Moreover, as the Save Darfur advocacy movement exemplified, R2P provides a moral code that motivates activists to take up a cause and offers a common language around which popular action can be mobilized. In this regard, R2P can act as the common denominator for a heterogeneous set of organizations—from human rights organizations to religious groups—and thus forms the glue that holds such advocacy coalitions together.

Darfur also demonstrates that R2P is not automatically applied when mass violence occurs. It needs to be activated through a narrative that frames a situation as relevant in terms of the norm. A narrative that clearly designates the victims and the perpetrators of mass attrocities creates a compelling need for intervention in accordance with R2P. This was the case in the Darfur conflict, which shot to fame after being framed as a genocidal campaign against African civilians perpetrated by an Arab-Islamist government and its local Arab henchmen. R2P began to lose its pertinence when the narrative shifted, as Darfur was increasingly viewed as a complex civil war. This shift demonstrates that the presence or absence of a compelling narrative, in which R2P is embedded, is decisive in whether R2P dominates the international response to a given conflict.

The way narratives are used by R2P advocates also raises a dilemma, which the Darfur case brought to the fore. A compelling communication strategy that translates the R2P agenda into practice is needed to raise public attention and galvanize action in the face of mass atrocities. The narratives that gain the most traction are those that clearly and unambiguously explain why mass atrocities are occurring, who is responsible, who is suffering, and what action should be taken. However, such narratives also risk distorting the way a conflict is viewed, for example, by framing it in racial terms. In Darfur, for example, the Arab vs. African frame has increased societal polarization and rendered difficult the emergence of an all-Darfur opposition alliance. Advocacy to save strangers may also resort to sensationalism, but this ultimately desensitizes the public and fosters compassion fatigue. Therefore, communicating effectively, while avoiding distortion and sensationalism, is a key challenge for R2P advocates.

The book further argues that political agency in countries experiencing mass atrocities is critical to understanding R2P implementation. Local actors are not passive recipients of norms but are active agents who shape the norm-diffusion process. In the case of Darfur, the Sudanese government played this role, as the main perpetrator of violence and the target of the norms campaign. It reacted to R2P with a mixture of tactical concessions and defiance. It notably claimed that R2P was a smokescreen for Western imperialism. This discourse had some resonance, especially in relation to the ICC. Later, Khartoum applied its agency to deactivate R2P by countering the dominant narrative and providing incentives that helped to shift priorities among the countries that cared most about Darfur.

R2P had also has a strong influence on opposition forces. On the one hand, R2P is a strategic tool, especially for militarized opposition forces to gain legitimacy and exert pressure on the government. On the other hand, R2P shapes their worldview and expectations. Not wanting to jeopardize their reputation, rebel groups are more likely to respect international standards, including the laws of war. At the same time, a strong R2P discourse seems to foster maximalist posturing and intransigence in peace talks, as rebel leaders count on international intervention. Leaders are also lured away from the local level, as the international community begins to provide them with legitimacy and material support. This fragments them, and undermines their ability to garner sufficient military power to force meaningful concessions from the government.

Against this, the book argues that R2P had a significant impact in Darfur. Framing Darfur as a situation in which the world had a responsibility to protect the victims of mass atrocities has helped bring a previously forgotten conflict into the spotlight of international politics. It is plausible that the world's attention had a certain deterrence effect on the Sudanese government, as it reduced its use of mass violence, at least for some years. The world's attention also pressured the Sudanese government to allow humanitarian organizations and peacekeepers into Darfur. The latter did help to improve safety in some areas, especially displaced camps, but these gains were not sustainable. When international attention diminished, the government was again free to use indiscriminate violence against the rebels' civilian support base, and allied itself with local militias for that purpose. What is more, the R2P-inspired international response had some unintended negative consequences. It encouraged fragmentation among rebel groups and absorbed the political capital that could have been used to achieve a workable political settlement. Overall, the international push to save strangers failed to resolve the underlying issues that led to mass violence 16 years ago.

How this book is structured

Chapter 1 sets out the overall framework, first by anchoring it in the literature on humanitarian intervention and R2P. It outlines different theoretical perspectives and sheds light on the main debates on R2P. Based on this, the chapter identifies two gaps in the literature: the lack of understanding of how R2P unfolds in countries experiencing mass atrocities, and the puzzling variation between situations in which R2P is the primary framework that shapes the international response to atrocities and situations where R2P is largely ignored. The second section conceptualizes the core R2P norm and differentiates it from other conceptualizations of R2P, in particular sovereignty as responsibility. The third section lays out the research approach and methodology, explains the reasons for selecting Darfur as a case, and proposes an analytical framework for understanding how the core R2P norm is translated into practice.

Chapter 2 explains the activation of the core R2P norm in the context of Darfur. The first section provides background about why violent conflict broke out and shows how Darfur was transformed from a forgotten conflict to a global cause. This process was enabled by a comparison of Darfur with the 1994 genocide in Rwanda. The second section draws on an analysis of several hundred media reports to show how R2P became the main prism through which the world viewed the Darfur conflict, providing the discursive raw material for a narrative that rendered Darfur meaningful to the broader public. The third section makes sense of the large-scale advocacy movement to "save Darfur," which in North America, the UK, and France became the largest social movement in foreign affairs since the anti-apartheid campaign. Based on interviews with key figures in the movement, this section shows that R2P was the rallying cry that motivated people to adopt Darfur as a cause and provided the common denominator in a highly heterogeneous movement.

Chapter 3 looks at the implementation of R2P in the context of Darfur. The first section examines the strategies the Darfur activists employed to promote R2P implementation, moving from mass mobilization to advocating for specific policies. The second section sheds light on the discursive responses of policymakers to the construction of Darfur as a test case for R2P. It argues that the alignment of official discourses with the Darfur narrative paved the way for interventions later, including one of the world's largest peacekeeping missions—the United Nations-African Union Hybrid Operation in Darfur (UNAMID). As the third section shows, UNAMID emerged as the primary tool to implement R2P in Darfur. The fourth section examines how international criminal justice, in particular the ICC, became an additional tool to implement R2P in Darfur. It demonstrates how the discursive construction of Darfur as a genocide with clear victims and perpetrators paved the way for the involvement of the ICC and guided the actions of the prosecutor, in particular his decision to press charges against Sudanese president Omar al-Bashir.

Chapter 4 demonstrates how opposition forces engaged with the international push to save strangers in Darfur and what consequences their engagement had. The first section shows how the opposition participated in internationalizing the Darfur conflict, playing an active part in the formulation of the Darfur narrative with R2P at its core. The second section focuses on Darfur's military opposition. Interviews with representatives of rebel groups show how framing Darfur as a test case for saving strangers influenced their mindset and expectations: It fostered intransigent behavior in peace talks and increased the fragmentation of rebel groups, but it also helped to deter the use of mass violence. The third section considers Darfur's political opposition. It shows how Darfuri dissidents appropriated the saving strangers discourse to gain leverage in their struggle against the government and how, in turn, this discourse shaped their expectations. The third section also discusses the unintended consequences of appropriating the R2P narrative, which led to the politicization of human rights and justice advocacy and the alienation of Darfuri Arabs.

Chapter 5 deals with the main target of the Darfur campaigns—the Sudanese government. The first section outlines the functioning of the Sudanese state and considers the mindset and evolution of the National Congress Party regime that was headed by Omar al-Bashir from 1989 until his ousting in 2019. The second section focuses on the strategies employed by Khartoum in defiance of the R2P-inspired international response to the Darfur conflict between 2004 and 2010. Based on an analysis of several hundred articles published in Sudanese newspapers as well as interviews with key government representatives, it sheds light on Khartoum's strategy to counter the dominant narrative, thereby delegitimizing international intervention in Darfur and casting itself as the victim of a neo-colonial conspiracy. Third, the chapter looks at the behavioral repercussions of

R2P activation in Darfur. It shows how the Sudanese government reacted by making a number of tactical concessions to defuse the pressure created by Darfur's status as a global cause. Some of these measures had a positive impact, for example, in opening Darfur to humanitarian organizations. However, despite significant pressure, the NCP regime failed to change how it governed Darfur or dealt with dissent in Sudan's peripheries.

Chapter 6 traces Darfur's trajectory from a global cause back to a forgotten conflict. The first section gives an overview of developments in Darfur since 2011. It also analyzes media reports about Darfur, showing that public attention drastically decreased as the narrative unraveled. The saving strangers frame largely disappeared, resulting in the deactivation of R2P as the lens through which the Darfur conflict was understood and addressed. The second section examines the reasons why R2P was deactivated. It draws on political developments related to the independence of South Sudan, the conflict in Libya and, later, the 2014 refugee crisis in Europe—all of which helped to transform Khartoum from a perpetrator into a partner. The Sudanese government actively promoted the idea of itself as an ally and, to that end, restricted access to war-affected areas in Darfur to hinder reporting about human rights violations. Coupled with the demise of the advocacy movement, the Darfur campaigns could not be sustained. The third section looks at the consequences of Darfur's de-coupling from R2P: It paved the way for decisions to hibernate ICC investigations, partially lift US sanctions, and draw down the UN-AU peacekeeping force in Darfur.

The book concludes by synthesizing the overall findings, in particular, those revealed by the Darfur case about R2P implementation. By referencing current cases, such as Libya, Syria, and Yemen, it aims to contribute to a better understanding of why R2P is the dominant framework in some situations but largely absent in others. In this context, this chapter emphasizes the importance of framing as well as the agency of local actors in influencing such framing. It then considers a number of dilemmas related to the implementation of R2P, before evaluating its role over 16 years of armed violence in Darfur. While the push to save strangers paved the way for a far-reaching international response, it failed to protect civilians in Darfur, because it came too late, offered the wrong remedies, and was not sustained.

Note

1 For example, Gareth Evans asserted that Darfur was a test case for R2P: "Darfur and the Responsibility to Protect," *The Diplomat*, 1 August 2004.

References

Acharya, Amitav. 2013. "The R2P and Norm Diffusion: Towards A Framework of Norm Circulation." *Global Responsibility to Protect* 5: 466–479.

Evans, Gareth. 2008. *The Responsibility to Protect: Ending Mass Atrocity Crimes Once and for All*. Washington, DC: Brookings Institution Press.

Glanville, Luke. 2016. "Does R2P Matter? Interpreting the Impact of a Norm." *Cooperation and Conflict* 51: 184–199.

Paris, Roland. 2014. "The 'Responsibility to Protect' and the Structural Problems of Preventive Humanitarian Intervention." *International Peacekeeping* 21: 569–603.

Risse, Thomas, and Kathryn Sikkink. 1999. "The Socialization of International Human Rights Norms into Domestic Practices: Introduction." In *The Power of Human Rights: International Norms and Domestic Change*, eds. Thomas Risse, Stephen C. Ropp and Kathryn Sikkink. Cambridge: Cambridge University Press. 1–38.

United Nations. 2005. *World Summit Outcome*. A/RES/60/1. 16 September.

1 Understanding R2P

Saving strangers in a messy world

R2P: An idea whose time has come ... and gone?[1]

The origins and development of R2P

The end of the Cold War freed the United Nations (UN) of its paralysis and led to an intensification of collective security efforts, including military interventions and peace operations with enforcement elements (Seybolt 2007). This shift reinvigorated the long-standing discussion about humanitarian intervention, whose roots go back to the just war doctrine. Proponents of the doctrine argue that, under certain circumstances, the use of force can serve a good moral purpose (Walzer 1977). Thus, *jus ad bellum* (the right to wage war), materializes under certain conditions, for example, when innocent life is in imminent danger, when force is used to protect populations in danger, and when interveners have exhausted all peaceful means. The intervention also needs a reasonable prospect of success, and its anticipated benefits should be proportional to the expected harms of war (Boyle 2006).

Three cases came to dominate the debate about humanitarian intervention. The first was the genocide in Rwanda in 1994, during which around 800,000 people—primarily Tutsis—were killed over a few months. International actors failed to react, and when the genocide began, the UN Security Council (UNSC) even withdrew the peacekeepers it had deployed the previous year to oversee a ceasefire (Barnett 2002). The second case was Srebrenica, where Serbian forces killed more than 8,000 Bosnians despite the presence of UN peacekeepers (United Nations 1999). With Rwanda and Srebrenica, inaction in the face of mass atrocities came to be identified with moral failure, which added weight to the idea of humanitarian intervention as just and necessary.[2]

The third case was NATO's controversial military intervention in Kosovo, which triggered debates among policymakers and scholars about the nature and merits of humanitarian intervention (Schnabel and Thakur 2000). Liberal internationalists (Ignatieff 2000; Tesòn 2003; Weiss 2016) supported humanitarian intervention, seeing in it a potential to realize the intrinsic values of human rights and to achieve progress towards a Kantian cosmopolitan society. Solidarists equally promoted it, seeing in it a pathway to fulfill the idea of justice in international society (Wheeler 2000). Conversely, some scholars argued that

Interventions not authorized by the UN Security Council, such as the Kosovo intervention, were illegal and undermined international legal order (Chesterman 2001). Others raised objections, claiming that humanitarian arguments for war conceal the hegemonic interests of big powers (Chomsky 1999). English School pluralists opposed humanitarian intervention because it subverts sovereignty, jeopardizing the legitimacy of international society (Ayoob 2002) and even the stability of world order, which could lead to an increase in war (Jackson 2000).

In any case, the Kosovo intervention brought a dilemma to the fore. NATO responded to a situation of grave danger for civilian populations, but, due to the opposition of Russia and China, it was unable to get UN Security Council authorization for its action (Johnstone 2003). The finding of a commission of inquiry got to the heart of the problem. It qualified NATO's intervention as "illegal but legitimate" (Independent International Commission on Kosovo 2000, 4). The discrepancy between a morally justified but legally questionable course of action created a significant impasse for the UN.[3] In response, the Canadian government established the International Commission on Intervention and State Sovereignty (ICISS) and tasked it to clarify the scope of humanitarian intervention (Johnstone 2011, 71). Composed of a diverse mix of scholars and politicians,[4] the ICISS published its final report in December 2001. It proposed a new doctrine to resolve the dilemma: the Responsibility to Protect. R2P's core premise is "that sovereign states have a responsibility to protect their own citizens from avoidable catastrophe ... but when they are unwilling or unable to do so, that responsibility must be borne by the broader community of states" (ICISS 2001, viii).

R2P remained faithful to the core idea of humanitarian intervention to determine permissibility for the use of force based on the well-known criteria of the just war doctrine (ICISS 2001, xii–xiii). However, it re-conceptualized the doctrine in two ways. First, R2P redefined the relationship between humanitarian intervention and sovereignty in terms of complementarity rather than antagonism. Thus, the ICISS referred to Deng et al.'s (1996) idea of "sovereignty as responsibility," according to which states have a duty to shield their citizens from massive abuses (Cohen 2012). Only when states are unable or unwilling to fulfill this obligation does the onus of protection fall on international actors—a transfer of responsibility that, according to the ICISS, safeguards a country's sovereignty, rather than undermining it.[5] The second innovation of R2P is that it embedded atrocity prevention in a broader framework to protect vulnerable populations. Thus, R2P proposed a broad range of diplomatic, political, economic, and security measures to prevent conflict, to react when it breaks out, and to rebuild communities in its aftermath (Evans 2008b). In this context, the use of military force is an option of last resort (Arbour 2008).

These innovations intended to differentiate R2P from the controversial idea of humanitarian intervention. The success of this strategy was demonstrated by states' unanimous endorsement of R2P at the 2005 World Summit. Yet, to reach this level of consensus, a refinement and clarification of R2P was necessary, attenuating some of the more controversial aspects of the ICISS's proposition (Bellamy 2006; Strauss 2009). Whereas the ICISS emphasized protection in a broad range of situations ranging from civil war, insurgency, and state collapse, the scope of R2P in the World Summit Outcome Document was reduced to four specific atrocity crimes: genocide, crimes against humanity, war crimes, and ethnic cleansing (Scheffer 2008). The Outcome Document also raised the bar for international intervention, clarifying that protection is the primary responsibility of states and that R2P only applies when a government is "manifestly failing" to protect its population (United Nations 2005, para 139). Finally, the Outcome Document made it clear that coercive measures under R2P required UN Security Council approval (Welsh 2013, 376). This differed from the ICISS's proposition. It had suggested that if the Council would reject a proposal meeting the criteria for an R2P intervention, military action could be taken "by regional or sub-regional organizations under Chapter VIII of the Charter, subject to their seeking sub-sequent authorization from the Security Council" (ICISS 2001, xiii).

In 2008, UN Secretary-General (UNSG) Ban Ki-moon appointed Columbia University professor Edward Luck as his special adviser on R2P and, the following year, presented a report to the UN General Assembly. Drafted by Luck, the report confirmed the relatively narrow scope of R2P, based on the four crimes set out in the Outcome Document, and outlined a broad range of measures to implement R2P, with an emphasis on prevention and international assistance (United Nations 2009). Luck's "narrow, but deep" approach (Bellamy 2010, 146) proposed to operationalize R2P across three pillars. The first outlined the state's protection responsibilities for populations in its care. The second focused on international assistance to strengthen a state's capacity to offer protection. The third pillar focused on "timely and decisive response" if states failed to protect populations against atrocity crimes. The last pillar proposed mostly non-military measures, but also noted that "no strategy for fulfilling the responsibility to protect would be complete without the possibility of collective enforcement measures, including through sanctions and coercive military action in extreme cases" (United Nations 2009, para 56).

One such case emerged in Libya in early 2011 after protests broke out against the government of Muammar Gaddafi. When the government threatened to use mass violence against protesters in the city of Benghazi, the UN Security Council authorized the use of force to protect civilians. Therefore, "the UN mandated, for the first time in its history, military intervention in a sovereign state against the express will of that state's government" (Morris 2013, 1271). A coalition led by France, the UK, and the US started an airborne military operation, quickly rolling back Gaddafi's forces and preventing them from taking over Benghazi. In the words of ICISS co-chair Gareth Evans, the Libya intervention "seemed at the outset a textbook example of R2P working as it was supposed to."[6] However, the military campaign did not stop there, but continued in support of the Benghazi-based rebels until they had toppled the Gadhafi government. This drew strong criticism from emerging powers, in particular Russia and China, and accusations that the coalition had exceeded its mandate (Thakur 2013).

These countries "were appalled by what they saw as the abuse of the humanitarian argument of protecting civilians for the political goal of regime change" (Brockmeier et al. 2016, 121).

As a result, Russia and China became highly reluctant about authorizing coercive action for humanitarian protection purposes—a factor that contributed to the UN Security Council's timid response to the war in Syria (Morris 2013). The Libya controversy also shaped the debate about R2P. In November 2011, Brazil proposed a concept called Responsibility while Protecting (RwP) to address what many countries perceived as a flawed implementation of R2P in Libya (Kenkel 2012). The Brazilian proposal called for a stronger emphasis on preventive diplomacy and other non-coercive measures, clearer criteria for the use of force under R2P, and an increase in the accountability of intervening countries vis-à-vis the Security Council (United Nations 2011). According to Tourinho et al. (2016, 138), RwP helped de-polarize the debate about R2P in the aftermath of Libya, giving skeptics an outlet to voice concerns without attacking the R2P principle itself.

While Libya-type interventions have not occurred since, efforts to institutionalize R2P have advanced, in particular within the UN system. The function of the UNSG's special adviser has been formalized, and the UN General Assembly discusses the topic annually. By 2018, the Security Council had reaffirmed the R2P principle in its entirety four times and referred to it over 60 times in resolutions. More than 60 governments established national R2P focal points and several non-governmental organizations (NGOs) dedicated to R2P advocacy emerged (Bellamy and Luck 2018). Therefore, according to scholar and former UNSG special adviser on R2P Jennifer Welsh (2013, 378), "R2P became part of the world's diplomatic language." Crossley (2018, 415–16) likewise found "it is no longer possible to discuss atrocity prevention and intervention on humanitarian grounds without reference to the principle or without terminology associated with R2P jargon."

Four debates about R2P …

Despite its proliferation, different aspects of the R2P doctrine and its implementation in specific cases have remained subject to debate (Welsh 2013). At the same time, R2P has become the subject of a growing body of literature, including countless publications, research projects, a dedicated journal, a book series, and two handbooks.[7] Scholars covered new ground, looking at the various political, legal, and ethical aspects of R2P, and providing new empirical analyses. They also participated in the debate, sometimes re-producing and sometimes shaping political discussions about R2P (Crossley 2018). The following section highlights four debates in particular.

The first debate concerns the criticism that R2P constitutes a Trojan horse (Bellamy 2005) aimed at justifying neo-colonial interventions by the world's most powerful states. Thus, Mamdani (2009, 300) dismissed R2P as "a slogan that masks a big power agenda to recolonize Africa." One reason for this is that

R2P allows "for the legal normalization of certain types of violence (such as Western counterinsurgency efforts), while arbitrarily criminalizing the violence of other states as 'genocide'" (Mamdani 2010, 53). In the words of Chandler (2004, 60),

> Opponents of intervention, mainly non-Western states, have been skeptical of the grounds for privileging a moral justification for interventionist practices and have expressed concern that this shift could undermine their rights of sovereignty and possibly usher in a more coercive, Western-dominated, international order.

This argument received a boost when the US used humanitarian arguments to justify the 2003 war in Iraq, fostering the perception that R2P works as a "smokescreen for bullies" on the world stage (Weiss 2004, 142).

Countering the Trojan horse critique, Bellamy (2014, Chapter 6) argued that R2P has inbuilt checks and balances in the form of specific criteria and a high threshold for intervention. These criteria help to safeguard against big power interventionism, rather than fostering it (Evans 2008b). Looking at the empirical record since the 1990s, other scholars likewise argued that there were no indications that big powers had an appetite for imperialism and use R2P for this purpose (Goodman 2006; Peters 2009, 532).

A second related debate revolves around a critique that R2P subverts international law. For pluralist scholars, the idea of sovereign equality—the recognition that all states are equal subjects in international law—and the associated principles of non-intervention and domestic jurisdiction—the idea that interference in the internal affairs of a state is impermissible—constitute a wall of protection for small states against hegemonic interventions (Kirsch 2005). According to Cohen (2004, 3), by replacing existing international law grounded in sovereign equality with the cosmopolitan order that R2P articulates, "we risk becoming apologists for imperial projects." As Welsh (2010, 427–428) explained, the fear is to "move from a horizontal international system of sovereign states that demonstrate mutual respect to a hierarchical world system where their behavior is subject to oversight and punishment by an unspecified agent of the so-called international community." A related fear is that R2P undermines another core principle of international law, one that guarantees a peaceful world order: the non-use of force. According to O'Connell (2010, 48), by suggesting force can be used to protect human rights, "advocacy for R2P supports the new acceptability of war, prodding those who would otherwise argue for peace and respect for law to do the opposite."

This claim is again refuted by Bellamy (2014, 119–120): "Nearly a decade after R2P was agreed by UN Member States, has any Western state ever used R2P to justify armed intervention without a Security Council mandate in Africa or elsewhere? No." In this perspective, R2P reaffirms, rather than undermines international law in line with the Outcome Document, which makes clear that UN Security Council authorization is required for military intervention under

R2P. Moreover, according to the legal scholar Anne Peters (2009), the Security Council has a duty to shield humans from mass violence, which R2P helps to uphold. Another riposte to the pluralist critique of R2P emphasized that the sovereignty-conscious members of the African Union (AU) were the first to stipulate, in the Constitutive Act of the AU, a right to intervene in cases of genocide, crimes against humanity, and war crimes (Aning and Okyere 2016). This showed that R2P is not a license for interventionism, but rather a stabilizing factor that helps to safeguard international law.

A third debate concerns the effects in countries where R2P interventions take place. A number of scholars criticized R2P for fostering paternalistic attitudes. According to Cunliffe (2011), R2P has regressive effects on domestic politics in third world countries. It seeks to make states responsible *for* their people vis-à-vis the international community, as opposed to promoting states' responsibilities *to* their citizens as part of a local democratic order. This argument was echoed by Branch (2011), who claimed that the application of R2P in Africa undermines local democracy by replacing people's agency with responsibilities of the state or the international community. Mégret (2009) similarly cautioned that R2P, which is commonly described as a responsibility of the international community, may raise false expectations among populations in conflict areas and, as such, crowds out resistance and self-protection efforts at the local level.

ICISS member Ramesh Thakur (2016, 418) made a contrary claim that the R2P doctrine sought to make a deliberate shift from humanitarian intervention, which "privileges the perspectives and rights of the intervening states" to a new approach, which "addresses the issue from the perspectives of the victims." Therefore, R2P empowers, rather than subdues populations in countries experiencing mass atrocities.

A fourth debate pertains to the use of force in the R2P doctrine, which gave rise to variegated arguments. Some scholars argued that the Outcome Document sets the threshold for military intervention too high, as it requires UNSC authorization (Pattison 2010). This leaves the Kosovo dilemma unresolved and potentially leads to inaction in the face of mass atrocities. A contrary assessment comes from Pape (2012, 51), who argued that "R2P obligates the international community to intervene in almost any instance of human suffering, including natural disasters, disease, failed states, and collateral violence to civilians during civil wars." However, as several scholars (Bellamy 2014; Glanville 2016) pointed out, Pape's assessment refers to the ICISS report and ignores the more narrow R2P scope put forth in the Outcome Document.

In addition, since the inception of the doctrine, there have been few cases in which states used military force under the banner of R2P. One such case was, of course, Libya, which is at the center of Paris' (2014) analysis of the structural problems of non-consensual military interventions in the framework of R2P. According to Paris, interventions like NATO's in Libya conflate altruism and self-interest in a way that can foster cynicism. Such interventions often exceed their mandate, turning into regime-change missions out of the fear that withdrawal would lead to revenge against the very populations that R2P should safeguard. Related is the moral hazard problem identified by Kuperman (2009): R2P encourages rebel groups to escalate their struggle, hoping to provoke retaliation from the government. Retaliation, in turn triggers international intervention. Hence, a dilemma arises: R2P is criticized when there is no military intervention in the face of mass atrocities, as was the case in Syria where R2P appeared irrelevant. R2P is likewise criticized when an intervention does take place, as in Libya, because it has unintended consequences that contradict the values of the doctrine (Paris 2014, 570).

... *and two unanswered questions*

Despite the growing body of literature, R2P's practical application remains underexplored (Paris 2014, 572). Two aspects deserve particular attention. The first is R2P's implementation in specific cases. While the literature includes various case studies, these tend to focus on dynamics at the international level, including UN Security Council debates and international mechanisms devised to protect civilians.[8] Analyses of local political dynamics in countries experiencing mass atrocities are rare,[9] and R2P scholars tend to treat local agency superficially. Proponents of R2P (e.g., Evans 2008b) largely omit local agency, while critics make the assumption that R2P undermines local politics (e.g., Branch 2011; Cunliffe 2011). A more differentiated analysis is lacking, leaving the question unanswered of how local structures influence R2P implementation.

Answering this question is, however, critical. Two related bodies of literature confirm this need. One is research on peacebuilding, which has undergone a "local turn" in recent years (Mac Ginty and Richmond 2013), with analysis of how local actors resist, co-opt, or cooperate with international efforts and what this means for the prospect of peace (Autesserre 2010; Richmond 2010; Campbell 2018; Hellmüller 2018). Local dynamics have been a key theme in constructivist research more broadly. Different studies have showed how domestic political structures operate as filters for norm diffusion (Cortell and Davis 1996) and how international norms are re-negotiated and re-shaped as local actors incorporate them into their specific contexts (Acharya 2004). There is thus a need for the R2P literature to catch up and take local agency seriously. Local factors are indeed critical to understand the implementation of R2P: In the absence of a non-consensual military intervention, the key to improving the protection of civilians is to influence the behavior of domestic actors, in particular the government and insurgent groups, but also the population as a whole.

A second underexplored aspect pertains to the variation in the implementation of R2P in different situations of mass atrocities. This is a key challenge in the practical application of R2P, and it is decisive for R2P as a global political project. As the UNSG (United Nations 2009, para 62) highlighted, "the credibility, authority and hence effectiveness of the United Nations in advancing the principles of the Responsibility to Protect depend, in large part, on the consistency with which they are applied." However, despite states' commitment, the practice of R2P has remained inconsistent. Some situations of mass atrocities triggered a far-reaching international response, whereas international action in others was muted or insufficient. Scholars have often invoked the contrast between the international responses to the conflicts in Libya and Syria to make this point (Morris 2013).

Scholars disagree about why R2P is applied inconsistently and what this means for the doctrine. For Hehir (2013), inconsistency is a permanent condition of R2P, as states' decisions are based on their pragmatic interests rather than on principles. Likewise, Paris (2014) sees inconsistency as a structural problem that weakens the R2P doctrine. For Glanville (2016), inconsistency is not necessarily negative, but reflects the practical and ethical dilemmas that make effective response impossible in certain cases, given states' capabilities and interests. The common denominator of these studies is their reference to the diffuse notion of states' "interests," which align with interventions to prevent mass atrocities in some cases but not in others. This explanation is superficial, however, especially taking into account the well-established constructivist claim that interests are not exogenous, but are socially constructed through a process of intersubjective meaning-making (Wendt 1992; Hopf 2002). Finnemore (2003) thus showed that the increase in humanitarian interventions since the 1990s reflects the changing belief of states about the use of force, rather than exogenously defined interests.

Against this background, this study adopts a constructivist approach and explores how R2P is translated into practice in specific cases. In so doing, it investigates how interest in atrocity prevention is constructed at the international level and how situations differ in this respect, thus shedding light on the inconsistencies in international reactions. By investigating R2P's implementation, the study pays particular attention to local political dynamics in countries experiencing mass atrocities, showing how domestic actors have engaged with R2P and what this means for the protection of civilians on the ground.

R2P: What is in a norm?

What is your status?

R2P defines expectations for appropriate behavior and prescribes certain behaviors: States have a duty to protect populations from atrocity crimes and, failing this, the international community should take timely and decisive action. Underpinning this is an ambitious aim to stigmatize mass atrocities so that states, as a matter of values and identity, refrain from committing them and automatically act to prevent them. In short, R2P aspires to both behavior regulation and identity constitution. According to Katzenstein (1996), this is what makes a "norm," which is defined in this context as "collective expectations about proper behavior for a given identity" (Jepperson et al. 1996, 54). R2P is therefore understood as a norm for the purpose of this study.

Treating R2P as a norm has been popular in the literature in recent years. Many R2P scholars have relied on Finnemore and Sikkink's (1998, 1999) norm-diffusion model. The model distinguishes three consecutive phases in the life cycle of a norm. First, the norm emerges because of the determined action of norm entrepreneurs, challenging existing normative constellations. After a critical mass of states has endorsed the norm, it reaches a tipping point and subsequently becomes "institutionalized in specific sets of international rules and organizations" (Finnemore and Sikkink 1998, 892). Second, in the cascade phase, states adopt norms through a socialization process underpinned by peer pressure. The final phase constitutes internalization, when states' conformity to the norm becomes automatic (Finnemore and Sikkink 1998, 895). R2P advocates among scholars have typically traced the progressive evolution of R2P from "concept to norm" along the life cycle model (Badescu and Weiss 2010; Badescu 2011). Thus, the ICISS report marks the stage of norm emergence, while the World Summit's endorsement constitutes the tipping point. The creation of UN mechanisms, the advent of dedicated NGOs, and the increasing references in political bodies are signs that R2P is cascading and moving towards full acceptance. According to Bellamy (2014, 161), R2P has become "a norm utilised almost habitually." Likewise in 2011, Gareth Evans identified an "overwhelming consensus" and therefore the "end of the argument" about R2P.[10]

Hehir (2019, 4 and 1) countered this claim by diagnosing "a pronounced disjuncture" between states' frequent invocation of R2P and its decreasing impact in a world where "state sponsored oppression, and indeed atrocity crimes, are on the rise." For him, therefore, R2P is a "hollow norm" (Hehir 2019, 7). A different critique comes from norms scholars. When talking about Finnemore and Sikkink's life cycle model, Welsh (2010, 426) stated, "Part of the problem is the tendency to view the development of norms as a linear process, with institutionalization as a key step on the road to their entrenchment." Instead, norms develop in a dynamic way, with contestation and argument as integral parts of the process. The R2P norm "is particularly susceptible to contestation, given its inherently indeterminate nature, and the erroneous tendency to measure its impact in terms of whether or not military intervention occurs in particular cases" (Welsh 2013, 365). This resonates with theories of norm localization. For Acharya (2013, 469), norm diffusion is a two-way process, whereby global norms "are contested and localized to fit the cognitive priors of local actors," which in turn provide feedback "to modify and possibly defend and strengthen the global norm in question." He mentioned Brazil's RwP concept as an example of how such norm circulation functions. Elaborating on local feedback effects, Negrón-Gonzales and Contarino (2014) examined different national responses, showing that prior normative commitment to human rights has resulted in a positive attitude towards R2P. Conversely, states emphasizing anti-imperialism and non-interference have tended to constrain R2P. States with conflicting normative commitments, such as Brazil, have taken intermediate positions and "engaged in soft feedback as they have sought to modify the global norm" (Negrón-Gonzales and Contarino 2014, 270).

This helps to make sense of a seemingly paradoxical development: There is momentum around R2P, but important elements of the doctrine continue to meet resistance, and its application in specific cases remains controversial. This finding underscores the dynamic nature of norm diffusion and the complex normative trajectory of R2P. It also shows the need for studies that focus on the empirically assessable effects of the R2P norm. The present analysis subscribes to this approach.

A bundle of norms about sovereignty?

In order to study R2P, the content of the norm must be clarified: What kind of norm is R2P, what does it prescribe, and what are the core beliefs underpinning R2P? Bellamy and Luck (2018, 37) pointed out that R2P is not a singular norm, but rather a bundle of norms in the form of "a composite of different rules and principles relating to the domestic behavior of states and the responsibilities of the international community." On the one hand, R2P obliges states to protect their populations from mass atrocities and to refrain from committing them. On the other hand, R2P calls on the international community to prevent mass atrocities by assisting states in fulfilling their protection duties or, if they fail to do so or commit atrocities themselves, by taking direct remedial actions.

Many scholars have analyzed the bundle of R2P norms in the context of sovereignty. R2P thus seeks to change sovereignty norms by catalyzing new intersubjective meaning about what sovereignty entails (Reinold 2013). Included within sovereignty is the government's requirement to protect its population from mass atrocities. Failing this, international intervention is permitted and, consequently, does not violate but rather helps to uphold sovereignty. In explaining the emergence of R2P, Gareth Evans (2008a, Chapters 1 and 2) traced the evolution from the dark ages of Westphalian sovereignty, when states faced no restrictions in how they treated their citizens, to the enlightened times of the post-Cold War period, when the notion of sovereignty as responsibility took hold. By highlighting the historic antecedents of the doctrine, Glanville (2014) challenged the view that R2P sought to erode traditional sovereignty. For him, R2P's roots can be found in the various projects through which states' sovereign responsibilities were articulated alongside sovereign rights. These include the notion of popular sovereignty emanating from the French and American revolutions at the end of the eighteenth century and the idea of trusteeship that conferred a responsibility on European states to govern the peoples of the colonial world (Glanville 2011). Other authors (e.g., Bass 2008; Weiss 2016, 42) referred to the nineteenth-century interventions of European powers to protect Christian populations in the Ottoman Empire as the origin of humanitarian intervention and R2P as an idea.

However, the analysis put forth here contends that such accounts are state-centric and sovereignty-focused, while the normative essence of R2P is different. Revolutionary popular sovereignty, colonial governance, and nineteenth century humanitarian interventions have very little in common with and—considering the many atrocities committed by colonial powers—even blatantly contradict the spirit and values of the R2P doctrine. What is more, R2P's primary contribution is not to restrict sovereignty. As Luck (2009) explained, the consensus about R2P at the 2005 World Summit was achieved precisely by re-conceptualizing the doctrine so it accommodated the sovereignty concerns of both developing and powerful developed countries. The normative essence of R2P, therefore, is not to change sovereignty norms, but to de-legitimize the use of mass atrocities as a political instrument. The founders of R2P thus aimed to accelerate the process through which committing atrocities would be transformed from a normal to a broadly stigmatized practice in world politics. Serrano (2010) captured this dynamic, stating that "while sovereign claims are still frequently upheld, not a single government can now easily afford to stand up and argue for inaction in the light of atrocity upheavals." However, this does not mean that effective action is always taken or that the principle of state sovereignty has been superseded. Instead, rather than opposing sovereignty as an institution, R2P seeks to preclude using sovereignty as a pretext to justify mass atrocities.

The core of R2P: the Saving Strangers Norm

Within the analysis presented, the core of R2P is constituted by the Saving Strangers Norm. This norm, also later referred to as the "core R2P norm," comprises three interrelated beliefs, through which the intersubjective meaning of the norm is constructed. First, mass atrocities are morally wrong, regardless of where or by whom they are committed. Second, action should be taken to protect the victims of mass atrocities, regardless of their nationality, religion, ethnicity, or social group. Third, there is no acceptable pretext to eschew such action based on considerations of national interest, stability, or sovereignty.

The three constitutive criteria clarify that R2P, as a normative project, is more closely aligned with efforts to prevent genocide or to promote human rights than it is with the articulation of sovereign responsibilities—for example, through the standards of civilization in colonial governance or through nineteenth century humanitarian interventions. As such, the core R2P norm is a relatively recent phenomenon. It emerged on the world stage through the R2P doctrine, but at the same time, it is the product of a long process of social construction. More specifically, the norm emerged from the convergence of three factors: structural enablers—changes in the normative structure of world politics; catalysts—the occurrence of historical events that triggered processes of norm innovation; and trailblazers—the presence of related norms onto which the core R2P norm was grafted.

First, the emergence of the core R2P norm was enabled by changes in the normative structure of world politics. This refers to the fundamental beliefs that underpin interactions in the international sphere. Most importantly, the idea of humanity has been universalized over the course of the last 100 years. Today, the basic proposition of the Universal Declaration of Human Rights that all human beings, regardless of their race or religion, are born free and equal in dignity and rights—is broadly recognized. This development was instrumental in de-legitimizing colonialism and in accelerating the disengagement of European powers from their colonies in the 1950s and the 1960s (Crawford 2002). It also discredited racial segregation as practiced by the apartheid regime in South Africa (Klotz 1995) and fostered a growing practice of humanitarian intervention (Finnemore 2003). Evidently, the universalization of humanity does not mean that oppression no longer occurs or that solidarity with the victims of such oppression arises automatically. However, universalization has created the potential to change existing practices and to develop new social norms. It has thus made it possible to generate compassion for populations in far-away war zones. This is the very foundation of the idea of saving strangers, which otherwise would be neither morally compelling nor politically feasible.

The second factor to understand the emergence of the core R2P norm pertains to historical catalysts. These are events in the sense of Sewell (2005, 101), which "bring about historical changes in part by transforming the very cultural categories that shape and constrain human action." As such, they trigger learning and norm innovation. For example, the Genocide Convention of 1948 developed at the initiative of the individuals and states who were convinced that something as horrifying as the Holocaust should never happen again.[11] The war in Bosnia from 1992 to 1995 and, most importantly, the Rwanda genocide in 1994 fulfilled a similar function, catalyzing the emergence of the Saving Strangers Norm and the related R2P doctrine. After the killings in Rwanda and Srebrenica, the general tone was that inaction in the face of mass atrocities was a serious moral and political mistake. Countless heads of state expressed remorse, while pleading that they would never again stand on the sidelines as genocide unfolded. By doing so, they affirmed that the failure to save strangers was incompatible with the values of the international community. This provided momentum for norm innovation. As the ICISS (2001, viii) wrote, "We want no more Rwandas, and we believe that the adoption of the proposals in our report is the best way of ensuring that." Rwanda and Srebrenica also galvanized an advocacy movement within civil society that was united by a vision of a world in which such crimes would no longer happen.

The third factor was the presence of catalyst norms onto which the idea of saving strangers was grafted. According to Price (1998, 617), "grafting" refers to associating a new norm with a broadly accepted pre-existing norm. Grafting creates discursive reference points, makes a new norm meaningful for larger audiences, and facilitates the building of coalitions of likeminded organizations that help to promote it. The core R2P norm exemplifies this process, as it was embedded in preexisting norms of protection (Kurtz and Rotmann 2016). In this way, R2P was anchored in a broader normative complex, which facilitated norm resonance and robustness (Welsh 2019, 68). The core R2P norm is thus linked to international human rights, which entitle individual citizens to demand certain actions be taken or omitted by their government (Donnelly 2007). Similar to R2P, the moral axis around which human rights turns is the individual. According to Forsythe (2000, 24–25), the emergence of human rights signifies that the "reference to the idea of state sovereignty no longer provides an automatic and impenetrable shield against international action on issues once regarded as essentially domestic." Not surprisingly, the members of the ICISS made countless references to human rights in their final report.

International efforts to prevent genocide represent another trailblazing norm. In a sense, the saving strangers idea first materialized in the Genocide Convention, as it defined genocide as a crime and obligated signatories to prevent it and punish its perpetrators. Therefore, the founders of R2P cited the Genocide Convention numerous times and included genocide as one of the crimes that triggers R2P. The fact that a number of anti-genocide activists, for example Elie Wiesel and Samantha Power, became active promoters of R2P lends further weight to the affiliation between preventing genocide and saving strangers.

The Saving Strangers Norm was also grafted onto international criminal justice norms, which have framed mass atrocities as crimes that can be prosecuted by international tribunals (Savelsberg 2010). The core R2P norm is aligned with this endeavor, which has gained significant momentum since the establishment of the International Criminal Court (ICC). As Scheffer (2008) explained, R2P is framed by atrocity crimes, which it tries to prevent by mustering international intervention, while international criminal justice seeks to punish its perpetrators. It is only logical, therefore, that Gareth Evans (2008b, 252–253) included the ICC as one instrument in his R2P toolbox. The UNSG also recommended that states ratify the Rome Statute and refer situations of mass atrocities to the ICC as measures to implement R2P (United Nations 2009, para 17, 19, and 54).

Finally, the Saving Strangers Norm is underpinned by norms emanating from international humanitarian law. This body of law distinguishes between combatants, who can be lawfully killed in the context of armed conflict, and non-combatants, who enjoy special protections. The principle of "protection of civilians" was generated from international humanitarian law to guide humanitarian action. It is important to distinguish the protection of civilians as a humanitarian principle from references to protecting civilians as a way of implementing R2P, for example in UN Security Council resolutions. However, the resemblance is not only semantic. The distinction between combatants and civilians and the idea that civilians ought to be protected is very much part of the saving strangers idea (Breakey 2012).

Approach and framework for studying R2P in Darfur

Research approach and methodology

Smith and Hollis (1991, 1) distinguished two basic epistemological approaches, or stories, of international relations research.

> One story is an outsider's, told in the manner of a natural scientist seeking to explain the workings of nature and treating the human realm as part of nature. The other is an insider's, told so as to make us understand what the events mean, in a sense distinct from any meaning found in unearthing the laws of nature.

This study adopts the latter approach, which draws on the concept of "Verstehen" developed by Max Weber (1968 [1922]). Thus, the role of the social scientist is to make sense of human action by interpreting the subjective meaning that people accord to their actions. For the purpose of the analysis presented here, the adoption of an interpretive epistemology implies, on the one hand, a focus on contextualized theorizing that is bounded by time and space, as opposed to universal claims (Price and Reus-Smit 1998, 273–275). On the other hand, it requires immersion in the research environment—the telling of an insider's story—and thus a focus on empirical research.

This study adopts a qualitative research strategy, with case-study research as the appropriate methodology. Focusing on historical analysis in political science research, George and Bennett (2005, 5) defined a case study as "the detailed examination of an aspect of a historical episode to develop or test historical explanations that may be generalizable to other events." Case studies consist of a relatively small number of in-depth analyses with the aim of making broader theoretical inferences. Therefore, case studies prioritize analytical depth over breadth. They allow for detail and context within a given case. As such, case-study methodology is well suited for empirical studies of international norms, not only to identify complex causal mechanisms, but also to grasp processes of intersubjective meaning-making.

To operationalize this approach, this study opted for a dual methodology that combines methods for constitutive analysis with those usually associated with causal analysis, as suggested by Lupovici (2009). It performed discourse analysis to understand the social construction of the context in which responses to mass atrocities occur, with a particular focus on the meaning-making role of the core R2P norm. In a second step, it used process-tracing in conjunction with counterfactual analysis to assess the specific policies that emerged from this context.

Discourse analysis is based on the belief that social reality is constructed and, as such, it "arise[s] out of interrelated bodies of texts—called discourses—that bring new ideas, objects and practices into the world" (Hardy et al. 2004, 20). Therefore, the task of discourse analysis "involves the systematic study of texts to find evidence of their meaning and how this meaning translates into a social reality" (Hardy et al. 2004, 20). For Cortell and Davis (2000, 58), analyzing discourse is essential in the study of international norms, because it explains why certain norms are salient in the domestic political context, while others are not. In this study, discourse analysis is used to show how meaning about situations of mass atrocities is constructed.

Once the context is established, the challenge is to explain why certain policy options were chosen in response to a given situation of mass atrocities, and how they were translated into practice. To this end, this study employed process-tracing, whereby "causation is established through uncovering traces of a hypothesized causal mechanism within the confines of one or a few cases" (Bennett and Elman 2007, 183). As a method, it is particularly suitable to account for the effects of ideas and normative frameworks (Jacobs 2015).

Concretely, process-tracers operate somewhat like detectives, as they meticulously reconstruct a sequence of events to make inferences about the causal links between them. Useful in this respect are counterfactual arguments: "the exploration of events that did not happen" (Lupovici 2009, 203). This requires demonstrating that if the context or specific variables had been different, an alternative outcome would have been observed than the one that came to pass. Counterfactual analysis thus increases the plausibility of the explanation about causal mechanisms put forward and, as such, forms an essential tool for process-tracers.

Why Darfur?

Given the research approach, this study selected the conflict in Darfur as a single case to investigate how R2P was implemented. The choice of a single case was motivated by the exploratory dimension of the research, which required significant empirical detail and analytical depth. The chosen methodology is ambitious from an empirical point of view. Both discourse analysis and process-tracing require large amounts of data that are both time and resource intensive to obtain and analyze. They also require cultural competence and an immersion in the study environment through field research.

Darfur is the right case to study R2P for three reasons. The first is that the discourse of R2P was very present in international discussions about the conflict (Smith 2010, Chapter 7). As explained in the introduction, when the magnitude of violence in Darfur became clear, many observers called it a test case for the R2P doctrine. In a resolution adopted in August 2006, Darfur was the first country-specific context in which the UN Security Council mentioned R2P (Gifkins 2016b). Darfur also gave rise to an advocacy movement motivated by the values of the core R2P norm (Lanz 2009). Finally, R2P framed the academic debate about the international response to the war in Darfur (Bellamy 2005; Hehir 2008; Badescu and Bergholm 2009; Mamdani 2009; Mills 2009; Verhoeven et al. 2016).[12] Scholars fundamentally disagreed about the nature, motivation, and consequences of international intervention in Darfur, but they agreed that R2P was an important factor. Therefore, Darfur became a relevant case to study how the norm was implemented.

The second reason is the way the implementation of R2P influenced Sudanese domestic politics through the various international interventions in Darfur. Armed conflict in Sudan has been heavily affected by international incentives, alliances, and discourses, which influenced dynamics on the battlefield (Gabrielsen Jumbert 2010). This was particularly the case for Darfur, as highlighted by different scholars. The international push to stop atrocities in the name of R2P had a strong impact on the ruling party within the Sudanese government (IDF and Assal 2010) as well as on the rebel groups in Darfur (Belloni 2006; De Waal 2007). Therefore, Darfur is a useful case to study the importance of local structures in R2P implementation, which is one of the underexplored questions in R2P research.

The third reason is the international response to Darfur, which is ideal for an exploratory single case study. R2P had a significant impact, but it did not generate an exceptional response, unlike the situation in Libya in 2011, for example, where a non-consensual intervention took place. The effects of the international response to the Darfur conflict were ambiguous, which makes it a typical case of international intervention in armed conflicts. Moreover, Darfur exhibits important and rather puzzling variations over time. At the outset of the conflict, it was almost completely ignored in the international arena, before suddenly being transformed in April 2004 into a highly publicized global issue. Since 2011, however, Darfur has largely fallen off the radar. These variations make Darfur the ideal case to study the inconsistency of R2P implementation by comparing different periods of international engagement and investigating the changes in the international response.

The Darfur conflict erupted in 2003, but the international response to it began in 2004, before states endorsed the R2P concept at the World Summit in 2005. Some scholars therefore argued that Darfur is not a suitable case to study R2P (e.g., Gifkins 2016a, 717). However, R2P as a concept, and certainly the core R2P norm as set out in this analysis, had emerged prior to the World Summit. Indeed, as Chapter 2 shows, when Darfur became a global issue in April 2004, it was primarily viewed through the lens of saving strangers. The most important international interventions—the ICC indictments and the UN-AU peacekeeping mission—occurred after 2005. Finally, although the World Summit Outcome Document narrowed the scope of R2P, Darfur would have qualified as an R2P situation *in any case*, given the magnitude of the violence and atrocity crimes committed. It therefore presents a pertinent case to study the effects of the R2P norm.

For the empirical analysis, research was conducted through expert interviews in order to gain insights into how people make sense of the world and into their opinions, perceptions, and values (Meuser and Nagel 2005). In addition, expert interviews have a unique advantage in providing insights into decision-making processes, motivations, and sequences of events. In total, the author conducted 110 interviews with experts who had played a role in the international response to the Darfur conflict, with representatives of the Sudanese government and opposition forces, as well as with experts of Sudanese politics.[13] The author conducted most interviews in person during several field trips, in addition to 14 phone interviews.

Apart from interviews, the research also drew on a variety of written sources. For the discourse analysis, it particularly relied on editorials published in major newspapers in Western countries and Sudan. Editorials are suitable to assess discursive processes, as they are influential, easily accessible, and illustrate the formation of public opinion. They are, in short, repositories of discourses. In addition to editorials, the book used primary data from a number of other texts, including official documents, transcripts of speeches and interviews, books and articles written by key figures, campaign material, cartoons, photos, and films. The research also drew on secondary sources, such as blog posts, newspaper articles, policy reports, and academic literature.

Analytical framework

This study drew on Risse and Sikkink's (1999) "spiral model" of norm diffusion to explore the implementation of the core R2P norm in Darfur. The model focuses on international human rights, but is valid for other norms, including R2P. Its starting point is when domestic actors bring to light the abusive practices of governments, triggering the involvement of transnational advocacy networks. These networks, with the support of sympathetic states, then mount campaigns to denounce the violations. Governments targeted by campaigns typically reject them as interference in internal affairs. However, when international pressure is upheld, norm-violating governments are compelled to make tactical concessions. Domestic groups thus redouble their actions, which eventually leads governments to adapt their discourse, change repressive practices, and, finally, to incorporate international norms into domestic jurisdiction.

Scholars have criticized the spiral model for not taking the agency of norm takers into account and for ignoring how norms change as they are transmitted from the sender to the receiver (Acharya 2004). Indeed, the concept of "translation" captures the effects of norms more accurately than "diffusion." According to Stritzel (2011, 344–346), translation implies a transfer of meaning from one context into another. It also entails a process of construction as meaning is re-articulated in a new context, and it involves localization as meaning is appropriated and incorporated in a new locale. Mindful of this, it is possible to devise an analytical framework to study R2P in Darfur by distinguishing three processes of norm translation. These are how norm entrepreneurs conceptualize R2P in campaigns, how states respond to these campaigns, and what reactions they elicit among domestic actors. For each step, it is possible to formulate questions for empirical research along with propositions from the literature to understand how norm translation works. It is also possible to identify factors that contribute to the resonance of R2P, or lack thereof, in a particular case.

The first process concerns the role of norm entrepreneurs, in particular international activists and advocacy groups, which have played an important role in Darfur. Questions include: How have activists translated the core R2P norm into practice in the case of Darfur? What strategies have they used and what remedies have they suggested to protect civilians? And what was the role of domestic opposition groups in Sudan? In answering these questions, the analysis drew on the research on norm entrepreneurs who operate through transnational advocacy networks. Keck and Sikkink (1998, 16–25) identified different types of resources that norm entrepreneurs utilize to translate norms into practice: They hold states accountable for their previously expressed policies and principles, generate politically usable information, and call upon symbols and narratives to make sense of a situation for far-away audiences. Norm entrepreneurs create cognitive frames with the aim of "rendering events or occurrences meaningful ... to organize experience and guide action, whether individual or collective" (Snow et al. 1986, 464).[14] They are thus meaning-makers in the sense of Barnett and Finnemore (2004, 33): "Events ... do not have an objective meaning but must be made meaningful by actors, and actors compete to affix meaning to these events because doing so creates boundaries of acceptable action."

Not all norm-based campaigns gain traction with policymakers or in public opinion. Research on transnational advocacy movements highlights the importance of broadly recognized organizations or individuals—so-called gatekeepers—in decisions about whether an issue is adopted (Bob 2005; Carpenter 2007). Other research points to the authority and the trustworthiness of norm promoters as key factors for adoption (Johnston 2001; Hero 2015). In cases of mass atrocities, this would mean that R2P is more likely to gain traction when the advocacy push is led by influential personalities who are perceived to be credible and authoritative. When gatekeeper norm entrepreneurs are absent, R2P has less resonance.

The second process of norm translation concerns the role of states, acting to prevent atrocities on their own or through multilateral organizations. Questions include: How have states responded to atrocity crimes in Darfur? How have they reacted to activist campaigns that promoted saving strangers in Darfur? And what measures did states propose to protect civilians? Relevant to understand how states respond to mass atrocities are the frames associated with a particular conflict. According to Autesserre (2009, 252), "Frames can account for what shapes the international understanding of the causes of violence and of the interveners' role, and how this understanding makes certain actions possible while precluding others." Frames thus influence the appropriate international response to a situation of violence. For example, the label "post-conflict" implies that elections should be held (Autesserre 2010). For R2P to play a significant role, conflict frames would need to emphasize mass atrocities and the possibility to prevent or stop these atrocities through concerted action.

The literature puts forward different explanations of why frames are more or less successful in mobilizing masses and galvanizing policy change. Four factors of resonance are relevant for R2P. The first is completeness: Frames that provide a comprehensive account of a problem are more compelling. This includes frames of causal and treatment responsibility, explaining who is responsible and who should take action to stop it (Iyengar and Simon 1993). A second factor refers to the simplicity of the frame—its ability to generate clear-cut images of good and evil. Iyengar (1991, 136) found that frames that attribute the responsibility of a problem to the actions of individuals or groups, rather than to structural causes, tend to be more effective in generating resonance. A third resonance factor lies in the coherence of the frame in the absence of competing frames. In their study of public opinion formation, Chong and Druckman (2010, 665) argued that "in competitive environments—where individuals are exposed concurrently to each side's strongest frame ...—the frames tend to cancel out and exert no net effect." Therefore, framing is more effective when one frame prevails over alternative arguments.

The fourth resonance factor goes beyond the narrative itself and looks at the broader context. As Benford and Snow (2000, 628) argued, framing "does not occur in a structural or cultural vacuum. Rather, framing processes are affected by a number of elements of the socio-cultural context in which they are embedded." Acharya (2009, 21) confirmed this, arguing that the localization of a new norm depends on its resonance with "cognitive priors," defined as "an existing set of ideas, belief systems, and norms, which determine and condition an individual's or social groups' receptivity to a new norm." This would mean that R2P's impact is likely to be stronger if it is embedded in an all-encompassing meaning-making narrative that resonates with existing interpretative frames and political interests.

The third process of norm translation pertains to local actors. Questions include: How has the Sudanese government, the main culprit of violence in Darfur, reacted to the core R2P norm? How has it engaged with international responses to protect civilians? Did it change its behavior? What was the reaction of the domestic opposition in Sudan? And how have rebel movements in Darfur engaged with international efforts to save strangers? According to Checkel (1999, 87), reactions to norm campaigns depend on the "cultural match" of a norm: "a situation where the prescriptions embodied in an international norm are convergent with domestic norms, as reflected in the discourse, the legal system, and bureaucratic agencies." The expectation is therefore that the reaction of a government responsible for mass atrocities will be conditioned by the cultural references and historical experiences that the Saving Strangers Norm evokes. As far as opposition groups are concerned, Bob (2005) refers to the "marketing of rebellion" to describe the ability of insurgents to create a narrative that arouses sympathy for their struggle. Those groups that frame their struggle in a way that resonates with Western advocacy networks will be most successful in popularizing their cause. In cases where R2P primarily targets the government, there is therefore a strong expectation that opposition groups will refer to the norm to seek external support for their struggle.

Chapter findings

Three main findings emerge from this chapter, laying the foundation for the analysis that follows. First, the case of Darfur presents valuable insights into two underexplored areas of R2P research. One, existing research has not paid sufficient attention to the political dynamics in countries experiencing mass atrocities, thereby neglecting the agency of local actors as they engage with international efforts to save strangers. Two, existing research does not sufficiently explain the inconsistent application of R2P, which forms the dominant framework in some cases of atrocities but not in others.

Second, the analysis presented suggests that the normative core of R2P is *not* to curtail state sovereignty. As the 2005 World Summit Outcome Document shows, broad acceptance of the norm was only achieved by re-conceptualizing the doctrine so that it accommodated the sovereignty of a broad range of states. Normatively speaking, the main aim of R2P is to stigmatize the use of mass atrocities. Therefore, the norm comprises three interrelated beliefs: One, mass atrocities are morally wrong, regardless of where and by whom they are committed.

Two, action should be taken to protect non-citizens that are victims of mass atrocities, regardless of their nationality, religion, ethnicity, or social group. Three, there is no acceptable pretext to eschew such action based on national interest, stability, or sovereignty.

The third finding concerns the question of how something as abstract as R2P manifests itself in the real world. It is best understood as a process of translation, whereby different actors promote, appropriate, and contest the application of the R2P norm. Thus, translation happens at three levels: in campaigns conceived by norm advocates, in states' responses to those campaigns, and in the reaction of domestic actors—primarily the government and opposition groups. Together, they constitute the effects of R2P in a given context.

Notes

1 This is the title of an article by one of the founders of the R2P concept, former Australian foreign minister Gareth Evans (2008a).
2 This sentiment is captured particularly well in Samantha Power's (2002) book *A Problem from Hell* and in the book *Shake Hands with the Devil* by Roméo Dallaire (2004), the force commander of the UN peacekeeping mission stationed in Rwanda during the genocide.
3 This was articulated by Kofi Annan in the essay "Two Concepts of Sovereignty," published in *The Economist* on 18 September 1999.
4 The ICISS was diverse in terms of the nationalities of the commissioners, who hailed from Algeria, Australia, Canada, Germany, Guatemala, India, the Philippines, Russia, South Africa, Switzerland, and the United States. However, there was only one woman among the 12 commissioners.
5 On sovereignty as responsibility, see the accounts of the ICISS co-chairs Gareth Evans and Mohamed Sahnoun (2002) and ICISS member Ramesh Thakur (2002).
6 Quote by Gareth Evans given in an interview with *The World Today* at Chatham House on 5 October 2012. Text of the interview available online at www.globalr2p. org/media/files/gareth-evans-on-responsibility-to-protect-after-libya.pdf (accessed 8 June 2019).
7 This refers to the journal *Global Responsibility to Protect* published by Brill and the book series *Global Politics of R2P* published by Routledge. The two handbooks were published by Routledge (Knight and Egerton 2012) and Oxford University Press (Bellamy and Dunne 2016).
8 See, for example, the case studies in Bellamy's and Dunne's (2016) *Oxford Handbook of R2P*, chapters 37–48.
9 Two exceptions of studies examining the local dynamics of R2P are Piccolino's (2012) analysis of Côte d'Ivoire (2012) and Kurtz and Jaganathan's (2016) of Sri Lanka. Both studies analyze the strategies and discourses mobilized by governments in an attempt to neutralize international pressure generated by R2P.
10 Gareth Evans, "End of Argument," Foreign Policy online article, 28 November 2011, available at https://foreignpolicy.com/2011/11/28/end-of-the-argument/ (accessed 8 June 2019).
11 On the role of Rafael Lemkin and Hersch Lauterpacht in pushing for the legal recognition of the crime of genocide, see Sands (2016).
12 In addition to the cited works, the book *The International Politics of Mass Atrocities: The Case of Darfur*, edited by Black and Williams (2010), provides a useful collection of contributions covering different aspects and perspectives of R2P in the context of Darfur.

13   More specifically, the author conducted 22 interviews with Darfur activists in the US, France, and the UK, nine with UN officials, nine with diplomats, three with international journalists, five with representatives of international humanitarian organizations, eight with different experts working for international NGOs, foundations and lobby groups, 13 with people affiliated with the Sudanese government, three with representatives of Sudanese opposition parties, 11 with representatives of Sudanese civil society groups, 16 with Sudanese academics and 11 with representatives of Darfur rebel groups and affiliated members of the Darfur Diaspora. Given the sensitive nature of the research, the interview quotes are anonymous, unless expressly authorized by the interviewee. However, to allow the reader to differentiate anonymous sources, interviews are labeled in chronological order—starting with AA, AB, AC … and ending with ED, EE—as well as by their location and date.

14   The classic text on the analysis of frames in social science is Goffman (1974).

References

Acharya, Amitav. 2004. "How Ideas Spread: Whose Norms Matter? Norm Localization and Institutional Change in Asian Regionalism." *International Organization* 58: 239–275.

Acharya, Amitav. 2009. *Whose Ideas Matter? Agency and Power in Asian Regionalism.* Ithaca, NY: Cornell University Press.

Acharya, Amitav. 2013. "The R2P and Norm Diffusion: Towards A Framework of Norm Circulation." *Global Responsibility to Protect* 5: 466–479.

Aning, Kwesi, and Frank Okyere. 2016. "The African Union." In *The Oxford Handbook of the Responsibility to Protect*, eds. Alex J. Bellamy and Tim Dunne. Oxford: Oxford University Press. 355–371.

Arbour, Louise. 2008. "The Responsibility to Protect as a Duty of Care in International Law and Practice." *Review of International Studies* 34: 445–458.

Autesserre, Severine. 2009. "Hobbes and the Congo: Frames, Local Violence, and International Intervention." *International Organization* 63: 249–280.

Autesserre, Severine. 2010. *The Trouble with the Congo: Local Violence and the Failure of International Peacebuilding.* Cambridge: Cambridge University Press.

Ayoob, Mohammed. 2002. "Humanitarian Intervention and State Sovereignty." *The International Journal of Human Rights* 6: 81–102.

Badescu, Cristina G. 2011. *Humanitarian Intervention and the Responsibility to Protect: Security and Human Rights.* Milton Park: Routledge.

Badescu, Cristina G., and Linnea Bergholm. 2009. "The Responsibility to Protect and the Conflict in Darfur: The Big Let-Down." *Security Dialogue* 40: 287–309.

Badescu, Cristina G., and Thomas G. Weiss. 2010. "Misrepresenting R2P and Advancing Norms: An Alternative Spiral?" *International Studies Perspectives* 11: 354–374.

Barnett, Michael. 2002. *Eyewitness to a Genocide: The United Nations and Rwanda.* Ithaca, NY: Cornell University Press.

Barnett, Michael, and Martha Finnemore. 2004. *Rules for the World: International Organizations in Global Politics.* Ithaca, NY: Cornell University Press.

Bass, Gary Jonathan. 2008. *Freedom's Battle: The Origins of Humanitarian Intervention.* New York: Alfred A. Knopf.

Bellamy, Alex J. 2005. "Responsibility to Protect or Trojan Horse? The Crisis in Darfur and Humanitarian Intervention after Iraq." *Ethics & International Affairs* 19: 31–54.

Bellamy, Alex J. 2006. "Whither the Responsibility to Protect? Humanitarian Intervention and the 2005 World Summit." *Ethics & International Affairs* 20: 143–169.

Bellamy, Alex J. 2010. "The Responsibility to Protect—Five Years On." *Ethics & International Affairs* 24: 143–169.

Bellamy, Alex J. 2014. *The Responsibility to Protect: A Defense*. Oxford: Oxford University Press.

Bellamy, Alex J., and Tim Dunne, eds. 2016. *The Oxford Handbook on the Responsibility to Protect*. Oxford: Oxford University Press.

Bellamy, Alex J., and Edward C. Luck. 2018. *The Responsibility to Protect: From Promise to Practice*. Cambridge: Polity Press.

Belloni, Roberto. 2006. "The Tragedy of Darfur and the Limits of the 'Responsibility to Protect'." *Ethnopolitics* 5: 327–346.

Benford, Robert D., and David A. Snow. 2000. "Framing Processes and Social Movements: An Overview and Assessment." *Annual Review of Sociology* 26: 611–639.

Bennett, Andrew, and Colin Elman. 2007. "Case Study Methods in the International Relations Subfield." *Comparative Political Studies* 40: 170–195.

Black, David R., and Paul D. Williams, eds. 2010. *The International Politics of Mass Atrocities: The Case of Darfur*. Milton Park: Routledge.

Bob, Clifford. 2005. *The Marketing of Rebellion: Insurgents, Media, and International Activism*. New York: Cambridge University Press.

Boyle, Joseph. 2006. "Traditional Just War Theory and Humanitarian Intervention." In *Humanitarian Intervention*, eds. Terry Nardin and Melissa S. Williams. New York: NYU Press. 31–57.

Branch, Adam. 2011. "The Irresponsibility of the Responsibility to Protect in Africa." In *Critical Perspectives on the Responsibility to Protect: Interrogating Theory and Practice*, ed. Philip Cunliffe. Milton Park: Routledge. 103–124.

Breakey, Hugh. 2012. "The Responsibility to Protect and the Protection of Civilians in Armed Conflict: Overlap and Contrast." In *Norms of Protection*, eds. Angus Francis, Vesselin Popovski and Charles Sampford. Tokyo: UN University Press.

Brockmeier, Sarah, Oliver Stuenkel, and Marcos Tourinho. 2016. "The Impact of the Libya Intervention Debates on Norms of Protection." *Global Society* 30: 113–133.

Campbell, Susanna. 2018. *Global Governance and Local Peace: Accountability and Performance in International Peacebuilding*. Cambridge: Cambridge University Press.

Carpenter, Charli. 2007. "Studying Issue (Non)-Adoption in Transnational Advocacy Networks." *International Organization* 61: 643–667.

Chandler, David. 2004. "The Responsibility to Protect? Imposing the 'Liberal Peace'." *International Peacekeeping* 11: 59–81.

Checkel, Jeffrey T. 1999. "Norms, Institutions, and National Identity in Contemporary Europe." *International Studies Quarterly* 43: 84–114.

Chesterman, Simon. 2001. *Just War or Just Peace? Humanitarian Intervention and International Law*. Oxford: Oxford University Press.

Chomsky, Noam. 1999. *The New Military Humanism: Lessons from Kosovo*. London: Pluto Press.

Chong, Dennis, and James N. Druckman. 2010. "Dynamic Public Opinion: Communications Effects over Time." *American Political Science Review* 104: 663–680.

Cohen, Jean L. 2004. "Whose Sovereignty? Empire Versus International Law." *Ethics & International Affairs* 18: 1–24.

Cohen, Roberta. 2012. "From Sovereign Responsibility to R2P." In *The Routledge Handbook of the Responsibility to Protect*, eds. Andy W. Knight and Frazer Egerton. Milton Park: Routledge. 7–21.

Cortell, Andrew P., and James W. Davis. 1996. "How Do International Institutions Matter? The Domestic Impact of International Rules and Norms." *International Studies Quarterly* 40: 451–478.

Cortell, Andrew P., and James W. Davis. 2000. "Understanding the Domestic Impact of International Norms: A Research Agenda." *International Studies Review* 2: 65–87.

Crawford, Neta. 2002. *Argument and Change in World Politics: Ethics, Decolonization, and Humanitarian Intervention.* Cambridge: Cambridge University Press.

Crossley, Noele. 2018. "Is R2P Still Controversial? Continuity and Change in the Debate on 'Humanitarian Intervention'." *Cambridge Review of International Affairs*: 415–436.

Cunliffe, Philip, ed. 2011. "A Dangerous Duty: Power, Paternalism and the Global 'Duty of Care'." In *Critical Perspectives on the Responsibility to Protect: Interrogating Theory and Practice*, ed. Philip Cunliffe. Milton Park: Routledge. 51–70.

Dallaire, Roméo. 2004. *Shake Hands with the Devil: The Failure of Humanity in Rwanda.* New York: Carroll & Graf Publishers.

De Waal, Alex. 2007. "Darfur and the Failure of the Responsibility to Protect." *International Affairs* 83: 1039–1054.

Deng, Francis Mading, Sadikiel Kimaro, Terrence Lyons, Donald Rothchild, and I. William Zartman. 1996. *Sovereignty as Responsibility: Conflict Management in Africa.* Washington, DC: Brookings Institution Press.

Donnelly, Jack. 2007. *International Human Rights.* 3rd ed. Boulder, CO: Westview.

Evans, Gareth. 2008a. "The Responsibility to Protect: An Idea Whose Time Has Come … and Gone?" *International Relations* 22: 283–298.

Evans, Gareth. 2008b. *The Responsibility to Protect: Ending Mass Atrocity Crimes Once and for All.* Washington, DC: Brookings Institution Press.

Evans, Gareth, and Mohamed Sahnoun. 2002. "The Responsibility to Protect." *Foreign Affairs* 81: 99–110.

Finnemore, Martha. 2003. *The Purpose of Intervention: Changing Beliefs About the Use of Force.* Ithaca, NY: Cornell University Press.

Finnemore, Martha, and Kathryn Sikkink. 1998. "International Norm Dynamics and Political Change." *International Organization* 52: 887–917.

Finnemore, Martha, and Kathryn Sikkink 1999. "International Norms and Political Change." In *Exploration and Contestation in the Study of World Politics*, eds. Peter J. Katzenstein, Robert O. Keohane and Stephen D. Krasner. Cambridge, MA: MIT Press. 247–278.

Forsythe, David P. 2000. *Human Rights in International Relations.* Cambridge: Cambridge University Press.

Gabrielsen Jumbert, Maria. 2010. *The Internationalization of the Sudanese Conflicts: from South Sudan to Darfur.* PhD thesis, Institut d'études politiques de Paris.

George, Alexander L., and Andrew Bennett. 2005. *Case Studies and Theory Development in the Social Sciences.* Cambridge, MA: MIT Press.

Gifkins, Jess. 2016a. "Darfur." In *The Oxford Handbook of the Responsibility to Protect*, eds. Alex J. Bellamy and Tim Dunne. Oxford: Oxford University Press. 717–733.

Gifkins, Jess. 2016b. "R2P in the UN Security Council: Darfur, Libya and beyond." *Cooperation and Conflict* 51: 148–165.

Glanville, Luke. 2011. "The Antecedents of 'Sovereignty as Responsibility'." *European Journal of International Relations* 17: 233–255.

Glanville, Luke. 2014. *Sovereignty and the Responsibility to Protect: A New History.* Chicago: Chicago University Press.

Glanville, Luke. 2016. "Does R2P Matter? Interpreting the Impact of a Norm." *Cooperation and Conflict* 51: 184–199.

Goffman, Erving. 1974. *Frame Analysis: An Essay on the Organization of Experience.* Cambridge, MA: Harvard University Press.

Goodman, Ryan. 2006. "Humanitarian Intervention and Pretexts for War." *American Journal of International Law* 100: 107–141.

Hardy, Cynthia, Bill Harley, and Nelson Phillips. 2004. "Discourse Analysis and Content Analysis: Two Solitudes?" *Qualitative Methods: Newsletter of the American Political Science Association Organized Section on Qualitative Methods* 2: 19–22.

Hehir, Aidan. 2008. *Humanitarian Intervention after Kosovo: Iraq, Darfur and the Record of Global Civil Society.* Basingstoke: Palgrave Macmillan.

Hehir, Aidan. 2013. "The Permanence of Inconsistency: Libya, the Security Council, and the Responsibility to Protect." *International Security* 38: 137–159.

Hehir, Aidan. 2019. *Hollow Norms and the Responsibility to Protect.* Cham: Palgrave Macmillan.

Hellmüller, Sara. 2018. *Partners for Peace: The Interaction between Local and International Peacebuilding Actors.* Cham: Palgrave Macmillan.

Hero, Annie. 2015. "Norm Entrepreneurs Advocating the Responsibility to Protect, and Peacekeeping Reform Proposals." In *Perspectives on Peacekeeping and Atrocity Prevention,* eds. David Curran, Trudy Fraser, Larry Roeder and Robert Zuber. Cham: Springer. 41–57.

Hollis, Martin, and Steve Smith. 1991. *Explaining and Understanding International Relations.* Oxford: Clarendon Press.

Hopf, Ted. 2002. *Social Construction of International Politics: Identities & Foreign Policies, Moscow, 1955 and 1999.* Ithaca, NY: Cornell University Press.

IDF, and Munzoul Assal. 2010. "The National Congress Party and the Darfurian Armed Groups." In *The International Politics of Mass Atrocities: The Case of Darfur,* eds. David R. Black and Paul D. Williams. Milton Park: Routledge. 27–48.

ICISS. 2001. *The Responsibility to Protect. Report of the International Commission on Intervention and State Sovereignty.* Ottawa: International Development Research Centre.

Ignatieff, Michael. 2000. *Virtual War: Kosovo and Beyond.* New York: Metropolitan Books.

Independent International Commission on Kosovo. 2000. *The Kosovo Report: Conflict, International Response, Lessons Learned.* Oxford: Oxford University Press.

Iyengar, Shanto. 1991. *Is Anyone Responsible? How Television Frames Political Issues.* Chicago: University of Chicago Press.

Iyengar, Shanto, and Adam Simon. 1993. "News Coverage of the Gulf Crisis and Public Opinion: A Study of Agenda-Setting, Priming, and Framing." *Communication Research* 20: 365–383.

Jackson, Robert H. 2000. *The Global Covenant: Human Conduct in a World of States.* Oxford: Oxford University Press.

Jacobs, Alan M. 2015. "Process Tracing the Effects of Ideas." In *Process Tracing: From Metaphor to Analytic Tool,* eds. Andrew Bennett and Jeffrey T. Checkel. Cambridge: Cambridge University Press. 41–73.

Jepperson, Ronald M., Alexander Wendt, and Peter J. Katzenstein. 1996. "Norms, Identity, and Culture in National Security." In *The Culture of National Security: Norms and Identity in World Politics,* ed. Peter J. Katzenstein. New York: Columbia University Press. 33–75.

Johnston, Alastair Iain. 2001. "Treating International Institutions as Social Environments." *International Studies Quarterly* 45: 487–515.

Johnstone, Ian. 2003. "Security Council Deliberations: The Power of the Better Argument." *European Journal of International Law* 14: 437–480.

Johnstone, Ian. 2011. *The Power of Deliberation: International Law, Politics and Organizations.* New York: Oxford University Press.

Katzenstein, Peter J. 1996. "Introduction: Alternative Perspectives on National Security." In *The Culture of National Security: Norms and Identity in World Politics*, ed. Peter J. Katzenstein. New York: Columbia University Press.

Keck, Margaret E., and Kathryn Sikkink. 1998. *Activists Beyond Borders: Advocacy Networks in International Politics.* Ithaca, NY: Cornell University Press.

Kenkel, Kai Michael. 2012. "Brazil and R2P: Does Taking Responsibility Mean Using Force?" *Global Responsibility to Protect* 4: 5–32.

Kirsch, Nico. 2005. "International Law in Times of Hegemony: Unequal Power and the Shaping of the International Legal Order." *European Journal of International Law* 16: 369–408.

Klotz, Audie. 1995. *Norms in International Relations: The Struggle Against Apartheid.* Ithaca, NY: Cornell University Press.

Knight, Andy W., and Frazer Egerton, eds. 2012. *The Routledge Handbook of the Responsibility to Protect.* Milton Park: Routledge.

Kuperman, Alan J. 2009. "Rethinking the Responsibility to Protect." *The Whitehead Journal of Diplomacy and International Relations* 10: 33–43.

Kurtz, Gerrit, and Madhan Mohan Jaganathan. 2016. "Protection in Peril: Counterterrorism Discourse and International Engagement in Sri Lanka in 2009." *Global Society* 30: 94–112.

Kurtz, Gerrit, and Philipp Rotmann. 2016. "The Evolution of Norms of Protection: Major Powers Debate the Responsibility to Protect." *Global Society* 30: 3–20.

Lanz, David. 2009. "Save Darfur: A Movement and its Discontents." *African Affairs* 108: 669–677.

Luck, Edward C. 2009. "Sovereignty, Choice, and the Responsibility to Protect." *Global Responsibility to Protect* 1: 10–21.

Lupovici, Amir. 2009. "Constructivist Methods: A Plea and Manifesto for Pluralism." *Review of International Studies* 35: 195–218.

Mac Ginty, Roger, and Oliver P. Richmond. 2013. "The Local Turn in Peace Building: A Critical Agenda for Peace." *Third World Quarterly* 34: 763–783.

Mamdani, Mahmood. 2009. *Saviors and Survivors: Darfur, Politics, and the War on Terror.* New York: Pantheon Books.

Mamdani, Mahmood. 2010. "Responsibility to Protect or Right to Punish?" *Journal of Intervention and Statebuilding* 4: 53–67.

Mégret, Frédéric. 2009. "Beyond the 'Salvation' Paradigm: Responsibility To Protect (Others) vs the Power of Protecting Oneself." *Security Dialogue* 40: 575–595.

Meuser, Michael, and Ulrike Nagel. 2005. "ExpertInneninterviews—vielfach erprobt, wenig bedacht. Ein Beitrag zur qualitativen Methodendiskussion." In *Das Experteninterview: Theorie, Methode, Anwendung*, eds. Alexander Bogner, Beate Littig and Wolfgang Menz, 2nd ed. Wiesbaden: VS Verlag für Sozialwissenschaften. 71–94.

Mills, Kurt. 2009. "Vacillating on Darfur: Responsibility to Protect, to Prosecute, or to Feed?" *Global Responsibility to Protect* 1: 532–559.

Morris, Justin. 2013. "Libya and Syria: R2P and the Spectre of the Swinging Pendulum." *International Affairs* 89: 1265–1283.

Negrón-Gonzales, Melinda, and Michael Contarino. 2014. "Local Norms Matter: Understanding National Responses to the Responsibility to Protect." *Global Governance* 20: 255–276.

O'Connell, Mary Ellen. 2010. "Responsibility to Peace: A Critique of R2P." *Journal of Intervention and Statebuilding* 4: 39–52.

Pape, Robert A. 2012. "When Duty Calls: A Pragmatic Standard of Humanitarian Intervention." *International Security* 37: 41–80.

Paris, Roland. 2014. "The 'Responsibility to Protect' and the Structural Problems of Preventive Humanitarian Intervention." *International Peacekeeping* 21: 569–603.

Pattison, James. 2010. *Humanitarian Intervention and the Responsibility to Protect: Who Should Intervene?* Oxford: Oxford University Press.

Peters, Anne. 2009. "Humanity as the A and Ω of Sovereignty." *European Journal of International Law* 20: 513–544.

Piccolino, Giulia. 2012. "David against Goliath in Côte d'Ivoire? Laurent Gbagbo's War against Global Governance." *African Affairs* 111: 1–23.

Power, Samantha. 2002. *"A Problem from Hell": America and the Age of Genocide.* New York: Harper Collins.

Price, Richard. 1998. "Reversing the Gun Sights: Transnational Civil Society Targets Land Mines." *International Organization* 52: 613–644.

Price, Richard, and Christian Reus-Smit. 1998. "Dangerous Liaisons?" *European Journal of International Relations* 4: 259–294.

Reinold, Theresa. 2013. *Sovereignty and the Responsibility to Protect: The Power of Norms and the Norms of the Powerful.* Milton Park: Routledge.

Richmond, Oliver P. 2010. "Resistance and the Post-liberal Peace." *Millennium—Journal of International Studies* 38: 665–692.

Risse, Thomas, and Kathryn Sikkink. 1999. "The Socialization of International Human Rights Norms into Domestic Practices: Introduction." In *The Power of Human Rights: International Norms and Domestic Change*, eds. Thomas Risse, Stephen C. Ropp and Kathryn Sikkink. Cambridge: Cambridge University Press. 1–38.

Sands, Philippe. 2016. *East West Street.* New York: Alfred A. Knopf.

Savelsberg, Joachim J. 2010. *Crime and Human Rights: Criminology of Genocide and Atrocities.* London: Sage.

Scheffer, David. 2008. "Atrocity Crimes Framing the Responsibility to Protect." *Case Western Reserve Journal of International Law* 40: 111–135.

Schnabel, Albrecht, and Ramesh Thakur. 2000. *Kosovo and the Challenge of Humanitarian Intervention.* Tokyo: UN University Press.

Serrano, Monica. 2010. "Implementing the Responsibility to Protect: The Power of R2P Talk." *Global Responsibility to Protect* 2: 167–177.

Sewell, William H. 2005. *Logics of History: Social Theory and Social Transformation.* Chicago: Chicago University Press.

Seybolt, Taylor B. 2007. *Humanitarian Military Intervention: The Conditions for Success and Failure.* Stockholm: SIPRI.

Smith, Karen E. 2010. *Genocide and the Europeans.* Cambridge: Cambridge University Press.

Snow, David A., E. Burke Rochford Jr., Steven K. Worden, and Robert D. Benford. 1986. "Frame Alignment Processes, Micromobilization, and Movement Participation." *American Sociological Review* 51: 464–481.

Strauss, Ekkehard. 2009. *The Emperor's New Clothes? The United Nations and the Implementation of the Responsibility to Protect.* Baden-Baden: Nomos.

Stritzel, Holger. 2011. "Security, the Translation." *Security Dialogue* 42: 343–355.

Tesòn, Fernando R. 2003. "The Liberal Case for Humanitarian Intervention." In *Humanitarian Intervention: Ethical, Legal and Political Dilemmas*, eds. J.L. Holzgrefe and Robert O. Keohane. Cambridge: Cambridge University Press. 93–129.

Thakur, Ramesh. 2002. "Outlook: Intervention, Sovereignty and the Responsibility to Protect: Experiences from ICISS." *Security Dialogue* 33: 323–340.

Thakur, Ramesh. 2013. "R2P after Libya and Syria: Engaging Emerging Powers." *The Washington Quarterly* 36: 61–76.

Thakur, Ramesh. 2016. "The Responsibility to Protect at 15." *International Affairs* 92: 415–434.

Tourinho, Marcos, Oliver Stuenkel, and Sarah Brockmeier. 2016. " 'Responsibility while Protecting': Reforming R2P Implementation." *Global Society* 30: 134–150.

United Nations. 1999. *Report of the Secretary-General: the Fall of Srebrenica.* A/54/549. 15 November.

United Nations. 2005. *World Summit Outcome.* A/RES/60/1. 16 September.

United Nations. 2009. *Report of the Secretary-General: Implementing the Responsibility to Protect.* A/63/677. 12 January.

United Nations. 2011. *Letter dated 9 November 2011 from the Permanent Representative of Brazil to the United Nations addressed to the Secretary-General.* A/66/551–S/2011/701. 11 November.

Verhoeven, Harry, Ricardo Soares de Oliveira, and Madhan Mohan Jaganathan. 2016. "To Intervene in Darfur, or Not: Re-examining the R2P Debate and Its Impact." *Global Society* 30: 21–37.

Walzer, Michael. 1977. *Just and Unjust Wars: A Moral Argument with Historical Illustrations.* New York: Basic Books.

Weber, Max. 1968 [1922]. *Economy and Society: An Outline of Interpretive Sociology.* New York: Bedminster Press.

Weiss, Thomas G. 2004. "The Sunset of Humanitarian Intervention? The Responsibility to Protect in a Unipolar Era." *Security Dialogue* 35: 135–153.

Weiss, Thomas G. 2016. *Humanitarian Intervention: Ideas in Action.* 3rd ed. Cambridge: Polity.

Welsh, Jennifer M. 2010. "Implementing the "Responsibility to Protect": Where Expectations Meet Reality." *Ethics & International Affairs* 24: 415–430.

Welsh, Jennifer M. 2013. "Norm Contestation and the Responsibility to Protect." *Global Responsibility to Protect* 5: 365–396.

Welsh, Jennifer M. 2019. "Norm Robustness and the Responsibility to Protect." *Journal of Global Security Studies* 4: 53–72.

Wendt, Alexander. 1992. "Anarchy Is what States Make of it: The Social Construction of Power Politics." *International Organization* 46: 391–425.

Wheeler, Nicholas J. 2000. *Saving Strangers: Humanitarian Intervention in International Society.* Oxford: Oxford University Press.

2 Activating R2P

The social construction of Darfur as a test case for saving strangers

They say Darfur is a simple civil war. We are saying it is not a civil war! It is a war against civilians!

Jacky Mamou (founder of the *Collectif Urgence Darfour*)[1]

There was a sense that we are going to be remembered for what we did on Darfur. We did not want Samantha Power to have to add another chapter to her book!

Student activist[2]

Darfur's trajectory from forgotten conflict to global cause

Setting the stage for conflict

A centralized state emerged in Darfur around the year 1500. In 1680, the Fur Sultanate was established and subsequently became one of the pre-eminent states in the region (O'Fahey 2008). To consolidate its power, the successive rulers of the Fur Sultanate adopted Islam and established markets along the east–west and north–south trans-Saharan trade routes. The Fur Sultanate attracted newcomers through a particular system of land concessions, which remains relevant today (Tubiana 2007). The Fur tribe was the dominant force in the sultanate—hence the name *Dar Fur*. However, the territory of the sultanate was divided into different homelands (*dar*), at the helm of which were leaders, usually of the predominant tribe within that area, who were responsible for governing and paying taxes in exchange for collective land ownership. Included within the *dar* were different patches of land (*hawakir*, singular *hakura*), which the sultan could distribute to individuals at his discretion. This system created a hierarchy of tribes in Darfur, as some tribes possessed a homeland, others claimed a *hakura*, and some—for example, the camel nomads in the north—were left landless (Abdul-Jalil 2006). In spite of this hierarchy, the "moral geography" of Darfur allowed for shared land use between nomads and pastoralists regardless of whether they had a homeland (De Waal 2005, 189–190).

In the beginning of the nineteenth century, "the Fur sultanate was the most powerful state within the borders of modern-day Sudan" (Flint and De Waal 2008, 22). However, the advent of Turkish–Egyptian rule in Sudan in 1821 was the beginning of Darfur's fall from being a regional power center to becoming a neglected region on the margins of the larger Sudanese state. It was only during the First World War that Darfur was definitively incorporated into Sudan as a result of the British colonial conquest. Darfur thus became a victim of two persistent realities of the Sudanese state. One was the concentration of power and wealth in Sudan's center, the capital Khartoum (Collins 2008, Chapter 2). In governing Sudan, the British colonial power relied on local elites from the Nile valley. The second and related reality was that the regions on the margins of the Sudanese state were characterized by "institutionalized neglect" on the part of colonial rulers (Daly 2010, Chapter 6). This neglect particularly affected Darfur, where numerous revolts took place in the 1920s and 1930s (Al-Karsani 1987). According to Darfur's former governor, Ahmed Ibrahim Diraige,

> The colonial powers considered Darfur to be a rebellious area. Therefore, they ruled it as a military zone, and most colonialists were military men. They were interested in security rather than development so there were no health services, roads, education.[3]

To govern Darfur, the British applied "indirect rule" through a native administration (Abdul-Jalil et al. 2007).

The marginalization of Darfur, as a byproduct of concentrating power and wealth in the center, continued after Sudan became independent from Britain in 1956. Darfur's share of state development funds was marginal, despite its considerable contribution to the state's export revenues through the export of livestock and gum arabic. Almost no Darfuris were included in Sudan's nascent civil service, leading to their extreme underrepresentation in government structures. Political life in Darfur was organized along tribal lines, which prevented the establishment of a united front. Local leaders were incorporated into Khartoum-based political parties, in particular the Umma Party, which emerged from the 1958 elections as the most popular political force in Darfur (El-Battahani 2009, 57–58). But despite marginalization, Darfur was relatively peaceful, not least because the native administration had devised an effective system of conflict management that was predicated on tribal reconciliation and the payment of blood money (*diyya*) (El-Battahani 2002; Mohamed 2009).

However, violent conflict became more frequent in Darfur in the 1970s and early 1980s during the rule of Jaafar Nimeiry. A contributing factor was Nimeiry's attempt to undermine the native administration and replace it with a Khartoum-controlled bureaucracy (Abdul-Jalil et al. 2007). The native administration's importance as a social institution was preserved, but deprived of resources and political leverage, its ability to manage conflict and govern at the local level was diminished.[4] A second factor was the environmental changes that affected Darfur. As rainfall became less frequent, the desert in North Darfur began encroaching on the nomadic communities living in the area. Compounded with the increase in human and livestock populations, competition for resources and the violent conflict over them became more frequent (Suliman 1996). The famine and the consequent resource depletion prompted many communities in the north, especially the Zaghawa camel herders, to migrate southward—often resulting in conflict with native communities (Young et al. 2005, 26–28). A third conflict-enabling factor was regional politics, which had an impact on local processes. Colonel Muammar Gaddafi, who came to power in Libya in a coup in 1969, used Darfur as a rear base for his interventions in the Chadian civil war (Burr and Collins 2008). The presence of Libyan soldiers contributed to the spread of arms and changed the balance of power among local tribes. As Marchal (2007, 179) noted, "Arab tribes ... benefited from generous military supplies, which helped militarize land disputes and social contradictions in Darfur."

Conflict escalated in the late 1980s. One factor was the 1984 famine, which profoundly disrupted the norms of communal co-existence and increased local disputes, in particular between nomads and farming communities (De Waal 1989). In 1986, after Nimeiry was disposed in a popular uprising, the new government led by Sadiq al-Mahdi from the Umma Party was insolvent and in desperate need of outside support, which Gaddafi's Libya generously provided. In exchange, al-Mahdi turned a blind eye to Libya's activities in Darfur. Thus, Gaddafi used Darfur as a staging ground for his campaigns against Hissène Habré in Chad and even contemplated the idea of annexing Darfur (Prunier 2007, 58–67). To this end, the Libyans promoted pan-Arabism and provided arms to local Arab tribes. This fostered the emergence, in 1987, of the Arab Gathering (*tajammu al-Arabi*), which claimed the supremacy of Arab tribes in Darfur (Flint and De Waal 2008, 47–56). In reaction, the Fur formed self-defense militias with some support from Habré. Conflict in Darfur was also fostered by Sadiq al-Mahdi's efforts to recruit a tribal militia—the so-called *murahalin*—in the fight against John Garang's Sudan People's Liberation Movement/Army (SPLM/A) in the south (Young et al. 2005, 22). Against this background, violence broke out between Arab tribes and the Fur. The war lasted from 1987 to 1989 and caused several thousand casualties (Harir 1994).

In June 1989, General Omar al-Bashir took power in Khartoum in a coup supported by the National Islamic Front (NIF), led by Hassan al-Turabi. The Islamists, including a significant number of Darfuris, soon dominated the civil service, the army, and the police. The Islamists were popular among Darfuri elites, who had been disaffected by the Umma Party (El-Affendi 1991). This helped calm down the situation in Darfur. Another appeasing factor was that Idriss Déby, operating from Darfur with support from Khartoum, took power in N'Djamena in 1990 (Burr and Collins 2008, Chapter 12), ending the Chadian civil war and its spillover into Darfur. These developments notwithstanding, the policy of the NIF regime towards Darfur planted the seeds of the rebellion in the early 2000s. A determinant was the regime's continued of the region neglect in terms of education, health, and infrastructure. The Islamists also favored Arab tribes, relying on them as a counter-insurgency force.[5] Moreover, the government undertook a number of structural reforms geared toward undercutting potential opponents and dividing Darfur into three states—North,

South, and West Darfur—that made the Fur a minority in each of them. These divisions also re-structured the tribal hierarchy, essentially creating a parallel system that depended on patronage from Khartoum.[6] The stage was set for the upcoming conflict.

In the early 2000s, a region-wide rebellion emerged in Darfur (Salih 2006). But Darfur's structural marginalization raises the question of why this occurred then and not earlier. The Darfur insurgency consisted of two distinct rebellions, whose convergence provides the rationale for the outbreak of the conflict. One insurgency had its roots in the farming communities of non-Arab tribes. Under threat since the 1980s, they began to form into tribally-based self-defense militias. Different groups eventually joined forces, rallying around a discourse denouncing the marginalization of Darfur. Thus, three Fur students, Abdelwahid al-Nur, Ahmad Abdel Shafi, and Abdu Abdalla Ismail, founded a clandestine Darfuri-based organization in Khartoum in the 1990s. In 2001, they linked up with Zaghawa and later Masalit leaders and, under the banner Darfur Liberation Front, staged their first attack on an army garrison in February 2002 (Flint and De Waal 2008, 83). In 2003, the group chaired by Abdelwahid was able to step up its attacks owing to training and arms provided by the SPLM, which had been engaged in peace talks with the Sudanese government at the time and wanted to increase its leverage over Khartoum. The SPLM cadres also helped the Darfur rebels write a political manifesto and suggested the group rename itself the Sudan Liberation Movement/Army (SLM/A) (International Crisis Group 2004, 20; Flint and De Waal 2008, 87–94).

The second rebellion originated within the elite politics of Khartoum. At the end of 1999, the Sudanese Islamist movement split when President al-Bashir sided with members of the security cabal to oust their former mentor al-Turabi from the regime (see Chapter 5). Subsequently, al-Bashir purged the government of alleged al-Turabi supporters, many of whom were Zaghawa Islamists from Darfur. According to Roessler (2011, 55),

> the regime conflict took on an ethno-regional dimension and therefore tended to split the Islamic Movement between *awlad al-bahr* (sons of the river), the area along the Nile River Valley from where Sudan's traditional ruling class comes, and *awlad al-gharib* (sons of the west), those from Darfur and other parts of western Sudan.

The split destroyed the network on which the government had previously relied to quell unrest in Darfur. It also led many disaffected Darfuri Islamists to join the Justice and Equality Movement (JEM) (El-Din 2007), which entered the political scene in May 2000 by publishing the Black Book: "a political and economic anatomy of Sudan that detailed the marginalization of most of Sudan's citizens" (Flint and De Waal 2008, 102).[7] JEM, under the leadership of Khalil Ibrahim, later became an armed movement operating from Darfur, although it lagged behind the Sudan Liberation Army in military strength at first.

From a forgotten conflict …

The SLA and JEM irrevocably launched the Darfur rebellion on 25 April 2003 when they jointly attacked the airport of El Fasher. The attack was a resounding success for the rebels. They destroyed half a dozen military aircrafts and captured an air force general. The Sudanese government, controlled by the National Congress Party (NCP), which the NIF had morphed into in the 1990s, realized that the Darfur rebels were a force to be reckoned with. The NCP regime became particularly alert, because at the time it had been making far-reaching concessions to the SPLM at the peace negotiations in Kenya, and it did not want to encourage resistance movements in other peripheral areas. The government could not rely on its army, the Sudanese Armed Forces (SAF), as doing so would have required an unfeasible amount of redeployment and training. A government official described an additional consideration: "40% of the armed forces were from Darfur so the army could not be used in Darfur."[8] The Khartoum security establishment thus opted for "counter-insurgency on the cheap" (De Waal 2004, 25). This meant arming local Arab militias, infamously known as the *janjawid*, and supporting their operations with airstrikes. Many of the *janjawid* came from camel-herding Arab tribes in North Darfur, but as many of Darfur's other Arab tribes were not involved, the *janjawid* were not an all-Arab phenomenon (Haggar 2007).

The aim of the counterinsurgency campaign, which was in full swing within a few months of the rebels' attack on El-Fasher airport, was to destroy the rebels' civilian support base. This gave rise to a scorched earth campaign directed against Darfur's non-Arab population, which led to killings and displacements of massive proportions (De Waal 2004). An international journalist, who crossed into Darfur from the Chadian border in early 2004, described what he saw:

> There was no intact village. It was the same pattern over and over: one village was burned, and its fountains and grain storage facilities were destroyed. This produced black smoke, which was the signal for the people in the surrounding villages to flee.[9]

A Human Rights Watch (2004) report confirmed the systematic and large-scale nature of the violence committed by a combination of militia and SAF troops against the civilian population in Darfur. The violence peaked between mid-2003 and mid-2004, resulting in the destruction of at least 395 mostly non-Arab villages[10] and the displacement of approximately 1.2 million Darfuris[11] during that time. According to the Belgium-based Centre for Research on the Epidemiology of Disasters (CRED), more than 120,000 people died as a direct result of the Darfur conflict between September 2003 and December 2004.[12]

It is difficult to imagine a clearer case for R2P than Darfur during the initial phase of the conflict. Nonetheless, the world ignored Darfur. At the outset of the conflict in 2002, there were only a handful of relief NGOs in the region. There were no media reports in major newspapers, and Darfur was off the radar of the diplomatic community, which had been focusing on the conflict between the SPLM and the Sudanese government. The reason for this lack of attention was not an absence of information. There was, in fact, ample knowledge of the conflict, which would have allowed the international community to react as violence was breaking out or even to prevent the conflict before it escalated. Observers who were familiar with the situation in the 1980s and 1990s knew that Darfur was conducive to mass atrocities, both in the context of intercommunal conflict and region-wide rebellion. Many interviewees in Sudan confirmed this fact. When asked if he had been surprised when the conflict escalated in 2003, a senior police officer who had been stationed in Darfur until 2002 answered, "No! At the time, there was chaos in Darfur. There was a lot of suffering, a lot of tribal fights."[13] Darfuris working for relief organizations were also aware of the precarious situation. According to one expert, "The conflict was predictable. In 2002 I would have said that conflict is about to break out. There was violence and there were indications that something more serious was about to happen."[14] Sudanese researchers, such as Hassan Abdel Abdi and Mohamed Suliman, who were examining the effects of environmental changes, also highlighted the potential for violent conflict in Darfur.[15] However, there is no evidence that international actors gave early warning, let alone acted in response to the growing potential for large-scale conflict in Darfur before 2003. Therefore, as far as conflict prevention is concerned, R2P failed in Darfur.

When violence escalated, a few international NGOs raised red flags. Amnesty International reacted first, partly because its first official mission to Sudan in January 2003 coincided with the outbreak of the Darfur conflict. In a press release on 21 February, Amnesty International spoke of attacks by nomads against farmers and urged the Sudanese government to improve protection and establish an independent commission of inquiry in Darfur.[16] These interventions were followed by a report on 30 June, calling on the government to "attempt to resolve the conflict by discussions among leaders of different ethnic groups and civil society in Darfur" (Amnesty International 2003). The International Crisis Group (ICG) also reacted but with somewhat different language. The lead analyst at the time, Suliman Baldo—a well-known Sudanese human rights advocate with an extensive network of local contacts—recalled, "I regularly received information from Darfuris. They showed me photos taken on cell phones of displaced people, of people on the run. These impressions flowed into our reports."[17] In June 2003, ICG (2003, 1) published a report, warning that the "massive military response threatened by the government in Darfur would take a tremendous toll on the civilian population." A subsequent report, written in the second half of 2003, provided a detailed account of how the government's counterinsurgency campaign operated.

Apart from international NGOs, many Sudanese were trying to raise awareness about the violence in Darfur. Representatives of the rebel movements were calling Sudan researchers and human rights activists with their Thuraya satellite phones. Likewise, members of the Darfuri Diaspora, including some in high academic positions, NGOs, and the UN, were also trying to alert the world. According to Suliman Baldo,

> The shock of the first reports about Darfur in 2003 provoked a major reaction within the Darfur Diaspora. In North America, Europe, and the Middle East, they got organized to make known what was happening in Darfur and to help their communities back home.[18]

Some Darfuris also connected with Western activists, for example Eric Reeves, a professor of English literature at Smith College in Massachusetts. He started writing about the Darfur conflict on his blog as early as November 2003, calling it genocide and comparing it with Rwanda.[19]

However, these efforts were to no avail and, again, not for lack of information. By the fall of 2003, it was clear that mass atrocities were taking place. However, Darfur was absent in the media. Until January 2004 no Western newspaper had published a substantive report about the conflict. Diplomats also continued to see Darfur as a secondary issue. A notable exception was the UN's Resident and Humanitarian Coordinator in Sudan, Mukesh Kapila. Starting in mid-September he sent internal memos to UN headquarters documenting *janjawid* crimes (Kapila 2013). The following month, Kapila travelled to different Western capitals in an attempt to place Darfur on the agenda of the UN Security Council. In November 2003, he spoke publicly about the deteriorating humanitarian situation in Darfur.[20] Kapila eventually found some allies, in particular Jan Egeland, a former Norwegian foreign minister and, at the time, head of the UN Office for the Coordination of Humanitarian Affairs (UNOCHA). Based on Kapila's reports, Egeland stated at a press conference, "the humanitarian situation in Darfur has quickly become one of the worst in the world."[21] In late 2003 and early 2004, he asked the ambassadors of UN Security Council member states to include Darfur on the Council's agenda (Traub 2010, 6).

Neither Kapila's nor Egeland's efforts were successful. In December 2003, UNSG Kofi Annan said he was "alarmed" by reports of abuses against civilians in Darfur,[22] but UN leadership fended off attempts to make Darfur a political issue, viewing it primarily as a humanitarian crisis. A statement by a senior UN official is telling in this regard: "People were dealing with Iraq, Liberia, the north-south peace talks in Sudan.... There was no deliberate covering up, but people were busy elsewhere. There was little discussion about Darfur at the time."[23] Not only the UN Secretariat, but also the members of the UN Security Council refused to consider Darfur. As Jan Egeland explained,

> I met with every presidency [of the Security Council]. And I said, "The worst humanitarian disaster in the world is Darfur, and I am prepared to be invited to the Security Council to talk about it." But the US and UK pursued a line vis-à-vis me and others, which was "We're not going to

have this on the Security Council agenda." The Norwegians took the same view. The three were so obsessed with getting a north-south agreement.

(quoted in Traub 2010, 6)

The US government also failed to prioritize Darfur. Similar to the UN, there were attempts from within the government to do so, but they were rebuffed. The main figure was Roger Winter, a former president of the US Committee for Refugees, who began to work in Sudan in the 1980s and who had forged a personal friendship with SPLM leader John Garang.[24] As Winter explained,

> when Darfur broke out USAID quickly had a humanitarian operation running. We pushed to get this component recognized and for the US government to invest some political capital in these operations. The diplomats were focused on the north–south agreement. But I argued that we can walk and chew gum at the same time.[25]

The willingness to act increased after USAID Administrator Andrew Natsios travelled to Darfur in October 2003. An employee recalls,

> Natsios saw the villages burning. He was fired up and championed a big push from USAID to make Darfur an issue. The pushback came from the State Department, and it prevailed in interagency consultations in early 2004. It was decided to stay focused on the north-south talks and to treat Darfur as a humanitarian crisis.[26]

In sum, despite attempts to draw attention to Darfur, it remained a forgotten conflict. There was no category to make sense of Darfur and, as a result, the broader public was not aware that a problem even existed. Darfur simply did not register as a relevant situation in terms of R2P.

... to global cause

In early 2004, ignorance about the conflict in Darfur began to erode. The role of humanitarian organizations present on the ground in Darfur or in refugee camps in Chad was notable in this regard. These agencies were confronted day-to-day with the destructive impact of the violence, bringing many of their staff members to a breaking point. Moreover, the Sudanese government, which was obviously complicit in the violence, imposed numerous access restrictions on humanitarian workers. A debate ensued within Médecins sans frontières (MSF) over how to deal with this situation. Some advocated for complete withdrawal, while others wanted to go public.[27] As a result, in January and February, MSF published two press releases in which it drew attention to the deteriorating conditions in Darfur. The latter mentioned "catastrophic mortality rates," but refrained from naming the perpetrators of the violence.[28]

Advocacy organizations also became more involved. Human Rights Watch was silent at first, but Amnesty International and ICG kept talking about Darfur. Furthermore, in a newsletter from the first week of January, the Committee of Conscience of the US Holocaust Memorial Museum gave new emphasis to its "genocide warning" for Sudan because of the conflict in Darfur. Moreover, in late February, the Washington Post ran an opinion editorial by Eric Reeves, which it had rejected several times before.[29] Titled "Unnoticed Genocide," the editorial accused the Sudanese government of wanting to exterminate Darfur's African populations. Reeves concluded with the following recommendation, "Immediate plans for humanitarian intervention should begin. The alternative is to allow tens of thousands of civilians to die in the weeks and months ahead in what will be continuing genocidal destruction."[30] Essentially, Reeves linked the situation in Darfur with R2P. However, this effort failed at the time. The turning point only came a few weeks later.

On 19 March 2004, Mukesh Kapila said in an interview with BBC Radio 4,

> I was present in Rwanda at the time of the genocide, and I've seen many other situations around the world and I am totally shocked at what is going on in Darfur. This is ethnic cleansing, this is the world's greatest humanitarian crisis, and I don't know why the world isn't doing more about it.[31]

A few days later, on 22 March, he told news channels, "the only difference between Rwanda and Darfur now is the numbers involved."[32] The idea that something as heinous as the Rwanda genocide—the tenth anniversary of which was to be commemorated only a few weeks later—was again being ignored had a massive impact. Kapila's statement was immediately picked up by newspapers, for example by Nicholas Kristof, who wrote an editorial titled "Ethnic Cleansing, Again." In the following weeks, the media coverage of Darfur skyrocketed. Within five weeks, the *New York Times* and the *Washington Post* alone published ten opinion editorials about Darfur[33]— a level of attention that African foreign policy issues very rarely attain.

Kapila's statement also provoked the kind of reactions from governments and the UN that he had been seeking for months. On 1 April 2004, the EU called for the establishment of a no-fly zone in Darfur (Traub 2010, 7). On 2 April, Jan Egeland was finally allowed to address the UN Security Council, telling members that "a coordinated, 'scorched earth' campaign of ethnic cleansing was taking place" in Darfur, resulting in "widespread atrocities and grave violations of human rights."[34] On 7 April, US President Bush spoke out for the first time and condemned the atrocities in Darfur.[35] On the same day—the tenth anniversary of the Rwanda genocide—Kofi Annan gave a speech at the UN Commission on Human Rights laying out an action plan for genocide prevention. In his speech, he explicitly addressed Darfur:

> It is vital that international humanitarian workers and human rights experts be given full access to the region and to the victims, without further delay.

If that is denied, the international community must be prepared to take swift and appropriate action. By "action" in such situations, I mean a continuum of steps, which may include military action.[36]

Annan's speech, which was more antagonistic towards the Sudanese government than any other statement before, was controversial within the UN. Annan had to assert himself vis-à-vis his staff, many of whom were worried about potential fallout.[37]

In summary, Kapila's public statement comparing Darfur with Rwanda meant that one of the most marginal areas of the world became a global cause that received major coverage in the media and incited policymakers across the world to make strongly worded statements. In essence, Kapila's statement discursively constructed Darfur as a morally relevant issue and, more specifically, a test case for R2P.

Why Darfur became a global cause

Why did the transformation from forgotten conflict to global cause happen in the case of Darfur? More specifically: Why did it occur in March and April 2004, one year after violence escalated? First, Kapila's statement was effective because it employed a "bridge-building metaphor." This concept has been developed in communication studies research, notably in Dervin's (1992, 1999) work on sense making. The general idea is that people overcome cognitive gaps in understanding the world by invoking metaphors in the form of ideas, values, stories, or narratives. Thus, Kapila used the 1994 Rwanda genocide as a bridge-building metaphor, which meant that people began to make sense of the Darfur conflict in the context of Rwanda. The effect of this was powerful: It conveyed a sense of urgency and signaled that passivity would be unacceptable in Darfur (Brunk 2008; Gifkins 2016). By invoking Rwanda, Kapila reminded leaders of their commitment to "never again" let something as horrible as genocide happen and shamed them into speaking up about Darfur. He thus created opportunities for policymakers to redeem themselves for their failures in Rwanda by acting resolutely on Darfur.

The second factor derives from the framing literature cited in Chapter 1: the absence of competing frames creates conducive conditions for frame resonance. Indeed, Darfur was a blank slate for public opinion. This made it easy for a narrative to be grafted onto Darfur. No conflicting interests or interpretation existed that could have challenged Kapila's claim that ethnic violence was engulfing the region. The seclusion and mysteriousness of Darfur made it even more plausible that something as horrible and savage as genocide could take place there.

A third factor pertains to Mukesh Kapila himself. He had experience in Rwanda in the aftermath of the 1994 genocide. As a UN official, he was presumed to be impartial. He was also a representative of the humanitarian community in Sudan, which had firsthand experience of the situation on the ground. Based on this, people attributed high credibility and integrity to Kapila as a person. These characteristics made him an effective norm entrepreneur. Therefore, when he blew the whistle, it was taken more seriously than previous attempts to frame Darfur as genocide.

But what was the role of R2P in making Darfur a morally relevant issue in world politics? R2P prompted people like Kapila, Egeland, and Annan to take up the Darfur issue despite the professional and political risks involved. Darfur became a matter of norm entrepreneurship for them. Kapila and Annan were both marked by the Rwanda genocide and subsequently professed their commitment to the R2P doctrine.[38] Egeland had been committed to human rights from the outset of his career.[39] Moreover, R2P provided the moral code on which Kapila's bridge-building metaphor was based. The power of associating Darfur with Rwanda was derived from using the Rwanda genocide as the prime example of why R2P is a moral necessity. Finally, the activation of R2P enabled a semantic move away from Darfur being seen as humanitarian crisis—something many people see as naturally occurring and thus take a passive position towards—toward being viewed as mass atrocities carried out by a clearly identifiable group of perpetrators that could be stopped with sufficient political will. This was a key aspect of the mass mobilization that came later on.

Making Darfur "meaning-ful": the emergence of a narrative to save strangers

Constitution of the Darfur narrative

To elicit a reaction, Darfur needed to be rendered "meaning-ful" to the broader public. This happened via a meaning-making narrative—the "Darfur narrative"—which came to dominate the public discourse about Darfur in the Western world and for which R2P provided the normative underpinning. The analysis of 233 editorials published about Darfur between 2003 and 2005—the time during which Darfur emerged as a global issue—in 10 major newspapers in North America and Western Europe,[40] revealed four interrelated frames through which the Darfur narrative was constructed.

The first frame pertained to the identities given to victims and perpetrators of violence in Darfur. As explained in Chapter 1, this is a central condition of R2P, which is only relevant if there are both perpetrators and victims of violence (in contrast to victims of natural disasters, for example). Moreover, international law differentiates ethnically targeted violence, such as genocide, from other forms of violence. In editorials about Darfur, most authors used ethnic labels. Thus, the victims of the conflict were the "African" tribes and the "black" or "darker-skinned" populations of Darfur. The ethnicization of identity was even stronger for the perpetrators. Almost without exception, the editorials attributed the violence to the activities of marauding "Arab" *janjawid* militias or referred to it as being supported by the "Arab-dominated" central government in Khartoum. The role of "African" rebel groups in connection with the violence was seldom exposed, while Arab victims of the conflict were almost completely unmentioned. *The Toronto Star* tellingly wrote, "all the victims belong to one race and all the perpetrators to another race."[41] The images of victims and perpetrators also reveal the narrative's gender dimensions. Accordingly, the most victimized group was made up of "black women whose husbands and children have been murdered, and who themselves have been gang raped by the Janjaweed."[42] Stories of rape were very present in reports about Darfur. About half of the editorials mentioned the rape of women and girls. Apart from one single editorial in the *Globe and Mail*, which highlighted the role of Arab women in encouraging atrocities against African tribes,[43] the perpetrators were depicted as men.

The second frame answers the question of why violence happened in Darfur. The logical counterpart to the ethnicization of victims and perpetrators was describing the violence in Darfur as ethnic cleansing or genocide. Around 70 percent of the examined editorials used such labels, suggesting that the violence was caused by Arabs wanting to rid Darfur of its African tribes. Many articles did not provide context and simply presented the violence as a projection of evil. In one editorial, Nicholas Kristof challenged the conservative TV anchor Bill O'Reilly to accompany him on a trip to Darfur. He wrote, "You'll have to leave your studio, Bill. You'll encounter pure evil. If you're like me, you'll be scared. If you try to bully some of the goons in Darfur, they'll just hack your head off."[44] A number of authors acknowledged that rebel groups instigated the Darfur conflict, but the violence they were describing was usually dissociated from the civil war and linked instead to the government's ethnic cleansing campaign.

The third frame compared the conflict in Darfur with episodes of violence elsewhere. This comparison closely relates to the bridge-building metaphor that was crucial in the initial activation of R2P. Authors systematically associated Darfur with previous genocides, in particular the 1994 Rwanda genocide. Tellingly, Roméo Dallaire, the famous force commander of the UN peacekeeping mission in Rwanda, wrote several editorials titled "Looking at Darfur, Seeing Rwanda." Similar to Mukesh Kapila, he claimed,

> I've seen it all happen before ... Sudan, an underdeveloped, orphan nation, with no links to colonial masters of its past, is essentially being left to its own devices. The Islamic Janjaweed militias of Darfur, with the complicit approval of the government, are bent on ridding the region of its residents, primarily black Africans.[45]

Moreover, many authors argued that the legacy of Rwanda, and the international community's inaction during the genocide there, created a moral responsibility to stop violence in Darfur. One of Samantha Power's editorials was called "Remember Rwanda, but Take Action on Sudan."[46] Many editorials also compared the violence in Darfur with the civil war in southern Sudan, presenting it as the latest episode of atrocities perpetrated by the Sudanese government against its people: "It perfected the art of ethnic cleansing in its long war against the country's southern rebels, and it has expertly repeated the process in Darfur."[47]

The narrative's fourth frame pertains to remedies to the violence in Darfur. Here, the link with R2P was most explicit. Drawing on a recurrent theme among proponents of R2P, the vast majority of editorials emphasized the international community's need to pressure the Sudanese government into changing the situation in Darfur. A wide range of measures was proposed for this purpose: travel bans, asset freezes, arms embargos, economic sanctions, and referring the situation to the ICC. A *Washington Post* editorial described the logic behind these recommendations,

> Time and again, Sudan's dictatorship has proved that it will bend to pressure: It expelled Osama bin Laden, it negotiated peace with the country's southern rebels, and it has improved humanitarian access to Darfur's camps. This time will be no exception, provided that the pressure is sufficient.[48]

Many editorials also advocated for direct action to protect the victims of violence in Darfur, including by deploying peacekeepers. Some authors also advocated for the establishment of a no-fly zone and humanitarian corridors. In contrast, few observers supported peace talks, arguing that the government would use them as a diversion:

> For 15 years, the international community has negotiated with this regime, soft-pedaling human-rights concerns in order to keep it at the negotiating table. This has played directly into the hands of the government's strategy, which has been to maintain endless negotiations as a means to deflect international pressure.[49]

In spite of this, calls for a full-fledged humanitarian intervention were relatively rare. Of 233 editorials, only 15 explicitly called for a non-consensual military intervention in Darfur, while four of them explicitly talked about the need for regime change in Sudan.[50]

Understanding the resonance of the Darfur narrative

The Darfur narrative was successful on many accounts. It ensured continuous media coverage of a region that did not normally receive attention in the mainstream media of North America and Western Europe. For five years, from 2004 to 2009, Darfur was one of the most reported African foreign policy issues. At certain moments, it was on par with the world's most prominent foreign policy issues.

One approach is to attribute the resonance of the Darfur narrative to the contributions of norm entrepreneurs: people with a special commitment to R2P who saw Darfur as a test case for putting R2P into practice. Darfur's early promoters—Kapila, Egeland, and Annan—have already been mentioned. Another was *New York Times* journalist Nicholas Kristof, who has long promoted human rights causes and is sensitive to the issue of genocide, in part because of his Armenian origins.[51] He has written prolifically about Darfur and played an important part in diffusing the Darfur narrative. Likewise, Nat Hentoff—a socially conservative columnist, strong advocate for humanitarian intervention, and supporter of the US-led war in Iraq in 2003 on humanitarian grounds—perpetuated the narrative in his many *Washington Times* editorials. Moreover, representatives of the NGOs explicitly mandated to promote R2P wrote about Darfur, drawing attention to the need to protect civilians. Some examples are John Prendergast from the International Crisis Group and, later, the Enough Project and James Smith from the British genocide-prevention NGO Aegis Trust. Similar contributions stemmed from other well-known R2P advocates, such as Roméo Dallaire, Samantha Power, Gayle Smith, and Susan Rice. These individuals applied their agency to promote the Darfur narrative.

Going beyond agency, aspects related to the quality of the narrative itself are also important in understanding the resonance of the Darfur issue. Chapter 1 laid out four factors of framing resonance. As for the first—completeness—the examined editorials indeed revealed that Darfur was comprehensively framed. This included a clear-cut causal responsibility: The Darfur conflict constituted a genocide comparable with Rwanda that was committed by Arabs against Africans. Treatment responsibility was straightforward as well: Darfuris needed to be saved through an external intervention. An activist accurately stated, "People viewed Darfur as a problem to be fixed. An issue they could do something about."[52] The completeness of the narrative ensured that Darfur was portrayed as an unambiguous problem, for which the actions of an identifiable group were responsible and for which feasible remedies existed.

As for the second resonance factor—simplicity—Darfur is a case in point. Many of the activists confirmed that the narrative's simplicity was crucial as it set Darfur apart from other conflicts.[53] A US-based journalist said,

> In sum, the conflict in Darfur, although extremely complicated, could be boiled down to a story of good guys and bad guys. Other places, like the DRC, were closer to anarchy and therefore did not lend themselves to the same black-and-white narratives. In comparison to Darfur it is much harder to explain in one sentence what happens in the DRC.[54]

Jacky Mamou made a similar argument:

> Why did we succeed in making Darfur a cause célèbre? Because it was a simple case! If you take what is happening in the Congo, where there are many more people killed than in Darfur, there is a weak state in Congo, there is a multiplicity of interveners, and there is old rancor between ethnic groups etc. This is confusing. Darfur is a simple thing, although they tell us that it is more complex. In reality, what is it? It's a strong central state

consisting of an Arab minority in the Nile Valley that suppresses and massacres the inhabitants of the periphery that were unfortunate enough to rise up. And instead of fighting the rebels, they went after the civilian population. It is an exemplary case.[55]

The third resonance factor—coherence—was also present. As explained above, the framing of the Darfur conflict was exceptionally uniform and coherent, despite the appearance of two competing narratives in the media in the beginning. The first portrayed the conflict as a struggle instigated by Islamist rebels against a government that was cooperating with the US to counter international terrorism. A writer from the conservative *The Washington Times* put this position forward in a May 2004 editorial when the Darfur conflict was not yet conclusively framed.[56] However, only four days later, this frame was eclipsed by one of Nat Hentoff's editorials that made the usual calls for pressure on Khartoum to end the government-orchestrated genocide in Darfur.[57] The pro-Khartoum position was never again articulated in the period examined, not in *The Washington Times* or in any other newspaper. The second competing narrative highlighted the unintended consequences of international calls for humanitarian intervention. This position came to the fore in a number of editorials by British commentators who had opposed the 2003 Iraq war,[58] but it never significantly reverberated beyond this milieu. Although there are some differences between countries and news sources and across time, the vast majority of editorials (218 out of 233) were consistent with, or at least did not contradict the prevailing Darfur narrative that called for an end to genocide. The coherence of the framing effort meant that the nature of the problem was clear and ensured that advocacy groups did not have to justify their position vis-à-vis opposing views.

The fourth resonance factor goes beyond the narrative itself and is concerned with its anchoring in existing interpretative frames and political interests. Thus, the Darfur narrative resonated with the prevailing discursive and normative structure along five dimensions. First, the Darfur narrative invoked Orientalist images of the Middle East and of Sudan in particular. Two themes dominate colonial accounts of Sudan. One is the early 1880s revolt of the Mahdi, who was described in the British media as a formidable but, ultimately, subversive force whose defiance had to be quelled. In 1885, when the British hero General Gordon was defeated and killed by the Mahdi's forces in Khartoum, shockwaves went through the British public. It strongly supported the re-conquest of Sudan in 1898 to avenge Gordon's death at the hands of rebellious desert fighters.[59] But even before that, Sudan had been well known to the British public from British anti-slavery activist campaigns. The activists led a "war on slavery." Sudan, where the practice was common in the nineteenth century, was one of their foremost battlegrounds. The activists denounced the northern Sudanese traders and made their case for ending the slave trade by force—a call that the British government eventually heeded (Scroggins 2003). The editorials about Darfur indirectly tapped into these Orientalist images of Sudan. For example, James Smith of Aegis Trust remarked that the "enslavement of blacks by Arabs in Sudan is as old as history."[60] In the collective consciousness, Sudan is a place where horrible, inhuman things happen, which made the notion that genocide was happening in Darfur plausible.

Second, the Darfur narrative aligned itself with colonialist stereotypes about Africa. Postcolonial scholars have long criticized the Western tendency to view African societies and politics primarily as a function of the struggle between supposedly homogenous ethnic groups (e.g., Mamdani 1996). Such "tribalism" is particularly prevalent in media reports about Africa, which, according to Carruthers (2003), tend to reify perceptions of "African savagery" versus "Western humanitarianism." These images are frequently invoked to understand armed conflict in Africa as battles between ethnic groups that hold deep-seated hatred against each other (Fair 1993; Neumann 2004). The Darfur narrative aligned itself with these images by framing Darfur as a conflict between tribes (Campbell 2007). The implication is that the conflict was rooted in naturally irreconcilable or even biological differences between ethnic groups in Darfur. By drawing on these long-established interpretive criteria, the Darfur narrative facilitated moral and analytical clarity, which contributed to its resonance.

The third alignment pertained to the "war on terror." Since the September 11 attacks, the general public in Western societies has been exposed to extensive media coverage of Islamic terrorism. The Darfur narrative tapped into this discourse by systematically qualifying the perpetrators of the violence as Arab or Islamic, creating resonance with the political and discursive context of the war on terror.

Fourth, when the Darfur conflict broke out, Sudan was already a public policy issue in the US and, to a lesser extent, in European countries like France. With anti-slavery groups and Christian evangelists at its helm, an advocacy campaign emerged in the 1990s that drew attention to the civil war in southern Sudan (Hertzke 2004, Chapter 7). Its framing was unmistakable: The Arab Islamic north was deliberately targeting African Christian populations in the south, in order to maintain their exclusive grip on power, spread Islam, and steal the southern oil. The similarities with the Darfur narrative are obvious. Thus, Darfur was grafted onto the South Sudan issue. Sudan was the place where Arabs victimize Africans. In this context, it was entirely plausible that another incidence of this pattern was playing out in Darfur and that African victims again needed protection from Arab oppressors.

Fifth, the Darfur narrative aligned itself with discourses about gender roles in war. According to the narrative, the impact of the violence was different for men and women: "Villages have been burned, crops uprooted, men murdered, women raped, and children abducted."[61] Other authors provided horrific details of the rape of women and girls, often citing the use of rape as a weapon of war. These stories confirmed deeply rooted perceptions of gender roles in war— Women are victims of wars fought by men. According to Carpenter (2006, 31), these gender essentialisms translate into a prescriptive claim: "If women can be assumed to be civilians and are innocent and vulnerable, it is they in particular (along with children, the elderly, and the disabled) who must be protected." This was precisely the message that many editorials conveyed about Darfur. The frequent rape references—roughly half of the editorials mentioned sexual violence in Darfur—gave the public a well-known framework through which to interpret the violence in Darfur. It also galvanized women's rights activists and organizations that were working on gender issues and the impact of armed conflict on women.

Tackling a "problem from hell": the emergence of the Save Darfur movement

Save Darfur! The genesis of the Darfur advocacy movement

The construction of Darfur as a pressing moral issue laid the foundation for a subsequent step in the norm activation process: the institutionalization of the discourse on Darfur in the form of an advocacy movement. How did the Darfur advocacy movement emerge? Who participated in it and why? What was the role of R2P?

From the outset, private activists like Eric Reeves and NGOs like Amnesty International and ICG worked to raise awareness about the conflict in Darfur. However, an overarching advocacy movement only emerged in the summer of 2004, a few months after Darfur had become a global issue. It was, therefore, a consequence rather than a cause of Darfur's emergence as a pressing public policy issue. The first push came from within the South Sudan activist community, which was already mobilized and saw the Darfur conflict as a repetition of Khartoum's brutalization of southerners. The activists staged protests and mobilized political networks, which led to the unanimous adoption on 22 July of a joint resolution by the US House of Representatives and Senate declaring Darfur a genocide (Hamilton and Hazlett 2007).

Beyond South Sudan, a new advocacy alliance emerged around Darfur, led by Ruth Messinger, the president of the American Jewish World Service, a charity associated with Reform Judaism—a progressive-liberal Jewish denomination. Together with the US Holocaust Memorial Museum, she initiated a Darfur emergency summit for Jewish organizations interested in the issue. The summit took place on 14 July 2004, with the ICG's John Prendergast and Holocaust survivor Elie Wiesel as keynote speakers and representatives of more than 40 NGOs in attendance. The outcome was the foundation of the Save Darfur Coalition (SDC), whose members issued on 2 August a statement of unity that

> the emergency in Sudan's western region of Darfur presents the starkest challenge to the world since the Rwanda genocide in 1994. A government-backed Arab militia known as Janjaweed has been engaging in campaigns to displace and wipe out communities of African tribal farmers.[62]

In an accompanying call to action, the coalition members appealed to "people of conscience everywhere to take any and all actions permitted by each individual's and organization's ability and constraint to encourage worldwide efforts to stop the displacement and end the crimes against humanity."[63] By September 2004, over 100 organizations had signed up to the SDC Unity Statement.[64]

In the fall of 2004, the Darfur advocacy campaign gained momentum and became one of the most popular social causes among students, with volunteer advocacy groups springing up across North American college campuses. These groups were loosely connected as chapters of Students Take Action Now: Darfur (STAND). Many of the student leaders benefited from the support of well-known personalities, who themselves were active in the Darfur campaign. For example, Gayle Smith helped the Swarthmore College students that founded the Genocide Intervention Network (GI-Net).[65] Through continuous rallies, protests, and lobbying as well as writing letters and opinion editorials, the advocates ensured that Darfur was omnipresent in public debates. These efforts were supported by celebrities like George Clooney, Mia Farrow, Don Cheadle, and Matt Damon, who had adopted Darfur as their cause. Consequently, by 2006, the Darfur advocacy movement had become the largest foreign affairs social movement in North America since the anti-apartheid campaign in the 1980s (Flint and De Waal 2008, 183).[66]

In Western Europe, Darfur did not achieve the same resonance, and the Darfur advocacy movement there was not institutionalized to the degree that it was in the US. However, in the UK and France, significant advocacy movements developed around Darfur. In the UK, although NGOs like Amnesty International and Oxfam led individual campaigns on Darfur, a coordinated advocacy push emerged in 2005. On 31 March of that year, a number of British NGOs launched the Protect Darfur Campaign, with a call by over 100 MPs for a peace-enforcement operation to protect people in Darfur. The campaign was financed by the Pears Foundation—a Jewish family foundation—and included an alliance similar to the one in the US, which saw Jewish groups, human rights NGOs, and some members of the Sudanese Diaspora joining forces to protect Darfur.

In France, the Collectif Urgence Darfour was set up on 8 February 2005 at the initiative of Jacky Mamou, former president of the humanitarian organization Médecins du Monde. The French movement also attracted public intellectuals who were early supporters of humanitarian intervention. Bernard-Henri Lévy, Bernard Kouchner, and André Glucksman all provided leverage for the Darfur campaign, which gained momentum in 2006 and culminated in the context of the 2007 French presidential elections.

Outside North America and Western Europe, activism on Darfur was more limited. In Africa, an amalgam of about 50 mostly human rights NGOs that were concerned about the violence in Darfur formed the Darfur Consortium in 2004. Likewise, in 2008, civil society organizations from 18 Arab countries formed the Arab Coalition for Darfur. Both groups were autonomous creations, although the US-based SDC provided advice and significant financial support.[67] The Consortium and the Arab Coalition actively made their voices heard, but they did not reach a critical mass and their influence was ultimately limited. Their greatest constraint was that the discursive context of their actions was not conducive to the rise of a mass movement. Public opinion in the Arab world, to the extent that it was aware of Darfur, largely saw it through the lens of the US-led war in Iraq, which had been justified with human rights arguments (Høigilt 2010). In African countries, South Africa in particular, the discourse on Darfur vacillated between human rights and anti-imperialism (Nathan 2011), which did not resonate with the Darfur narrative being promoted by the activists.

Understanding the Save Darfur movement

What motivated different organizations and individuals to adopt Darfur as their cause? This section argues that the common denominator and driving force of the movement was a normative commitment to saving strangers. The core R2P norm was thus the rallying cry of the Darfur advocacy movement and the glue that held its different parts together.

Saving strangers as a matter of faith and identity

Jewish organizations were an important driving force of the movement in North America, the UK, and France. Darfur struck a chord, not because of the Arab and Islamic character of the conflict's protagonists, but rather because it resonated with a collective commitment to prevent genocide. Revealing in this regard is the speech given by Elie Wiesel at the founding meeting of the Save Darfur Coalition:

> As a Jew who does not compare any event to the Holocaust, I feel concerned and challenged by the Sudanese tragedy. We must be involved. How can we reproach the indifference of non-Jews to Jewish suffering if we remain indifferent to another people's plight?
>
> It happened in Cambodia, then in former Yugoslavia, and in Rwanda, now in Sudan. Asia, Europe, Africa: Three continents have become prisons, killing fields, and cemeteries for countless innocent, defenseless populations. Will the plague be allowed to spread?
>
> "Lo taamod al dam réakha" is a Biblical commandment. "Thou shall not stand idly by the shedding of the blood of thy fellow man." The word is not "akhikha," thy Jewish brother, but "réakha," thy fellow human being, be he or she Jewish or not. All are entitled to live with dignity and hope. All are entitled to live without fear and pain.
>
> Not to assist Sudan's victims today would for me be unworthy of what I have learned from my teachers, my ancestors and my friends, namely that God alone is alone: His creatures must not be....
>
> Should the Sudanese victims feel abandoned and neglected, it would be our fault—and perhaps our guilt.
>
> That's why we must intervene.[68]

The speech shows that Wiesel had anchored the project to save strangers in both Jewish faith and Jewish group identity. Wiesel demands solidarity, not because the victims are fellow believers, but because they are human beings. This is tantamount to the universalization of humanity, which lies at the core of R2P, as explained in Chapter 1. On the same grounds, Aaron Dorfman and Ruth Messinger (2010, 61) put forward "a Jewish argument for the responsibility to protect." Accordingly, Jewish text and tradition stipulate:

> the principle that Jews must not only refrain from committing crimes of violence against others or from being complicit in those crimes as passive bystanders but also that Jews must actively intervene when confronted with the knowledge that such crimes are being committed. While many of the laws and stories that constitute this literature of intervention are cast narrowly around protecting Jewish victims, we argue ... that the overall ethic is a universal one and, certainly in our time, must be universally applied.
>
> (Dorfman and Messinger 2010, 61)

Another argument is that, having lived through the horrors of the Holocaust, Jews should work to prevent other peoples from falling victim to genocide. This was crucial for their Darfur engagement. According to a Jewish member of STAND:

> The notion of "never again" has particular resonance since the Holocaust for obvious reasons. Traditionally, "never again" was applied to Jews exclusively, instilling a sense of both resistance and victimhood in the Jewish community. Progressively, the notion of "never again" underwent a process of universalization in the sense it provided a moral argument not just to prevent genocide against Jews, but genocide against any people. This development underpins Jewish activism on behalf of Darfur and for the prevention of genocide more generally.[69]

Rabbi Harold Schulweis articulated this vision in one of his sermons:

> What have we to do with a people we do not know, in a land we have not visited? What have we to do with people of another faith, another culture, another civilization? Have we Jews not sufficient burdens of our own? ...
>
> We Jews see with ancient eyes. We have seen the torture, the starvation, the death by disease, the rapes, the abandonment by the civilized world before. We Jews possess a terrible knowledge, an awesome wisdom we gained not out of books, but out of our own bodies. A knowledge out of the testimony of numbers seared into the skin of living human beings and the stench of burned flesh. We see with ancient eyes: We are eye witnesses to the consequences of the callousness of lethal silence. We offer testimony to the morbid symptoms of apathy, the moral laryngitis that strangles the voice of protest.
>
> With ancient eyes we see Darfur with a shock of recognition. We experience a collective *deja vu* even as we speak.[70]

The idea that, by virtue of their history, Jews have a special obligation to prevent genocide had gained momentum, particularly among progressive Jews. Referring to Raphael Lemkin, the initiator of the Genocide Convention, one activist remarked: "The connection between Darfur and the Holocaust is genocide! Lemkin codified the lesson of the Holocaust in the Genocide Convention, not the Holocaust Convention! We have an obligation to act to prevent future genocides."[71] One expression of a special Jewish responsibility to prevent genocide is the US Holocaust Memorial Museum's former Committee on Conscience, now the Simon-Skjodt Center for the Prevention of Genocide. The Committee was indeed one of the most active players in the Darfur campaign.

Other religious communities were active in the Darfur campaigns as well. For Christian activists, the principle motivation for engaging in the Darfur campaigns was likewise related to the Saving Strangers Norm, even if it was cast as a matter of faith rather than one of group identity. As one Christian activist said,

> For Christian groups, core values of peace and justice are at stake in Darfur. Showing compassion and solidarity for the victims of Darfur is a testimony to the decency of humanity.... The situation in Darfur is precarious. There are vulnerable populations that need to be protected. This captured people's imagination.[72]

Particularly revealing is a booklet on "biblical reflections on the mission to end genocide in Darfur and beyond." It served as the Christian companion to John Prendergast and Don Cheadle's book on Darfur, *Not on Our Watch*, and prominently referenced Pope Benedict XVI's support for R2P. As a metaphor for why Christians should care about Darfur, the authors cited the Bible parable of the Good Samaritan who saved a stranger lying injured by the side of the road after other travelers had passed by without helping:

> Jesus' point is, of course, that loving our neighbor is costly. Those passing by didn't want to get their hands dirty.... "Who knows?" they might have asked, "This naked victim might not be one of 'Us'. We'll have to confront discomforting realities of race religion, and ethnic conflict. Our own neighbors might think us 'unclean' ('sellouts') if we touch him...." It was the Samaritan, actually, (the "outsider" ...) who overcame prejudice and intervened. He risked ethnic insult to help out. He also sacrificed his money, time, and energy—not to mention his day's forgone business opportunity. He was, in other words, willing to get "stuck" with another guy's problem at significant cost to himself.
>
> (Leffel and Mefford 2008, 11)

The lesson for Christians in North America and Western Europe was that, despite the temptation to be passers-by, they must not ignore the fate of a far-away people. Instead, they must become Good Samaritans and save strangers in Darfur: "Inevitably, we'll be confronted by our own responsibility to act for

Darfur. We are stewards of great wealth that can be used to relieve suffering. God trusts us to use it wisely" (Leffel and Mefford 2008, 13).

Tackling a "problem from hell"

R2P played an important role for student activists as well. Many of them referred to Samantha Power's book, in which she provided a detailed account of the US government's lack of response to situations of genocide in the twentieth century. She exposed how policymakers treated genocide as a "problem from hell," which they ostensibly could do nothing about. The purpose of the book, in line with R2P, was to challenge this notion and to galvanize action to prevent genocide. This provided a theory of change, which inspired many student activists. They referred to *A Problem from Hell* as a "huge motivator"[73] and even "our bible."[74] The Darfur advocacy movement thus represented an attempt to tackle a problem from hell as a way of building a world where genocide would be eradicated.

This calling resonated beyond the student advocacy community. Underlying it is a strong belief that genocide represents the ultimate stigma. According to one activist,

> I got involved because genocide is a peculiar type of horrible, the most heinous of acts that we have to do something against. In genocide, people are wiped out for who they are. Genocide calls into question the very identity of human beings. Even the most callous of hearts will recognize the evil of genocide.[75]

Insofar as genocide diminishes humanity, acting on Darfur would be a way to redeem humanity:

> Darfur is highly symbolic of an important question. If you exterminate all the Darfuris, about 6 million people, it is not at all relevant geopolitically. It's just a population of very poor farmers with no natural resources, nothing. You can kill them without anything. So what do you do? It's like exterminating the Jews from the Polish *Städtl*. It's not relevant geopolitically which means that one is confronted with one's humanity. Humanity is confronted with its own humanity. And the activists are confronted with a question that goes beyond the realm of the political. What do you do when a people that do not count at all on the plant are threatened of extermination? That's the basic question that Darfur posed.[76]

Related to the recognition that genocide represents the ultimate evil is a sense of guilt for not having done more to prevent previous genocides, above all the one in Rwanda. The discourse on Darfur tapped into this feeling and generated energy for the advocacy movement. One student leader at Harvard University recounted how he got involved in the Darfur campaign:

I remember that in sixth gradé I heard about the Holocaust. We read Anne Frank and we went to the Holocaust Memorial Museum with my class. I remember that I was moved by the inability of mankind to prevent genocide. But this sentiment was tucked away and I slept through Rwanda. I later found out about Rwanda and felt guilty for ignoring it. During my first semester at the Kennedy School, we watched a video about Rwanda in our ethics class. That was the moment! I stood up and asked fellow students if they wanted to do something about the ongoing genocide. Out of this group, the Harvard Darfur Action Group emerged.[77]

Darfur thus offered an opportunity for redemption for failing to take action on Rwanda, which had been defined a posteriori as the litmus test of R2P. This mechanism was important for celebrities as well. In a phone interview, Mia Farrow, who was a strong advocate and travelled to Darfuri refugee camps in Chad many times, explained her involvement:

I didn't know about the Rwandan genocide when it occurred. I have a private feeling that haunts me, a sense of human failure that I didn't know about it and that I didn't do anything to prevent it.... During the tenth anniversary of the genocide, I read an op-ed piece by Samantha Power. This was a jaw-dropping moment! I learned about horrible violations in a remote place that I have never heard of. Through my role as UNICEF ambassador I travelled to the region for the first time a few months later.[78]

Test case

Beyond genocide, many organizations and individual activists got involved because they saw Darfur as a test case for R2P. At stake was whether R2P was merely rhetoric or whether the international community would succeed in protecting vulnerable civilians in Darfur.[79] This frame made Darfur a priority cause for norm entrepreneurs, who were concerned with the overarching project of de-legitimizing the use of mass atrocities as a political instrument. Jacky Mamou, for example, described the purpose of his work,

I've always believed the right to intervene and the responsibility to protect was an essential question. I got engaged for Kosovo, for Chechnya when I worked for Médecins du monde at the time. So naturally I got engaged for Darfur as well.[80]

R2P resonated particularly with celebrities, who were cognizant of their impact in the media and felt that their status bestowed them a special responsibility to help vulnerable populations. Mia Farrow is the most telling example of this. Through her encounters with Darfuris in displaced camps, she internalized the notion of the responsibility to protect, both on a collective and personal level:

When I travelled to Darfur for the first time in 2004, I was given an amulet by a Darfuri woman by the name of Halima. Halima wore the amulet around her neck when she was attacked and she gave it to me to tell the world what happened to the people of Darfur. This eye-to-eye contact with Halima was really important for me.[81]

In a foreword to a book on Darfur, Farrow elaborated on what the encounter triggered in her:

On the plane heading home I tried to process all I had seen and learned. The family mantra "with knowledge comes responsibility," took on a new meaning. An inescapable knowledge of atrocities and immeasurable suffering was now mine. But what could *I do?* At this point, I knew only that I must honor my pledge to Halima and other courageous survivors and do my utmost to "tell the world what is happening" in Darfur, with the hope that good people everywhere, if only they knew, would rise to put an end to the killing.... My deepest conviction is that we have both a responsibility to remember and a responsibility to protect.
(quoted in Hamilton 2011, xi, emphasis in the original)

R2P was also important for George Clooney, who consistently advocated for action on Darfur. In September 2006, Clooney addressed the UN Security Council to convince members to authorize a robust peacekeeping force in Darfur. His statement revealed that he essentially saw Darfur as a test case for R2P:

I'm here to represent the voices of the people who cannot speak for themselves. And from our side, we're not so naive either. We know how difficult a task this is. We understand how many issues are in front of you this moment, each needing great care and attention. But you are the UN and this is a task that you have been given. You have to decide what's most urgent. You have responsibility to protect.

In the time that we're here today, more women and children will die violently in the Darfur region than in Iraq, Afghanistan, Palestine, Israel, or Lebanon.... It is the first genocide of the 21st century. And if it continues unchecked it will not be the last.

In many ways, it's unfair, but it is, nevertheless, true that this genocide will be on your watch. How you deal with it will be your legacy, your Rwanda, your Cambodia, your Auschwitz. We were brought up to believe that the UN was formed to ensure that the Holocaust could never happen again. We believe in you so strongly. We need you so badly.[82]

Casting Darfur as a test case for R2P made it appealing in philanthropic circles as well. The Darfur advocacy movement especially benefited from newly established foundations that worked specifically on the prevention of mass atrocities. The most important actor was Humanity United, led by Pam Omidyar. Not only did Humanity United become the major funder of the Darfur advocacy movement, supporting organizations like the Save Darfur Coalition and GI-Net, but Darfur became a matter of "personal conviction" for Pam Omidyar herself.[83] She became active in the campaigns, for example, by joining a hunger strike for Darfur initiated by Mia Farrow[84] and by forging personal relationships with those leading the advocacy effort, in particular Samantha Power and John Prendergast.[85]

In sum, the core idea of R2P—that mass atrocities are morally wrong, regardless of where or against whom they are committed, and that global citizens have a responsibility to prevent them from occurring—provided the common denominator of the Darfur advocacy movement. It motivated different groups to get involved and provided a common cause with which all proponents of the movement could identify and focus their efforts.

Chapter findings

Three findings can be identified in concluding this chapter. First, Darfur showed that situations of mass violence do not automatically register as morally relevant. As a case in point, during the most violent phase of the conflict in late 2003 and early 2004, the world largely ignored Darfur. Moral relevance needed to be "activated," and the core R2P played a crucial role in this regard. It provided a moral code for early advocates and a powerful interpretive frame, as exemplified by the framing of Darfur as another Rwanda.

Second, the activation of the R2P norm in Darfur involved several cascading steps. It started with a few early advocates framing of the situation as a "problem" of saving strangers. This elucidated a reaction, as a few gatekeeper journalists, NGO representatives, and policymakers took up the issue. Press coverage increased, leading to the formation of a discursive narrative, through which the broader public could make sense of the issue in the context R2P. The formation of advocacy campaigns entrenched and amplified this process, to the extent that the norm became the primary prism through which the Darfur issue was viewed.

Third, the endeavor to save strangers in Darfur became more compelling and more sustainable because it was embedded in a comprehensive discursive narrative. Such a narrative is essential in rendering far-away conflicts meaningful to public opinion. To enhance its impact, the narrative should be comprehensive, yet simple. It should provide unequivocal answers to the questions: Who should be saved? Why should they be saved? Who should save them? The narrative's resonance increases if it aligns with pre-existing narratives, normative projects, and interpretive categories.

Notes

1 Interview, Paris, November 2011 (interview in French, author's translation).
2 Interview (AT), Washington, DC, March 2010.
3 Interview with Ahmed Ibrahim Diraige, London, April 2011.

4 These findings are partly derived from a research project on the role of the native administration in Darfur that the author worked on as a researcher for the UN Mission in Sudan (UNMIS) in 2007. Brosché and Rothbart (2013, Chapter 4) also reflected on local elite conflicts as a contributing factor to violent conflict in Darfur.

5 Interview with a Darfuri academic (BT), Khartoum, November 2010.

6 For background on the genesis of the Darfur conflict in the 1990s, see Flint and de Waal (2008) and Prunier (2007).

7 The book *Darfur and the Crisis of Governance* by Hassan and Ray (2009) includes an English translation and a review of the Black Book by Abdullahi Osman el-Tom (2009), a leading member of JEM.

8 Interview (CB), Khartoum, November 2010.

9 Interview (DL), Zurich, November 2011 (interview in German, author's translation).

10 This refers to the number of villages destroyed until 2 August 2004. The number is derived from the US Department of State's Humanitarian Information Unit, which has compiled maps of destroyed villages in Darfur since 2004. Map available at https://commons.wikimedia.org/wiki/File:Villages_destroyed_in_the_Darfur_Sudan_2AUG2004.jpg (accessed 8 June 2019). Similar numbers are provided in an Amnesty International (2004) report published on 1 July 2004.

11 As of 1 July 2004, the UN Office of the Resident's Coordinator in its Darfur Humanitarian Profile No. 4 counted just over one million internally displaced persons (IDPs) in Darfur, in addition to 170,000 Darfuri refugees in Chad. Report available at https://reliefweb.int/sites/reliefweb.int/files/resources/B02B487627CD5CFB49256EF60004EDEE-unrc-sud-1jul.pdf (accessed 8 June 2019).

12 Numbers of excess deaths taken from Table 5 (Period 2+3) in Degomme and Guha-Sapir's (2010, 298) Lancet article about patterns of mortality in Darfur. For the whole period of examination, i.e., September 2003 to December 2008, the authors estimated excess deaths from the Darfur conflict at 300,000. While there are different and frequently contested death numbers, the US Government Accountability Office (2006), having examined various sources of mortality data, concluded that the numbers cited by CRED are the most reliable.

13 Interview (CU), Khartoum, December 2010 (interview in Arabic, interpretation into English by author's research assistant).

14 Interview (CJ), Khartoum, November 2010.

15 Hassan Abdel Ati confirmed this in an interview with the author held in Khartoum in November 2010. Mohamed Suliman published several works on the environment-conflict nexus in Sudan, including an analysis of Darfur (Suliman 1996).

16 Amnesty International, "Sudan: Urgent Call for Commission of Inquiry in Darfur as Situation Deteriorates," press release, 21 February 2003, www.amnesty.org.uk/press-releases/sudan-urgent-call-commission-inquiry-darfur-situation-deteriorates (accessed 8 June 2019).

17 Interview with Suliman Baldo, New York, March 2011.

18 Interview with Suliman Baldo, New York, March 2011.

19 Eric Reeves, "The Accelerating Catastrophe in Darfur (Sudan): Khartoum Fixes Upon a Policy of War and Civilian Destruction," 24 November 2003, http://sudanreeves.org/2004/12/17/the-accelerating-catastrophe-in-darfur-sudan-khartoum-fixes-upon-a-policy-of-war-and-civilian-destruction-november-24-2003/ (accessed 8 June 2019).

20 IRIN News, "Sudan: Concern Grows over Deteriorating Situation in Darfur," 14 November 2003, www.irinnews.org/Report/47250/SUDAN-Concern-grows-over-deteriorating-situation-in-Darfur (accessed 8 June 2019).

21 Quoted in UN News Centre, "Humanitarian and Security Situation in Western Sudan Reach New Lows, UN Agency Says," 5 December 2003, www.un.org/apps/news/story.asp?NewsID=9094&Cr1= (accessed 8 June 2019).

22 UN News Centre, "Annan Alarmed at Reports of Widespread Abuses of Civilians in Darfur, Sudan," www.un.org/apps/news/story.asp?NewsID=9137&Cr=sudan&Cr1= (accessed 8 June 2019).

23 Interview (DA), New York, March 2011.

24 On Roger Winter's involvement in Sudan, see Eliza Griswold, "The Man for a New Sudan," *New York Times Magazine*, 15 June 2008. USAID refers to the United States Agency for International Development.

25 Interview with Roger Winter, Washington, DC, February 2010.

26 Interview (AP), Washington, DC, March 2010.

27 Interview with MSF staff (DU), Paris, November 2011.

28 MSF, "Massive Aid Urgently Needed in Darfur, Sudan," press release, 16 February 2004, www.doctorswithoutborders.org/what-we-do/news-stories/news/massive-aid-urgently-needed-darfur-sudan (accessed 8 June 2019).

29 Phone interview with Eric Reeves, February 2010.

30 Eric Reeves, "Unnoticed Genocide," *Washington Post*, 25 February 2004.

31 Quoted in BBC News, "Mass Rape Atrocity in West Sudan," 19 March 2004, http://news.bbc.co.uk/2/hi/africa/3549325.stm (accessed 8 June 2019).

32 Quoted in IRIN News, "Sudan: Darfur is World's Greatest Humanitarian Disaster, Says UN Official," 22 March 2004, http://allafrica.com/stories/200403220078.html (accessed 8 June 2019). In a video on the occasion of the 2011 Holocaust Memorial Day, Kapila explained the motivations of his BBC statement: "Untold Stories, Mukesh Kapila," online video, www.hmd.org.uk/resource/untold-stories-mukesh-kapila/ (accessed 8 June 2019).

33 Chapter 6 (Figure 6.1) provides a complete account of editorials published about Darfur in the *New York Times* and the *Washington Post*.

34 UN News Centre, "Sudan: Envoy Warns of Ethnic Cleansing as Security Council Calls for Ceasefire," 2 April 2004, www.un.org/apps/news/story.asp?NewsID=10307&Cr=sudan&Cr1= (accessed 8 June 2019).

35 The White House, "President Condemns Atrocities in Sudan," 7 April 2004, http://georgewbush-whitehouse.archives.gov/news/releases/2004/04/20040407–2.html (accessed 8 June 2019).

36 Kofi Annan, "Risk of Genocide Remains Frighteningly Real', Secretary-General Tells Human Rights Commission as he Launches Action Plan to Prevent Genocide," 7 April 2004, https://www.un.org/press/en/2004/sgsm9245.doc.htm (accessed 8 June 2019).

37 Interview (DA), New York, March 2011.

38 Annan was head of the UN Department of Peacekeeping Operations (UNDPKO) during the Rwanda genocide (Traub 2006, Chapter 3) and he subsequently became a champion of R2P (see Chapter 1). Kapila was a civil servant in the UK government and, in this function, part of one of the first British teams to enter Kigali after the genocide in 1994. He is an active supporter of the R2P doctrine. See, for example, the video of a speech he gave on 25 January 2006, "Moving from Words to Action: The Responsibility to Protect," https://vimeo.com/4887869 (at 2:14, accessed 8 June 2019).

39 Egeland's (1988) PhD thesis lays out his liberal worldview and commitment to human rights.

40 The analysis drew on editorials published in: *Le Figaro* (France), *Globe and Mail* (Canada), *Guardian* (UK), *Irish Times* (Ireland), *Le Monde* (France), *New York Times* (US), *The Times* (London, UK), *Toronto Star* (Canada), *Washington Post* (US), *Washington Times* (US).

41 Richard Gwyn, "Canada waffling while Darfur burns," *Toronto Star*, 1 August 2004.

42 Nat Hentoff, "Stop a Repeat of Rwanda; The Silence on Darfur is Morally Deafening," *Washington Times*, 31 May 2004.

43 "The Rapes in Sudan," *Globe and Mail*, 21 July 2004.

44 Nicholas Kristof, "A Challenge for Bill O'Reilly," *New York Times*, 18 December 2005.

45 Roméo Dallaire, "Looking at Darfur, Seeing Rwanda," *Toronto Star*, 5 October 2004.

46 Samantha Power, "Remember Rwanda, but Take Action on Sudan," *New York Times*, 6 April 2004.

47 "300,000 Deaths Foretold," *Washington Post*, 7 June 2004.

48 "Hope in Darfur," *Washington Post*, 22 September 2004.

49 John Prendergast, "Sudan's Killing Fields," *Washington Times*, 7 September 2004.

50 See Peter Moszynski, "There Can Be No Quick Fix in Sudan," *Guardian*, 28 July 2004; Eric Reeves, "Regime Change," *Washington Post*, 23 August 2004; William Kristol and Vance Serchuk, "End the Genocide Now," *Washington Post*, 22 September 2004; Richard Gwyn, "Canada Must Resist 'Quickie' Show in Darfur," *Toronto Star*, 17 May 2005.

51 See the following blog post: Nicholas Kristof, "Speaking Not as an Armenian," 5 March 2010, http://kristof.blogs.nytimes.com/2010/03/05/speaking-not-as-an-armenian/ (accessed 8 June 2019). In 1990, Kristof and his wife, Sheryl WuDunn, won a Pulitzer Prize for their reporting of the 1989 student protests at Tiananmen Square, Beijing.

52 Interview (AT), Washington, DC, March 2010.

53 Interview (AF), Washington, DC, February 2010.

54 Interview (AS), Washington, DC, March 2010.

55 Interview with Jacky Mamou, Paris, November 2011 (interview in French, author's translation).

56 "Engaging Sudan," *The Washington Times*, 20 May 2004.

57 Nat Hentoff, "The Disgrace of the United Nations; Doing Nothing about Sudanese Slaughter," *The Washington Times*, 24 May 2004.

58 E.g., Simon Jenkins, "We Cannot Save Darfur at the Point of a Gun," *Guardian*, 28 July 2004.

59 Winston Churchill's (1899) account of the British re-conquest of Khartoum is particularly telling in this regard.

60 James Smith "Cleansing in Sudan May Soon Become Genocide," *The Times (London)*, 18 May 2004.

61 Kofi Annan and Alpha Oumar Konaré, "A Chance for Peace in Darfur," *Toronto Star*, 27 May 2005.

62 Unity Statement of the Save Darfur Coalition, 2 August 2004, http://web.archive.org/web/20040805182908/ http:/savedarfur.org/go.php?q=unityStatement.html (archived website accessed 3 July 2018).

63 Call to Action of the Save Darfur Coalition, 2 August 2004, http://web.archive.org/web/20040805004127/ http://savedarfur.org/go.php?q=callToAction.html (archived website, accessed 3 July 2018).

64 List of Signatories of the Unity Statement, 15 September 2004, http://web.archive.org/web/20041019180129/ www.savedarfur.org/go.php?q=listOfSignatories.html (archived website, accessed 3 July 2018).

65 Interview with student advocacy leader (AT), Washington, DC, March 2010.

66 For an insider's account of the genesis and development of the North American Darfur advocacy movement, see Hamilton (2011). For an academic analysis of the movement, see Budabin (2012).

67 Interview with SDC staff member (AM), March 2010.

68 Elie Wiesel, "On the Atrocities in Sudan," remarks delivered at the Darfur Emergency Summit, New York, 14 July 2004, www.ushmm.org/wlc/en/article.php?ModuleId=10007205 (accessed 8 June 2019).

69 Interview (AG), Washington, DC, February 2010.

70 Sermon of 26 August 2005, quoted in The Pears Foundation, "Darfur: A Jewish Response," 2007, http://jhub.org.uk/wp-content/uploads/2017/12/Darfur-Report-Final.pdf (accessed 8 June 2019), p. 21.

71 Interview (CY), Washington, DC, March 2011.

72 Interview (AF), Washington, DC, February 2010.
73 Interview (CY), Washington, DC, March 2011.
74 Interview (AG), Washington, DC, February 2010.
75 Interview (AH), Washington, DC, February 2010.
76 Interview (DW), Paris, November 2011 (interview in French, author's translation).
77 Interview (AI), Boston, March 2010.
78 Phone interview with Mia Farrow, February 2010.
79 See Evans, "Darfur and the Responsibility to Protect."
80 Interview with Jacky Mamou, Paris, November 2011 (interview in French, author's translation).
81 Phone interview with Mia Farrow, February 2010.
82 George Clooney, UN Security Council Address on Darfur, delivered on 14 September 2006, www.americanrhetoric.com/speeches/georgeclooneyunitednations.htm (accessed 8 June 2019).
83 Phone interview with former Humanity United employee (AV), March 2010.
84 "Darfur Fast for Life, Pam Omidyar rejoins the fast," 5 June 2009, http://fastdarfur.org/?cat=4 (accessed 8 June 2019).
85 Phone interview with former Humanity United employee (AV), March 2010.

References

Abdul-Jalil, Musa. 2006. "The Dynamics of Customary Land Tenure and Natural Resource Management in Darfur." *Land Reform, Land Settlement and Cooperatives*: 8–23.

Abdul-Jalil, Musa Adam, Adam Azzain Mohamed, and Ahmed A. Yousuf. 2007. "Native Administration and Local Governance in Darfur: Past and Future." In *War in Darfur and the Search for Peace*, ed. Alex De Waal. Cambridge, MA: Harvard University Press. 39–67.

Al-Karsani, Awad Al-Sid. 1987. "The Establishment of Neo-Mahdism in the Western Sudan, 1920–1936." *African Affairs* 86: 385–404.

Amnesty International. 2003. *Sudan: Looming Crisis in Darfur*. AFR 54/041/2003. London: AI. 30 June.

Amnesty International. 2004. *Sudan: At the Mercy of Killers, Destruction of Villages in Darfur*. 54/072/2004. London: AI. 1 July.

Brosché, Johan, and Daniel Rothbart. 2013. *Violent Conflict and Peacebuilding: The Continuing Crisis in Darfur*. Milton Park: Routledge.

Brunk, Darren. 2008. "Dissecting Darfur: Anatomy of a Genocide Debate." *International Relations* 22: 25–44.

Budabin, Alexandra Cosima. *Citizen's Army for Darfur: The Impact of a Social Movement on International Conflict Resolution*. PhD thesis, New School University, 2012.

Burr, Millard, and Robert O. Collins. 2008. *Darfur: The Long Road to Disaster*. Princeton, NJ: Markus Wiener Publishers.

Campbell, David. 2007. "Geopolitics and Visuality: Sighting the Darfur Conflict." *Political Geography* 26: 357 382.

Carpenter, Charli. 2006. *Innocent Women and Children: Gender, Norms, and the Protection of Civilians*. Hampshire: Ashgate.

Carruthers, Susan L. 2003. "Tribalism and Tribulation: Media Coverage of 'African Savagery' and 'Western Humanitarianism' in the 1990s." In *Reporting War: Journalism in Wartime*, eds. Stuart Allan and Barbie Zelizer. Milton Park: Routledge. 155–173.

Churchill, Winston. 1899. *The River War: An Historical Account of the Reconquest of the Soudan*. London: Longmans Green.

Collins, Robert O. 2008. *A History of Modern Sudan*. New York: Cambridge University Press.

Daly, M. W. 2010. *Darfur's Sorrow: The Forgotten History of a Humanitarian Disaster*. 2nd ed. Cambridge: Cambridge University Press.

De Waal, Alex. 1989. *Famine that Kills: Darfur, Sudan, 1984–1985*. Oxford: Clarendon Press.

De Waal, Alex. 2004. "Counter-Insurgency on the Cheap." *London Review of Books* 26: 25–27.

De Waal, Alex. 2005. "Who are the Darfurians? Arab and African Identities, Violence and External Engagement." *African Affairs* 104: 181–205.

Degomme, Olivier, and Debarati Guha-Sapir. 2010. "Patterns of Mortality Rates in Darfur Conflict." *The Lancet* 375: 294–300.

Dervin, Brenda. 1992. "From the Mind's Eye of the User: The Sense-Making Qualitative-Quantitative Methodology." In *Qualitative Research in Information Management*, eds. Jack D. Glazier and Ronald R. Powell. Englewood, CO: Libraries Unlimited. 61–84.

Dervin, Brenda. 1999. "On Studying Information Seeking Methodologically: The Implications of Connecting Metatheory to Method." *Information Processing & Management* 35: 727–750.

Dorfman, Aaron, and Ruth Messinger. 2010. "Towards a Jewish Argument for the Responsibility to Protect." In *Responsibility to Protect: The Global Moral Compact for the 21st Century*, eds. Richard H. Cooper and Juliette Voïnov Kohler. New York: Palgrave Macmillan. 61–75.

Egeland, Jan. 1988. *Impotent Superpower, Potent Small State: Potentials and Limitations of Human Rights Objectives in the Foreign Policies of the United States and Norway*. Oslo: Norwegian University Press.

El-Affendi, Abdelwahab 1991. *Turabi's Revolution: Islam and Power in Sudan*. London: Grey Seal.

El-Battahani, Atta. 2002. "Tribal Peace Conferences in Sudan: The Role of the Joudiyya Institution in Darfur, Western Sudan." In *Transformation of Resource Conflicts: Approach and Instruments*, eds. Günther Baechler, Kurt R. Spillmann and Mohamed Suliman. Bern: Peter Lang. 379–448.

El-Battahani, Atta. 2009. "Ideological Expansionist Movements versus Historical Indigenous Rights in the Darfur Region of Sudan: From Actual Homicide to Potential Genocide." In *Darfur and the Crisis of Governance in Sudan: A Critical Reader*, eds. Salah M. Hassan and Carina E. Ray. Ithaca, NY: Cornell University Press. 43–67.

El-Din, Ahmed Kamal. 2007. "Islam and Islamism in Darfur." In *War in Darfur and the Search for Peace*, ed. Alex De Waal. Cambridge, MA: Harvard University Press. 92–112.

El-Tom, Abdullahi Osman. 2009. "The Black Book: Imbalance of Power and Wealth in Sudan." In *Darfur and the Crisis of Governance in Sudan: A Critical Reader*, eds. Salah M. Hassan and Carina E. Ray. Ithaca, NY: Cornell University Press. 406–447.

Fair, Jo Ellen. 1993. "War, Famine, and Poverty: Race in the Construction of Africa's Media Image." *Journal of Communication Inquiry* 17: 5–22.

Flint, Julie, and Alex De Waal. 2008. *Darfur: A New History of a Long War*. London: Zed Books.

Gifkins, Jess. 2016. "Naming and Framing: Darfur, the Genocide Debate, and the Responsibility to Protect." In *The United Nations and Genocide*, ed. Deborah Mayersen. London: Palgrave Macmillan. 100–122.

Haggar, Ali. 2007. "The Origins and Organization of the Janjawiid in Darfur." In *War in Darfur and the Search for Peace*, ed. Alex De Waal. Cambridge, MA: Harvard University Press. 113–139.

Hamilton, Rebecca. 2011. *Fighting for Darfur: Public Action and the Struggle to Stop Genocide*. New York: Palgrave Macmillan.

Hamilton, Rebecca, and Chad Hazlett. 2007. " 'Not on Our Watch': The Emergence of the American Movement for Darfur." In *War in Darfur and the Search for Peace*, ed. Alex De Waal. Cambridge, MA: Harvard University Press. 337–366.

Harir, Sharif. 1994. "Arab Belt versus African Belt: Ethno-Political Conflict in Darfur and the Regional Cultural Factors." In *Short-Cut to Decay: The Case of the Sudan*, eds. Terje Tvedt and Sharif Harir. Uppsala: Nordic Africa Institute.

Hassan, Salah M., and Carina E. Ray, eds. 2009. *Darfur and the Crisis of Governance in Sudan: A Critical Reader*. Ithaca, NY: Cornell University Press.

Hertzke, Allen D. 2004. *Freeing God's Children: The Unlikely Alliance for Global Human Rights*. Lanham, MD: Rowman & Littlefield.

Høigilt, Jacob. 2010. *Darfur and Arab Public Opinion: Strategies for Engagement*. Working paper. Madrid: FRIDE. March.

Human Rights Watch. 2004. *Darfur Destroyed: Ethnic Cleansing by Government and Militia Forces in Western Sudan*. New York: HRW. May.

International Crisis Group (ICG). 2003. *Sudan's Other Wars*. Africa Briefing No. 14. Brussels: ICG. 25 June.

International Crisis Group (ICG). 2004. *Darfur Rising: Sudan's New Crisis*. Africa Report No. 76. Brussels: ICG. 25 March.

Kapila, Mukesh. 2013. *Against a Tide of Evil*. Edinburgh: Mainstream Publishing.

Leffel, Gregory P., and Bill Mefford. 2008. *The Not on our Watch Christian Companion: Biblical Reflections on the Mission to End Genocide in Darfur and Beyond*. Washington, DC: Enough Project.

Mamdani, Mahmood. 1996. *Citizen and Subject: Contemporary Africa and the Legacy of Late Colonialism*. Princeton, NJ: Princeton University Press.

Marchal, Roland. 2007. "The Unseen Regional Implications of the Crisis in Darfur." In *War in Darfur and the Search for Peace*, ed. Alex De Waal. Cambridge, MA: Harvard University Press. 173–198.

Mohamed, Adam Azzain. 2009. *Evaluating the Darfur Peace Agreement: A Call for an Alternative Approach to Crisis Management*. Claude Ake Memorial Papers No. 6. Uppsala: Department of Peace and Conflict Research, Uppsala University; Nordic Africa Institute.

Nathan, Laurie. 2011. "Interests, Ideas and Ideology: South Africa's Policy on Darfur." *African Affairs* 110: 55–74.

Neumann, Roderick P. 2004. "Moral and Discursive Geographies in the War for Biodiversity in Africa." *Political Geography* 23: 813–837.

O'Fahey, Rex Sean. 2008. *The Darfur Sultanate: A History*. New York: Columbia University Press.

Prunier, Gérard. 2007. *Darfur: The Ambiguous Genocide*. Ithaca, NY: Cornell University Press.

Roessler, Philip. 2011. *Political Instability, Threat Displacement and Civil War: Darfur as a Theory-Building Case*. Working Paper, published with SSRN e-library.

Salih, M. A. Mohamed. 2006. *Understanding the Conflict in Darfur*. Occasional Paper. Copenhagen: Centre for African Studies, University of Copenhagen.

Scroggins, Deborah. 2003. *Emma's War: Love, Betrayal and Death in the Sudan.* London: Harper Collins.

Suliman, Mohamed. 1996. "War in Darfur or the Desert versus the Oasis Syndrome." In *Environmental Degradation as a Cause of War, Vol. II*, eds. Günther Baechler and Kurt R. Spillmann. Chur: Verlag Rüegger. 145–179.

Traub, James. 2006. *The Best Intentions: Kofi Annan and the UN in the Era of American World Power.* New York: Picador.

Traub, James. 2010. *Unwilling and Unable: The Failed Response to the Atrocities in Darfur.* New York: Global Centre for the Responsibility to Protect.

Tubiana, Jérôme. 2007. "Darfur: A Conflict for Land?" In *War in Darfur and the Search for Peace*, ed. Alex De Waal. Cambridge, MA: Harvard University Press. 68–91.

US Government Accountability Office. 2006. *Darfur Crisis: Death Estimates Demonstrate Severity of Crisis, but Their Accuracy and Credibility Could Be Enhanced.* GAO-07–24. November.

Young, Helen, Abdul Monim Osman, Yacob Aklilu, Rebecca Dale, Babiker Badri, Abdul Jabar and Abdulla Fadul. 2005. *Darfur: Livelihoods under Siege.* Medford, MA: Feinstein International Famine Center. June.

3 Implementing R2P

The international response to the Darfur conflict

Supporters of the new norm must galvanize what has been a relatively passive and apolitical humanitarian contingent into an active bloc.

Samantha Power (2009, ix)

In the absence of a peace agreement the question becomes how the UN can contain the war. But we can't!

UNDPKO official[1]

Activist strategies to save strangers in Darfur

Saving strangers through mass mobilization

The driving force behind the international response to the Darfur conflict was the advocacy movement, which, as Chapter 2 showed, represented a push to implement the core R2P norm. In the beginning, the activists focused on galvanizing public opinion. According to the first coordinator of the Save Darfur Coalition, David Rubenstein, the focus in the beginning was on mass mobilization: "the closer we could get to a bumper sticker, the better we'd be as an organization" (Quoted in Hamilton and Hazlett 2007, 344). What was the rationale of this strategy? In the concluding chapter of *A Problem from Hell*, Samantha Power stated:

> The battle to stop genocide has thus been repeatedly lost in the realm of domestic politics. Although isolated voices have protested the slaughter, Americans outside the executive branch were largely mute when it mattered. As a result of this society-wide silence, officials at all levels of government calculated that the political costs of getting involved in stopping genocide far exceeded the costs of remaining uninvolved....
>
> It takes political pressure to put genocide on the map in Washington.... Because so little noise has been made about genocide, U.S. decision-makers have opposed U.S. intervention, telling themselves that they were doing all they could—and, most important, all they should—in light of competing American interests.

(Power 2002, 509)

The lesson is clear: The key to saving strangers was to make noise and thus create political will among decision makers. As mentioned in the epigraph above, Power called for the creation of a politically active constituency for atrocity prevention. The Darfur activists saw themselves as the vanguards of this effort. According to one activist, "Samantha Power's call for a domestic constituency against genocide was very powerful. The last ten pages of *A Problem from Hell* provided the theory of change for the Darfur advocacy movement!"[2] The activists saw it as their primary goal to mobilize people and raise awareness. They believed that this would foster political will and ensure that policymakers could not ignore Darfur or, for that matter, any other situation of mass atrocities. As Cheadle and Prendergast (2007, 10) phrased it with strong religious overtones, the challenge for the Darfur activists was to overcome the "Four Horsemen Enabling the Apocalypse: apathy, indifference, ignorance, and policy inertia."

Other activists explicitly linked the task of building political will with R2P:

> The R2P report is a tool; it's a framework for how to think about the issue of prevention of mass atrocities. What is missing is R2P 2.0, to get non-state actors involved in prevention. The R2P report was very persuasive for me and helped me persuade others as well. But it didn't tell us what we can do as citizens! The lesson from *A Problem from Hell* was not that governments took action, but that individuals through their agency did. These are your Dallaires, Lemkins etc.[3]

Implementing R2P through mass mobilization meant that activists put a lot of effort into framing Darfur in a way that would resonate with the largest number of people. One strategy was to communicate the cause through the personal stories of victims, usually Darfuri refugees forced to flee because of the fighting. To this end, photos of the war in Darfur were omnipresent. Activists used them to shock consciences and galvanize people's involvement in the campaign. One example is the *Darfur/Darfur* exhibit, which Humanity United sponsored, and the Save Darfur Coalition helped to set up.[4] The Darfur campaigns also promoted films like *Darfur Diaries*, *Darfur Now*, and *The Devil Came on Horseback*, as well as books like *The Translator* and *Tears of the Desert* that tell the stories of individual Darfuris who were victimized by the conflict.[5]

Related to personalization is a second feature of the campaigns: a focus on easily understandable categories, often clichés, to relay information about the conflict in Darfur. Interestingly, the categories employed in the Darfur narrative are closely related to Karpman's (1968) "drama triangle," which psychotherapists use to help patients re-enact and eventually deconstruct stereotypical roles in society (L'Abate 2009). The idea is that a basic story, for example a fairy tale, consists of three elementary roles: victim, persecutor, and rescuer. The interaction of these roles brings the norms of society to the fore and makes for a captivating drama.

The Darfur campaign clearly assigned these roles to certain groups. The persecutors of Darfur, in particular the *janjawid* fighters, were depicted as the projection of evil. John Prendergast, for example, called them "a grotesque mixture of the mafia and the Ku Klux Klan."[6] In stark contrast, the victims of genocide, Darfur's African populations, were portrayed as helpless and lacking agency—an impression reinforced in photos of Darfur that often showed destitute creatures marked by violence or illness, or people queuing for food aid in displaced persons camps. The role of the rescuer was reserved for the activists themselves selflessly fighting for the most vulnerable human beings. One example is a portrait of John Prendergast in Men's Vogue Magazine: "John Prendergast has talked back to tyrants, networked with Hollywood activists, and given hope to hundreds of thousands of refugees. Can one man save a country from itself?"[7]

These elements made for a compelling narrative, but they also created a discrepancy between the narrative and the infinitely more complex real world. Not surprisingly, this discrepancy drew criticism. The Sudan expert Julie Flint, for example, remarked on the activists. "For them, Darfur is not a place with a complex history; it's a moral high ground."[8] Similarly critical was the Save Darfur Accountability Project, a blog set up by former SDC employees, who were alienated by the organization's advocacy strategy and the opportunism behind the engagement of some of the movement's senior exponents.[9] The inflated casualty numbers cited by Darfur activists also drew criticism. This was especially the case after a verdict by the British Advertising Standards Authority. Its ruling obliged the Darfur activists to state the death tolls put forward in their ads as opinion rather than fact, thus handing a public relations victory to the Sudanese government.[10] As Chapter 6 shows, these elements later played a part in the deconstruction of Darfur as a relevant public policy issue.

The 3Ps to save strangers in Darfur

Some advocacy leaders were aware of the limitation of mass mobilization. One activist said,

> The idea was that political will had to be created and everything else would flow automatically. As a result, we paid little attention to policy content and the deeper issues of the Darfur conflict.... In hindsight, political will proved to be a necessary but insufficient condition to affect change in a place like Darfur.[11]

Rebecca Hamilton (2011, 193–194) came to a similar conclusion in her book *Fighting for Darfur*:

> It is not much of an oversimplification to say that most of those, myself included, who first got involved in advocacy for Darfur believed that it was our outcry that would mark the dividing line between life and death in Darfur.... The Darfur story, however, shows that this necessary outcry is not sufficient.

This realization had some impact on the Darfur advocacy movement in North America. The Save Darfur Coalition first focused on movement-building, operating with little resources and providing a platform for individual member organizations to campaign. In 2005 and 2006, the SDC became more established and funding multiplied. The peak was 2006, which saw revenues close to US$50 million following a large anonymous donation that the SDC had to spend on advertisements.[12] The SDC thus professionalized its operations and hired 30 to 40 employees, including a number of policy specialists. This coincided with the establishment of the Enough Project in 2007 with funding from Humanity United. The founders were John Prendergast and Gayle Smith, who both had experience in US foreign policy, in particular related to Africa. Also important was that the project focused on atrocity prevention in general, not just in Darfur. A former staffer explained the rationale of the organization:

> The Save Darfur Coalition's advocacy campaigns were successful but somewhat unsophisticated. This was the niche of the Enough Project: to be the 'Intel chip' of the advocacy movement by having inside knowledge of the policymaking process and reliable information from the field. Therefore, the Enough Project was conceived as a bridge between think tank and advocacy, a kind of hybrid structure.[13]

Once it was up and running, the Enough Project developed strategy papers with the aim of orienting Save Darfur's advocacy. An article by two staff members, Colin Thomas-Jensen and Julia Spiegel, referred to the R2P doctrine as the "theoretical and intellectual underpinning" of the Darfur advocacy movement, because it provided "a platform from which to address the difficult question of exactly *how* the international community should respond to the crisis in Darfur" (Thomas-Jensen and Spiegel 2007, 847–848, emphasis in the original). To implement R2P, the authors called on the US government "to aggressively pursue a three-pronged multilateral approach to end the Darfur crisis: serious peace negotiations, protection of innocent civilians, and accountability for those most responsible for crimes against humanity" (Thomas-Jensen and Spiegel 2007, 852). Indeed, this approach echoed a strategy paper by John Prendergast (2007, 14–15), in which he proposed a framework for resolving the Darfur conflict based on the "3Ps for confronting mass atrocities": protecting people, punishing perpetrators, and promoting peace.

What do the 3Ps entail? The first "P"—protection—refers to the interposition of external actors with the aim of deterring violence against civilians. According to Cheadle and Prendergast (2007, 212–213), this usually requires military force:

> Many of us peace and human rights advocates are rightly reluctant about the use of force. We need to get over it. There is such a thing as evil in this world, and sometimes the only way to confront evil is through the judicious use of military force.

In Darfur, this implied supporting the deployment of a robust peacekeeping force led by the UN. The second "P"—punishment—refers to international efforts to hold perpetrators accountable for past crimes. For Darfur, this meant supporting the ICC. The third "P"—peacemaking—refers to "a comprehensive peace deal that addresses the causes of the conflict in Darfur," according to Prendergast.[14]

John Prendergast underlined the unified nature of the 3Ps: "When we apply these 3Ps together, not one, not two of them, but all three together, usually solutions follow."[15] However, a closer look reveals that there are multiple contradictions between the 3Ps. One is an incompatibility between pushing towards a negotiated settlement in which conflict parties agree to share power and wealth, and, at the same time, prosecuting the senior leadership of the same parties in an international court. The second contradiction is between peace and protection: Imposing the foreign deployment of a foreign military force tends to antagonize the government of that country, regardless of the force's purpose. Therefore, it seems very difficult to use military force against the will of a government and, at the same time, to expect that government to make compromises at the negotiation table. Therefore, despite the rhetoric surrounding the 3Ps, the focus of the Darfur advocacy movement in implementing R2P was on protection and accountability, rather than peace talks.

Reaping what you sow: "doing something" to save strangers

The dynamics of "doing something"

Since the initial goal of the Darfur activists was to raise awareness without giving specific instructions as to what policies were needed, the response was made up of rhetorical declarations and symbolic gestures. Governments responded to the call to "do something" and, in that sense, the activists reaped what they sowed. Indeed, countless high-level representatives from governments and international organizations mentioned Darfur in speeches and traveled to Sudan to signal their concern. Almost all Darfur-related speeches were made after Kapila's Rwanda comparison in March 2004, and they usually adopted the mass atrocity frame Kapila had introduced. There is no doubt, therefore, that these actions were a direct consequence of the discursive construction of Darfur as a test case for R2P.

Within the UN, the impetus came from Kofi Annan, who, according to a UN official, had been "personally involved" in the Darfur issue since his April 2004 speech at the UN Commission on Human Rights.[16] Annan subsequently sent a high-level delegation to Sudan at the end of April, and he himself visited Darfur in June–July 2004. Darfur made it onto the agenda of the UN Security Council, which expressed "its utmost concern at the consequences of the conflict in Darfur on the civilian population."[17] The US also upped its rhetoric in relation to Darfur. Secretary of State Colin Powell visited Darfur together with Kofi Annan at the end of June 2004. A few weeks later, Congress called the situation in

Darfur genocide. Darfur became a prominent foreign policy issue in the 2004 US presidential elections. It was raised in several TV debates and candidates made repeated statements about Sudan. European leaders reacted to Darfur as well. Foremost among them was UK Prime Minister Tony Blair. In the summer of 2004, he talked about the possibility of sending troops to Sudan. He later backtracked on the statement, but affirmed: "we have a moral responsibility to deal with this and deal with it by any means we can."[18]

These declarations were a far cry from the intentions of the founders of R2P, but they did engender a number of processes that had an important impact on the ground. One immediate consequence was that governments began to fund humanitarian operations in Darfur. This was a form of "saving strangers on the cheap" for governments: They could "do something" to help the Darfuris as the activists were demanding, even if they were unwilling or unable to muster the political capital to intervene more forcefully. After Darfur became a global cause, funding opportunities multiplied for agencies working in Darfur and access opened up (see Chapter 5). Therefore, Darfur saw a significant influx of humanitarian organizations, especially in the major towns and IDP camps. In April 2004, 11 international NGOs, seven UN agencies, and the International Committee of the Red Cross (ICRC) were present in Darfur, employing a few hundred staff members and 37 expatriates. By May 2005, 79 NGOs, 13 UN agencies, and the ICRC were operational, employing 11,219 staff including 964 expatriates (numbers cited by Large 2011, 174). According to Fabrice Weissman of MSF, Darfur thus became "the largest humanitarian operation in the world."[19] Several epidemiological studies confirm that the influx of humanitarian aid had a significant impact. Nielsen et al. (2011) concluded that, between 2004 and 2005, global and severe acute malnutrition in Darfur decreased by 16 percent and 28 percent respectively.

The power of argumentative traps: the case of the US government

The rhetorical declarations by world leaders were also effective on another level. They engendered what Risse (1999, 531) called "argumentative self-entrapment." Thus, a decision maker issues a statement that, at the outset, has a purely symbolic value. Norm entrepreneurs seize on this to play accountability politics, pressing for further measures. Decision makers comply by making concessions. Thus, a cascade of measures is created, ultimately leading to significant policy engagement. Through process-tracing, the following sections show how this mechanism worked in the context of the US government's Darfur policy.

Towards Powell's genocide determination

As explained in Chapter 2, USAID's Andrew Natsios and Roger Winter had tried to make Darfur a foreign policy priority. Their efforts initially failed and those within the State Department who were focusing on the north–south peace talks prevailed. This changed in March–April 2004 when George W. Bush spoke about Darfur for the first time, condemning the atrocities committed against the civilian population. Bush's acknowledgement of the atrocities, even if purely rhetorical, galvanized senior officials in the State Department. In particular, Lorne Craner, Assistant Secretary for Democracy, Human Rights and Labor, and Pierre-Richard Prosper, US Ambassador at Large for War Crimes Issues, took up the cause. Craner and Prosper subsequently functioned as internal norm entrepreneurs. Craner had read *A Problem from Hell* and "viewed the US government's avoidance of 'the g-word' with shame, and committed not to repeat such a failure if he encountered an analogous situation."[20] After March 2004, Power's book "became the framework through which Craner began to filter information about Darfur" (Hamilton 2011, 31). Together with Prosper, he began to push for an investigation into whether the situation in Darfur constituted genocide. Initially, their call was not heeded. Colin Powell, along with other senior US government representatives, remained cautious. They did not talk about genocide.

In June, the pressure mounted. A drumbeat of media reports began calling the situation in Darfur genocide. Within the State Department, those championing a more assertive approach were gaining momentum. Andrew Natsios obtained the declassification and publication of NASA satellite images that had been acquired by the US government in April and showed the destruction of hundreds of non-Arab villages in Darfur (Natsios 2006). A few weeks later, Craner and Prosper achieved their goal: The US government established the Atrocities Documentation Team (ADT) to assess the nature of the violence in Darfur.[21] Although Prosper and Craner described it as a legal instrument, the creation of the ADT followed a political logic. According to de Waal (2005, 11), it was a "tactical maneuver designed to placate the anti-Khartoum lobbies circling around Congress ..., while buying time for those in the State Department committed to pushing a negotiated settlement [between the government and the SPLM]."

The following week, Powell travelled to Sudan. In an interview with National Public Radio's Michele Norris, he said,

> based on what we have seen, there were some indicators but there was certainly no full accounting of all indicators that lead to a legal definition of genocide, in accordance with the terms of the genocidal treaties. That's the advice of my lawyers.

When Norris insisted that "the reluctance to label this genocide hearkens back to Rwanda," Powell replied, "It isn't reluctance. I can assure you that if all of the indicators lined up and said this meets what the treaty test of genocide is, I would have no reluctance to call it that."[22] Despite his assurances to the contrary, Powell very much came across as reluctant. In fact, his statement made him look like a character in Samantha Power's book, engaging in semantic and legalistic hair-splitting in the face of mass atrocities. The anti-Khartoum lobby referred to by de Waal seized on this and, within three weeks, the US Congress unanimously adopted a resolution declaring Darfur genocide.

By insisting that genocide was a legal question, Powell provided a hook for the Darfur advocates within the State Department. In late August 2004, the final report of the ADT came out. Based on interviews with a representative sample of 1,000 Darfuri refugees in Chad, the report revealed the scale of the violence in Darfur: 81 percent of respondents saw the destruction of villages; 61 percent witnessed the killing of a family member; 31 percent heard racial epithets during attacks; and 16 percent experienced rape.[23] Confronted with these numbers, Powell discussed the report's implications with his staff. His legal advisor, William Taft IV, argued that the genocide determination was not clear-cut but would be defensible depending on the interpretation of the mens rea requirement, according to which perpetrators of genocide have to act with the specific intent to exterminate a group.[24] Given Powell's statement in Khartoum, Prosper—who was in favor of the determination—argued that the overwhelming targeting of African villages and the Sudanese government's simultaneous prevention of the delivery of humanitarian assistance and medicine indeed pointed to genocidal intent (Kostas 2006, 121–122).

This argument convinced Powell and overruled other concerns. At that point, given the evidence that the State Department had itself collected, those who believed the genocide declaration would undermine the north–south peace talks were in the minority. Also, as Hamilton (2011, 36) revealed, Powell's legal advisors banished the fear that the determination would require the US to take action on Darfur, in accordance with its obligations under the Genocide Convention. Colin Powell therefore made his decision. Informing President Bush two days before, he made the following statement before the Senate Foreign Relations Committee on 9 September 2004:

> When we reviewed the evidence compiled by our team …, we concluded, I concluded, that genocide has been committed in Darfur and that the Government of Sudan and the Jingaweit bear responsibility—and that genocide may still be occurring.
>
> Mr. Chairman, some seem to have been waiting for this determination of genocide to take action. In fact, however, no new action is dictated by this determination. We have been doing everything we can to get the Sudanese Government to act responsibly. So let us not be too preoccupied with this designation. These people are in desperate need and we must help them.[25]

Powell's statement was historic. For the first time the US government formally declared an ongoing conflict to be genocide. However, the declaration remained in the realm of rhetoric, especially because of Powell's caveat that no new action was required. Therefore, some observers believed the declaration was inconsequential (e.g., Strauss 2005) and even constituted "bullshitting" (Seymour 2014). The analysis in this book suggests otherwise. As illustrated in Chapter 2, Powell's statement inspired the emergence of an influential advocacy movement. It also provided a hook, which activists subsequently used to pressure the US government to take action on Darfur—often with success.

Towards an ICC referral

One of Powell's aims was for the genocide determination to spur other countries into action on Darfur.[26] To achieve this, the US took the matter to the UN Security Council. On the day following Powell's genocide declaration, the US tabled a draft resolution. On 18 September 2004, the Council adopted a resolution establishing a commission of inquiry, which was tasked to determine "whether or not acts of genocide have occurred, and to identify the perpetrators of such violations with a view to ensuring that those responsible are held accountable" (United Nations 2004, para 12). The Commission, which was led by the former president of the International Criminal Tribunal for the former Yugoslavia Antonio Cassese, conducted several field missions to Darfur to collect evidence. The Commission submitted its final report on 25 January 2005, concluding that "the Government of Sudan has not pursued a policy of genocide" even if "international offences such as crimes against humanity and war crimes that have been committed in Darfur may be no less serious and heinous than genocide" (United Nations 2005, 4).

The Commission's finding was controversial and revealed a range of legal and political disagreements about genocide and its application in the context of Darfur (Savelsberg 2015, 51–56). Most consequential was the Commission's recommendation that the UN Security Council refer the situation in Darfur to the ICC. Indeed, in view of a possible investigation, Cassese had submitted a sealed envelope to Kofi Annan with the names of 51 suspects—including rebels, *janjawid*, and government officials—who were implicated in the violence (Schabas 2010, 137). As a result, lengthy negotiations about follow-up actions ensued between UN Security Council members. The US government was in a difficult situation. It had initiated the Commission and faced a growing domestic constituency that demanded tough measures against Khartoum. At the same time, it had waged a campaign against the ICC, making it a central foreign policy issue for the Bush Administration. In the words of Samantha Power, "the Bush Administration can't decide what it dislikes more: genocide or the International Criminal Court."[27]

Condoleezza Rice, the new Secretary of State, tasked Pierre-Richard Prosper to find a way out of the dilemma. Prosper proposed the establishment of an ad hoc UN-AU hybrid tribunal for Darfur. The tribunal would be an extension of the International Criminal Tribunal for Rwanda in Arusha, with all its expenses—estimated between US$40 and 150 million annually—to be paid for by the US government (Kaufman 2005, 346–347). Those favoring the ICC option strongly criticized the hybrid court proposal, partly because it would have been more expensive than an ICC trial.[28] Most importantly, the Darfur activists referred to Powell's genocide declaration and thus played accountability politics. Nicholas Kristof remarked in a *New York Times* editorial:

> Mr. Bush's sympathy for Sudanese parents who are having their children tossed into bonfires shrivels next to his hostility to the organization that the

UN wants to trust with the prosecution: the International Criminal Court. Administration officials so despise the court that they have become, in effect, the best hope of Sudanese officials seeking to avoid accountability for what Mr. Bush himself has called genocide.[29]

European diplomats, who were pushing for the ICC referral, used the same trick: "The French believed that it would be difficult for the United States to veto a proposal on justice for a situation that they had labeled genocide" (Hamilton 2011, 62). Therefore, they threatened to table a resolution on Darfur. The US, fearing the reputational costs of a public veto and not wanting to jeopardize good relations with Europe, gave in and decided to abstain. This allowed the UN Security Council to pass a resolution on 31 March 2005 referring the situation in Darfur to the ICC. Two days before, the Council had already expanded its sanctions related to Darfur, imposing an arms import embargo on all belligerents, including the Sudanese government, and authorizing individual sanctions in the form of travel bans and asset freezes against those committing atrocities.[30]

The US government took two decisions on Darfur that were unprecedented: It declared an ongoing conflict to be a genocide, and it allowed the UN Security Council to refer a situation to the ICC. These decisions were enabled by the construction of Darfur as a case for saving strangers on par with Rwanda. It created opportunities for internal and external norm entrepreneurs and ensnared official actors in argumentative traps. It also helped to pull in those without a special commitment to R2P, but who had a tendency towards a moralistic worldview based on a distinction between good and evil. George W. Bush was so concerned about Sudan that some of his staff called him the "Sudan desk officer" (Stedjan and Thomas-Jensen 2010, 161). According to Jendayi Frazer, Assistant Secretary of State for African Affairs under Bush from 2005 to 2009, the reasons for the President's interests were "personal and humanitarian, rather than strategic." Therefore, "the President kept asking 'What do we do to protect innocent lives?' When the President is constantly on your ass about something, you know you've got to do something about it!"[31] This attitude made the US government susceptible to pressure from advocacy groups and led it to take measures on its own.

In spite of these measures and a context dominated by R2P, competing foreign policy priorities persisted for the US government. A particular focus remained on supporting the north–south peace agreement, securing Khartoum's cooperation in countering terrorism (see Chapter 5), and—beyond Sudan— reducing military engagement as violence was escalating in Iraq. These objectives meant that while options for military intervention in Darfur were "very seriously discussed," the Pentagon vetoed them, as it was dealing with too much fallout from the Afghanistan and Iraq wars.[32] This decision-making shows that while a context dominated by R2P can make atrocity prevention a priority, specific policy measures—especially costly ones—are still evaluated vis-à-vis other interests and thus have to meet the threshold for what is politically possible.

Vanguards of protection: peacekeepers to save strangers

Outsourcing protection: the African Union in Darfur

A few Darfur activists, foremost Eric Reeves, continuously called for a non-consensual military intervention. However, contrary to what critics (e.g., Funk and Fake 2009; Mamdani 2009) claimed, this never represented a mainstream position within the Save Darfur movement. The reluctance to support intervention may appear strange considering that the activists were painting a picture of Darfur as a site of horrific genocide, where thousands of innocent civilians were being brutally slaughtered. If this were actually happening, then surely Darfur would meet the threshold for humanitarian intervention? And if so, why did so few people call for military intervention?

In truth, observers knew that, in the post-Afghanistan and post-Iraq world, another US-led military intervention in a predominantly Muslim country was not in the cards. Nicholas Kristof's commentary is a case in point. In his editorials, he often gave graphic details of the most horrific atrocities. However, as far as remedies were concerned, he was pragmatic. "The U.S. is not going to invade Sudan. That's not a plausible option. But we can pass a tough UN Security Council resolution authorizing troops, as well as more support for African peacekeepers."[33] This shows a tendency on the part of the Darfur activists to marry their normative commitment to R2P and their moral outrage over Darfur with political realism and an understanding of the measures that were politically feasible. Against this background, peacekeepers became the main implementers of R2P in Darfur. Given that other, more forceful options to save strangers were not realistic, those advocating for Darfur had to settle for second best: peacekeepers provided by the African Union.

AU peacekeeping in Darfur materialized following the N'Djamena Humanitarian Ceasefire Agreement. Signed on 8 April 2004, a few days after Darfur registered on the radar of the international community (see Chapter 2), it led to the establishment of the African Union Mission in Sudan (AMIS)—a monitoring force. AMIS observers were first deployed to Darfur in June 2004. But AMIS had been mandated to monitor a ceasefire that had never really existed. To compensate, in October 2004 the AU Peace and Security Council (AUPSC) boosted the mission's strength to 2,200 armed personnel, including force protectors and civilian police. It also extended the AMIS mandate "in a way that responded to humanitarian appeals but at the same time satisfied the Sudanese host state, the AU membership and the foreign donors" (Badescu and Bergholm 2009, 297). Specifically, the AUPSC tasked AMIS with "protecting civilians whom it encounters under imminent threat and in the immediate vicinity, within resources and capability, it being understood that the protection of the civilian population is the responsibility of the government of Sudan" (quoted in Human Rights Watch 2006, 16). The mission continued to grow and, by September 2006, it had over 7,000 armed personnel operating in eight sectors across Darfur (Ekengard 2008).

AMIS received considerable international support and its budget was entirely covered by international donors. The EU got involved from the outset, contributing €300 million in total. The US government gave nearly US$300 million, the bulk of which went to the private contractors who built AMIS' bases (Badescu and Bergholm 2010, 106).[34] Canada's funding paid for helicopters rented from private contractors.[35] NATO helped by airlifting AU troops in and out of Darfur, while the EU provided military planning assistance and supported AMIS' civilian police component. The Darfur activists were also in favor of AMIS because they felt AU peacekeepers were "the only people who will stand between civilians and their killers on the ground in Darfur."[36] The activists even organized private fundraising campaigns for AU peacekeepers.[37] However, the activists had unrealistic expectations. For them, peacekeepers had to speak truth to power to Khartoum and offer full-fledged protection to Darfuris. For example, Roméo Dallaire said, with the help of NATO, the AU peacekeepers "could protect Darfur's displaced people in their camps and remaining villages, and eliminate or incarcerate the Janjaweed."[38]

Such assessments failed to appreciate the operational limitations of AU peacekeeping and the political realities of the African context. Thus, it is not surprising that different policy reports reached the conclusion that AMIS was limited in protecting civilians (Chin and Morgenstein 2005; O'Neill and Cassis 2005; International Crisis Group 2005b; Human Rights Watch 2006; Kagwanja and Mutahi 2007; Ekengard 2008). A variety of factors inherent to the mission contributed to this assessment. AMIS operated in an ongoing civil war and, with just a few thousand peacekeepers, had to cover a territory the size of Spain. It did not have significant force projection capability and, given the AU's limited peacekeeping experience, faced logistical and capacity constraints. It also had a mandate that obliged it to work with the Sudanese government.

Despite these constraints, AMIS did make a difference. Violence in Darfur diminished significantly during its presence on the ground. Even if this was primarily the result of shifting military strategies among the conflict parties, it is plausible that the presence of AMIS soldiers—as the eyes and ears of the international community—had a deterring effect. This was especially the case in areas where AMIS was physically present.[39] More concretely, AMIS developed a number of initiatives that directly improved security for Darfuris, especially those in IDP camps (O'Neill and Cassis 2005, 35–49).

Blue-hatting the peacekeepers

The African Union not only deployed peacekeepers in Darfur. It also mediated between the Sudanese government and the Darfur rebels, organizing multiple rounds of peace talks in Abuja for the purpose. The AU Special Envoy Salim Ahmed Salim, a former Tanzanian foreign minister, led the process. Its first success came in June 2005 when the Sudanese government and the Darfur rebels, represented by SLA and JEM, adopted a declaration of principles that set up the main parameters of a political settlement (Brooks 2008). However, the SLA subsequently split into two rival factions, one led by the original chairman Abdelwahid al-Nur and the other by Minni Minawi, a Zaghawa field commander. At the same time, the Western countries that had been funding the peace talks grew impatient and demanded a conclusion to the talks. Their impatience reflected a new policy priority that crystallized in early 2006 in the creation of a new UN peacekeeping mission with a Chapter VII mandate to protect civilians in Darfur. This was somewhat surprising because, throughout 2005, the Darfur activists, policymakers, and pundits continued to insist that strengthening AMIS was what was needed to protect civilians in Darfur.

The mood shifted towards the end of 2005. Negative reports multiplied about AMIS and its inability to prevent abuses against civilians. These reports were fueled by Brian Steidle, a US defense contractor who had worked for AMIS in 2004. In 2005, he published confidential pictures from his mission, joined the Save Darfur Coalition, and wrote a book based on his experience—*The Devil Came on a Horseback*—which was later made into a film. When AMIS soldiers were kidnapped and killed by rebel and *janjawid* forces, many disparaged the mission because it appeared incapable of protecting itself. There were also reports about AMIS soldiers dying of AIDS-related illnesses. The Western countries that were bankrolling AMIS had a change of heart, calling into question the system of voluntary funding that had financed the mission. The US Congress reduced its funding, as did the EU because of apparent irregularities in AMIS' accounting procedures.[40] Within a year, AMIS turned from a straw man for saving strangers in Darfur into an institution that embodied the world's inaction in the face of genocide. According to Mamdani (2007, 4) "The AU itself had quickly become a target both for the belligerents and for anybody agitated by the conflict."

The new silver bullet was the deployment of a UN peacekeeping force. According to Nicholas Kristof, "The most practical solution is to 'blue hat' the force, making it a UN peacekeeping force built around the African Union core."[41] The authors of a Refugees International report published in November 2005 explained the rationale of this approach: Blue-hatting regional peacekeeping missions had worked in Liberia and in Burundi, and so it was the right solution for Darfur as well (Chin and Morgenstein 2005, ii). An International Crisis Group report of March 2006, titled *To Save Darfur*, made the same recommendation. Subsequently, the call for deploying a robust UN peacekeeping force became the rallying cry of Darfur activists across the world. Policymakers heeded the call and began to lobby for its establishment. Feedback from the UN, however, was that a peacekeeping mission was only feasible if there was actually a peace to keep. Therefore, a Darfur peace agreement became the precondition to implement R2P via robust peacekeeping.

Against this background, international pressure to conclude the Abuja talks mounted on the African Union. Therefore, in early April 2006, the AU political leadership set a deadline for the talks to conclude by the end of the month (Nathan 2007). The mediators and their advisors drafted a comprehensive peace agreement for Darfur, which was first presented to the parties on 25 April (the

Arabic translation arrived on 28 April). International heavyweights, including US Deputy Secretary of State Robert Zoellick and Nigerian president Olusegun Obasanjo, travelled to Abuja to take over the process. They decided that the night of 4 May would see the end of the Abuja negotiations. The Sudanese government had signaled its willingness to sign an agreement, so the mediators focused on the rebels. Obasanjo and Zoellick invited the three rebel leaders into a room one by one and pushed them to sign the agreement. For example, Zoellick told Abdelwahid al-Nur, "I conclude that you are not serious about an agreement. Going forward, we are parting ways for good. If you think there is an alternative, you are dead wrong. And I mean dead wrong" (Quoted in De Waal 2007, 277). An observer in the room recounted what happened when the mediators asked Khalil Ibrahim to sign the agreement on behalf of JEM:

> Khalil didn't answer and instead launched out on a political speech. Obasanjo interrupted him, said "Who the hell do you think you are." Then Zoellick got the floor and said something to the effect of "You are not worth it, please leave." Khalil didn't know what to do, there was dead silence until Obasanjo clearly said "You go!"[42]

Despite these threats, Abdelwahid and Khalil Ibrahim refused to sign. Minni Minawi, however, decided otherwise. Therefore, on 5 May 2006, a ceremony was held, during which Minni and the government's lead negotiator signed the Darfur Peace Agreement (DPA). This terminated the Abuja negotiations.

The international community had managed to achieve the peace agreement that it needed to deploy UN peacekeepers, but the agreement itself had adverse consequences in Darfur. Only selective provisions of the DPA were implemented, and it certainly did not foster a political process that would resolve the conflict's underlying issues. Worse, the agreement led to further fragmentation among rebel groups. Some fighters joined the signatory camp, while others went with the non-signatories (Tanner and Tubiana 2007). As a result, fighting between rebel groups increased, and the security situation in Darfur deteriorated (Fadul and Tanner 2007). The failure of the Darfur Peace Agreement also compromised the neutrality of AMIS peacekeepers, who were obliged to defend an unpopular agreement that was rejected by many rebels. As a result, attacks on peacekeepers multiplied (Fadul and Tanner 2007).

The DPA's failure arose partly from this difficult context, but it was also a consequence of the international community's approach to implementing R2P in Darfur. Peace talks were not a priority, as activists were focusing on protection and punishment. Telling in this regard was a rally held for Darfur on 30 April 2006 in Washington, DC. It was one of the largest during the campaign. Few activists spoke about the Abuja talks, even though they were in their decisive final phase. Some activists booed Jendayi Frazer when she mentioned the US government's involvement in the talks.[43] On 10 May 2006, five days after the Abuja talks ended, Eric Reeves called the DPA "a meaningless piece of paper signed under genocidal duress."[44] The bottom line is that activists and policymakers saw peace negotiations as a means to an end—the deployment of UN peacekeepers with a robust protection mandate—rather than an end in itself. This attitude seriously undermined peacemaking attempts in Darfur.

UNAMID: a peacekeeping force to save strangers[45]

In January 2006, the donor countries of AMIS—in particular the EU and the US—made it clear that they would not keep footing the bill. Although hesitant, the Chairman of the AU Commission, Alpha Oumar Konaré, was forced to accept the transition of AMIS into a UN operation (Hamilton 2011, 79–80). The DPA had also helped overcome skepticism from within the UN and paved the way for UN Security Council resolution 1679, which recommended transitioning from AMIS to a UN operation. This was followed on 31 August 2006 by UNSC resolution 1706. It authorized expanding an existing UN peacekeeping force in Sudan that had been deployed in 2005 to oversee the implementation of the Comprehensive Peace Agreement (CPA) between the Sudanese government and the SPLM. UNSC resolution 1706 thus authorized an additional 17,000 soldiers and 3,300 civilian police to be deployed in Darfur and explicitly mentioned R2P.

To curtail Khartoum's hostility and to assuage the concerns of China, the resolution's drafters inserted a clause "inviting" Khartoum's consent for the mission's deployment. Khartoum seized on this and, as Chapter 5 shows, launched a campaign against resolution 1706. According to MacKinnon (2010, 80), "Khartoum's sustained opposition to the resolution won the day and the resolution was effectively shelved in November 2006." As a way out of the impasse, Kofi Annan proposed a new plan: a UN-AU hybrid mission in Darfur. Thus, after many months of protracted negotiations, the UN Security Council created the United Nations-African Union Hybrid Operation in Darfur (UNAMID) on 31 July 2007. Resolution 1769 authorized the deployment of up to 19,555 troops and 3,772 police officers and gave the mission an explicit Chapter VII mandate "to support early and effective implementation of the Darfur Peace Agreement … and protect civilians" (United Nations 2007, para 15).

UNAMID took over from AMIS in January 2008 and became one of the largest and the most expensive UN peacekeeping missions to date.[46] Given the nature of the veto politics surrounding UN peacekeeping, the creation of UNAMID was a highly significant development. It was enabled by three conditions that largely stemmed from framing Darfur as a test case for R2P. Counter-factual reasoning can be employed to underscore this finding.

The first condition relates to the presence of outside promoters. The UN Security Council will only create a peacekeeping force of the size and cost of UNAMID if a coalition of member states is willing to expend significant political capital in support of it. In the case of Darfur, the main impetus came from the US, supported by the UK and later France.[47] The experts interviewed who were involved in the negotiation process confirmed this fact. "The U.S. and especially Zoellick put strong pressure on the UN to come up with a peace operation in Darfur."[48] As explained above, the deployment of a protection force was, in fact, the cornerstone of the US Darfur policy in 2006 and 2007. It responded directly to calls from the Darfur advocacy movement, which had launched a multi-million ad campaign on this topic. But would a Republican US administration have been similarly committed to creating a peacekeeping mission in the absence of such advocacy or if public opinion had not viewed Darfur as a case of mass atrocities? It seems very unlikely given that UNAMID's creation required an investment of significant political capital over a sustained period of time.

The second condition was support within the UN Secretariat. At the outset, "there was significant resistance within UNDPKO about taking on a peacekeeping mission in Darfur."[49] The fear was that such a mission could lead the UN into the kind of unchartered waters that—according to the Brahimi Report—had led to the peacekeeping disasters of the 1990s. According to another UN official:

> UNAMID violates almost all of Brahimi's principles. First of all, it violates Brahimi's preference for light-footprint missions. Second, it violates the principle that the Security Council should be told what it needs, not what it wants to hear. A too optimistic picture was painted of UNAMID—the U.S. wanted to believe that the mission would make a difference; there was pressure from activist groups, and the UN Secretariat played along without thinking. A third point regarding Brahimi is that there was no lasting peace agreement in Darfur which UNAMID could help implement.[50]

It was Kofi Annan who made sure that internal resistance did not obstruct the process of creating UNAMID. He was personally invested in Darfur and cut short the critical voices within UNDPKO. One telling episode from an informal UN Security Council meeting in late 2006 involved Annan and the particularly critical head of UNDPKO, Jean-Marie Guéhenno. According to an observer:

> Guéhenno went on and on about how a UN peacekeeping mission in Darfur would be a screwdriver for a problem that requires a hammer; that it would be difficult to find troop contributors. After a while, Annan just cut him off and basically said "We are going to do this!" Guéhenno just shrunk. And this was the end of the discussion within the UN Secretariat. The message was very clear.[51]

Precluding internal resistance was an important factor. Allowed to run its course, opposition to the mission could have played into the hands of the Sudanese government and reinforced the position of other states that were reluctant to send UN peacekeepers to Darfur. What made the difference was Kofi Annan's personal commitment. Had Darfur not been framed as "another Rwanda," would Annan have taken the same position? Again, it seems unlikely. As a long-time UN official and former head of UN peacekeeping, Annan was normally receptive to the advice of his specialists. However, Darfur was a special case, and Annan was willing to overrule his staff.

The third condition was the absence of spoilers among the veto-holding permanent members of the UN Security Council—the P5. This primarily concerned China, which has a strong normative preference for non-interference and traditional peacekeeping. As Contessi (2010) demonstrated, Beijing repeatedly emphasized this position in UNSC discussions about peacekeeping in Darfur, and it was at China's insistence that the consent clause was included in resolution 1706. However, one year later, China dropped its resistance and even put pressure on Khartoum to accept the proposed hybrid mission (Richardson 2011). Without it, resolution 1769 would not have been possible.

What caused China to change its position? The Darfur campaigns played an important role. In 2007, a small group of Darfur activists around Eric Reeves and Mia Farrow turned their attention on China, seeking to highlight Beijing's role in supporting the NCP regime in Sudan. They coined the phrase "genocide Olympics"[52] and, with a US$500,000 grant from Humanity United, started the campaign Dream for Darfur.[53] The campaign quickly gained momentum. According to Jill Savitt, the campaign's coordinator, "We received so much press it was ridiculous."[54] The campaign hit China where it hurt the most. It connected China's prestige project, the 2008 Olympic Games in Beijing, with the stigma of genocide. In classic spiral model behavior, China first denied the activists' assertions and then made a series of tactical concessions, which included acquiescing to the deployment of a Chapter VII mission in Darfur (Budabin 2011). The counterfactual point is clear: Had it not been for the "genocide Olympics" campaign, there is no indication that China would have changed its position.

What difference did UNAMID make on the ground? Its positive contributions included regular patrols and other activities like community policing that have helped to improve the safety in and around IDP camps (Kahn 2008, 49–50). UNAMID also facilitated the delivery of humanitarian aid by carrying out road patrols between the main towns of Darfur. Some UN agencies, in particular the World Food Programme, travelled with peacekeepers for protection. NGOs that are reluctant about associating themselves with military actors often followed the patrols at a distance. The same was true for commercial trucks and local busses operating in Darfur. The presence of peacekeeping forces also seems to have increased physical protection. The level of violence in Darfur diminished from 2005. For example, from January 2008 to July 2009, a study of the Harvard Humanitarian Initiative reported 2,112 battle-related fatalities in Darfur, of which 585 were civilian casualties (De Waal et al. 2010, 6). This represents a stark decrease compared to 2003 and 2004. It thus plausible that the presence of peacekeepers deterred some attacks, even if the main driver was changing dynamics on the battlefield.

While there are positive examples, UNAMID's overall ability to protect civilians has been limited. It has certainly been a far cry from the aspirations of the R2P doctrine. There were indeed several cases where UNAMID blatantly failed to protect people under imminent threat.[55] There are different reasons for UNAMID's shortcomings, many of which had already afflicted its predecessor, AMIS. First and foremost, the number of military personnel was insufficient to provide comprehensive protection in a territory as large, as populated, and as unstable as Darfur.[56] The mission's equipment was also inadequate, in particular the absence of military utility helicopters. Another complicating factor was Darfur's highly volatile security situation that was characterized by banditry and crime. Security requirement thus drew significant resources, led to high staff turnover, and made it difficult for UNAMID staff to travel or interact with the local population. Another constraint was the restrictions imposed by the Sudanese government, which had undermined the mission from the outset. And as explained in Chapter 6, when international attention for Darfur waned, Khartoum faced little to no consequences for doing so.

In sum, R2P enabled the creation of one of the world's largest peacekeeping missions. Peacekeepers in Darfur have had a positive impact in some areas, but on the whole, have not been able to protect the vulnerable civilian population. As the primary instrument to implement R2P, peacekeeping fell short because of the structural difficulties that limit the effectiveness of peacekeeping missions in contexts like Darfur.

The ICC Factor: Criminal justice to save strangers

The International Criminal Court as a tool of R2P

In addition to peacekeeping, international criminal justice emerged as a main tool to implement R2P in Darfur. To understand the ICC's role in the international response to the Darfur conflict, it is important to consider the convergence of R2P and the ICC. Noteworthy in this context is Scheffer's (2008, 111) proposition of "atrocity crimes framing the responsibility to protect." Accordingly, R2P is triggered by a series of legally defined crimes. The same crimes constitute the core of the Rome Statute, which established the ICC and on which its involvement is based. Thus, R2P and the ICC go hand in hand and should be applied in conjunction—the former to bring about interventions to stop atrocities, and the latter to punish the perpetrators of those atrocities. Further illustrative is an essay by Cherif Bassiouni, the Chairman of the drafting committee of the Rome Statute, titled "Advancing the Responsibility to Protect through International Criminal Justice." For him, the essence of R2P is to spur early action so that atrocities can be prevented before they occur. Thus, international criminal justice helps to advance the goal of prevention

> on the assumption that the prosecution and punishment of decision-makers and senior perpetrators ... will produce deterrence. If this result is obtained, even in part, then prevention of crimes such as genocide, crimes against humanity, and war crimes will be achieved and the goals of R2P will be achieved. In this respect, international criminal justice can be seen as a corollary of R2P.
>
> (Bassiouni 2009, 33)

Bassiouni's vision explains the convergence of the ICC and R2P: By promoting the accountability of senior leaders, the ICC deters crimes and thus helps implement the R2P prevention agenda. In this context, Akhavan (2005, 419) clarified the underlying rationale of the ICC's contribution to conflict prevention:

> The interests of global justice include deterrence or general prevention not only through pragmatic considerations such as shifting the boundaries of legitimacy and thereby changing the cost-benefit calculus of using atrocities as an instrument of power, but also through the more subtle, but far-reaching, socio-pedagogical influence of judicial stigmatization to induce subliminal inhibitions against criminal conduct.

It is Akhavan's first consideration—that the ICC can affect a cost on perpetrators that makes them change their behavior—that is reflected in the R2P doctrine. According to Evans (2008), the ICC plays an important role in implementing R2P, both before and during conflicts. It can use the threat of international criminal prosecution to prevent the outbreak of conflict, and it can indict senior leaders as a form of intervention to stop ongoing atrocities. The same idea underpins the 3P approach. The aim of the second "P," punishment, is to create a cost for perpetrators by prosecuting them in an international court. This is why the Darfur activists promoted the ICC, providing strong support to the Court, in particular its prosecutor.

Apart from generating political support, the most important contribution of R2P was in providing an interpretive frame through which the ICC prosecutor at the time, Luis Moreno Ocampo, could make sense of the situation in Darfur and the ICC's role in it. This was crucial because, in spite of operating within the set legal framework of the Rome Statute, the Office of the Prosecutor has considerable leeway in its work. The prosecutor's most important responsibility, for which the Rome Statute provides limited guidance, is to decide against whom to press charges (Mahony 2012). This is where the prosecutor's interpretation of the nature of the conflict and its main actors plays an important role. According to the dominant narrative, the main culprits of the violence in Darfur were the NCP regime as well as its *janjawid* henchmen. It made sense, therefore, that Moreno Ocampo first pressed charges against a *janjawid* leader, Ali Muhammad Ali Abd-Al-Rahman (known as "Ali Kushayb"), and the former Sudanese interior minister, Ahmed Haroun. The prosecutor announced his decision on 27 February 2007—a decision, which de Waal (2008, 31) qualified as "politically astute" because Haroun "is a significant figure in the hierarchy with command responsibility ..., but not someone sufficiently senior nor well-connected to the highest leadership that he could not be sacrificed politically."

However, Khartoum showed no intention of extraditing the indictees and, as Chapter 5 shows, denounced the ICC as an instrument of neo-colonialism. Given Khartoum's lack of cooperation, Moreno Ocampo decided to move up the chain of command all the way to the top. On 14 July 2008, he applied for an arrest warrant against Sudan's president Omar al-Bashir on two charges of war crimes, five charges of crimes against humanity, and three charges of genocide in Darfur. After much deliberation, the Pre-Trial Chamber issued the warrant on 4 March 2009, at first excluding the genocide charges but then reinserting them in July 2010 upon Moreno Ocampo's appeal.

The decision sparked worldwide controversy and caused a backlash against the ICC in Africa (Mills and Bloomfield 2018). What compelled the prosecutor to charge al-Bashir despite knowing that an indictment against a sitting head of state would carry significant political risk? Moreno Ocampo's speeches shed light on his mission. In June 2008, a few weeks before announcing the charges against al-Bashir, Moreno Ocampo briefed the UN Security Council about the situation in Darfur:

> In Darfur, the evidence shows an organized campaign by Sudanese officials to attack civilians, in particular the Fur, Massalit and Zaghawa, with the objective to physically and mentally destroy entire communities....
>
> Sudanese officials protect the criminals and not the victims. Denial of crimes, cover up and attempts to shift responsibility have been another characteristic of the criminal plan in Darfur. We have seen it before.
>
> The Nazi regime invoked its national sovereignty to attack its own population, and then crossed borders to attack people in other countries....
>
> The evidence shows that the commission of such crimes on such a scale, over a period of five years, and throughout Darfur, has required the sustained mobilization of the entire Sudanese state apparatus....
>
> It takes a lot to commit massive crimes. It takes planning and organization. It takes commanders and many executioners. But mostly, it requires that the rest of the world look away and do nothing. This Council, when it requested my Office to intervene in Darfur, acted in a decisive way, thinking of the Darfuris, but remembering also Rwanda, and Srebrenica. At the Council's request, my Office will present new evidence exposing the facts and identifying those most responsible.[57]

This speech reveals Moreno Ocampo's strong normative position, in line with R2P, that inaction in the face of mass atrocities is morally wrong. He also made sense of Darfur as a case of genocide on par with previous genocides, such as the Holocaust and Rwanda, where the state launched a centrally planned and systematically executed campaign to eliminate a group within its population. Accordingly, in his application for an arrest warrant against al-Bashir, Moreno Ocampo stated, "His pretext was a 'counterinsurgency'. His intent was genocide. The goal was not simply to defeat a rebellion, but to destroy those ethnic groups whose members challenged his power" (International Criminal Court 2008, 7).

Viewing the situation in Darfur primarily through the prism of saving strangers informed Moreno Ocampo's prosecutorial strategy in two ways. First, it explains why he targeted Omar al-Bashir: Insofar as the Sudanese state was the main culprit of genocide, it seemed logical that the ICC would pursue the person at its helm. Second, it elucidates Moreno Ocampo's use of "perpetration by means" or "indirect perpetration" as a basis of liability to create a connection between al-Bashir and the genocide crimes in Darfur. Indirect perpetration implies a high threshold of proof, especially for genocide. This meant not only that the direct perpetrator (the *janjawid* militia) and the indirect perpetrator (al-Bashir) acted with genocidal intent, but also that the latter controlled the will of the former (International Criminal Court 2008, 70–72). Other modes of liability would make prosecution easier. This is the case, for example, with "common purpose," when guilt is inferred from a person's involvement in an organization that committed crimes. However, this is a mode of secondary liability, which would not have been appropriate given that Moreno Ocampo saw al-Bashir as the main culprit of a genocidal campaign akin to that of the Holocaust or Rwanda.[58] The prosecutor's legal approach drew criticism, for example from Andrew Cayley (2008, 840), a former staff member of the Office of the Prosecutor, who wrote, "It is difficult to cry government-led genocide in one breath and then explain in the next why two million Darfuris have sought refuge around the principal army garrisons of their province."

Another aspect pertaining to R2P explains the vehemence with which the ICC prosecutor pursued the Darfur case. He wanted to help the victims of genocide by promoting accountability and justice. An editorial that Moreno Ocampo wrote in July 2010, after the Pre-Trial Chamber reinserted the genocide charges into the indictment against al-Bashir, is revealing:

> Bashir is attacking Sudanese citizens, the same people he has the duty to protect. Now the international community has a new opportunity to provide protection. There are countries that are not members of the treaty that created the ICC, but which are members of the genocide convention. The convention could apply in this situation, triggering the responsibility of these states to prevent and to suppress the acts of genocide. Humanity has a responsibility to protect the Darfuris.
>
> As the prosecutor of the ICC, my mandate is to ensure justice for these Darfuris, the victims of genocide.[59]

This demonstrates that Moreno Ocampo essentially saw the ICC as a tool of R2P in Darfur. In addition to promoting justice for victims, the prosecutor saw one ICC contribution as removing indictees from power and therefore stopping mass atrocities. After the Haroun indictment, he stated,

> My job is to help the people of Darfur here and now—to help stop the crimes. Haroun is threatening the victims. If he is removed from office, arrested and sent to The Hague, the system that produced the crimes will be broken.[60]

Taking this argument to its logical conclusion, an indictment against Sudan's head of state is tantamount to calling for regime change. Although the prosecutor did not make this explicit, it was one of the main reasons why the indictment was so controversial.

Strangers in jeopardy? The consequences of the al-Bashir indictment

When the ICC confirmed the arrest warrant against Omar al-Bashir on 4 March 2009, the government cancelled the licenses of three national NGOs and expelled 13 international aid NGOs.[61] Eleven of the 13 international NGOs came from the US, France, and the UK—countries that had taken a particularly strong stance on Darfur and supported the ICC's activities in Sudan. This suggests the expulsions were a form of retaliation against unfriendly governments. The consequences on the ground were serious. The expelled organizations made up 40 percent of aid workers in Darfur and were responsible for more than half of the total aid delivered. As the Humanitarian Policy Group (2009, 1) wrote a few weeks after the expulsion, "assistance to Darfur's 2.7 million-plus displaced people has been severely compromised, and a number of health-related crises are already emerging." Khartoum eventually allowed some of the NGOs back in, while UN agencies took over programs from the NGOs that were forced to leave. However, according to Jonathan Loeb (2013, 25–26), access for humanitarian organizations operating in Darfur, especially in rebel-controlled areas, deteriorated permanently. The indictment against al-Bashir also increased the government's obstruction and intimidation of aid workers and peacekeepers (Duursma and Müller 2019). Moreover, the quality of aid suffered, as it became very difficult to carry out activities related to protection, human rights, and gender-based violence.[62]

Apart from the immediate consequences of the expulsions, the humanitarians operating in Darfur were divided by the ICC's intervention. Some rejected the court, while others saw it as a positive development and even put evidence at its disposal. Most aid groups had supported the ICC's creation, and many were even members of the Coalition for the International Criminal Court. However, as the ICC started operating in conflict regions, the attitude of aid NGOs towards the Court took an ambiguous turn. While few have an official policy of cooperating with the ICC, "the vast majority of NGOs ... prefer to choose on a case-by-case basis between humanitarian action and collaborating with the ICC to fight impunity" (Weissman 2009, 3). This ambivalence stems from the contradiction between the pragmatism of delivering aid to as many victims as possible, which ICC cooperation could hinder, and a principled commitment to justice, which ICC cooperation could promote.

It is precisely this conflict between principles and pragmatism that the al-Bashir indictment brought to the fore. The case of MSF is telling in this regard. Officially, "all MSF sections have adopted a binding internal policy refraining from any cooperation with the ICC."[63] However, the reality is more complex. MSF's Darfur engagement is characterized by several contradictions and individual acts of resistance against this policy. At the outset of the crisis, MSF-France was one of the first organizations to talk publicly about the crisis in

Darfur. It thus turned the light of international attention onto the crisis, which put the Sudanese government under heavy pressure. Moreover, on 8 March 2005, as the negotiations about a possible ICC referral by the UN Security Council were in full swing, MSF-Holland published a report on rape crimes in Darfur. The timing of its publication was not likely a coincidence, especially since the report called for "end[ing] the impunity of the rapists and their accomplices."[64] Indeed, the issue of rape was taken up by Kofi Annan when lobbying for the ICC referral. Even if he did not expressly mention MSF, it was clear from his remarks that his information stemmed from the report.[65] The Sudanese government evidently thought so too. In May 2005, it arrested two MSF-Holland employees, accusing them of undermining national security.[66]

When the expulsions happened, the consequences of MSF's ambiguity became evident. The message became all the clearer when the Sudanese government forced out the French and Dutch sections but allowed the less outspoken Belgian and Spanish sections to stay. This triggered extensive debates within MSF, which culminated in an editorial by its International Council president, Christophe Fournier, published in the *New York Times*. He clarified that

> humanitarian assistance is not necessarily compatible with punishing war criminals or, for that matter, the armed protection of civilians. The crisis in Darfur highlights the need for aid organizations to acknowledge these contradictions and dispel any doubts about what their priority is and what they will or will not do. While Doctors Without Borders respects the ICC, we have not cooperated and will not cooperate with the court or relay any information to it, a position we have publicly and privately affirmed both to the ICC and to the Sudanese authorities since 2004. Making clear the role of humanitarian aid and demonstrating a commitment to impartiality and neutrality allows groups to work on both sides of the frontline not only in Darfur but in other conflicts as well.[67]

The tone of Fournier's editorial indicates that those advocating for a policy of non-cooperation with the ICC prevailed in the internal debate.[68] However, there was significant internal dissent, as some staff members criticized MSF for undermining punitive action for war crimes, which they saw as an integral part of humanitarian assistance.[69]

In sum, the intervention of the ICC as an instrument of saving strangers in Darfur had two problematic effects on humanitarian organizations. First, insofar as a number of NGOs supported the ICC, they were drawn closer to the politics of international intervention perceived by the Sudanese government as highly subversive. As a result, humanitarian organizations became vulnerable to retaliations, like the expulsion and expropriation seen in March 2009. Second, the ICC fostered a conflict within aid organizations. Those humanitarians favoring a pragmatic approach in order to maximize access were pitted against those advocating for a principled approach based on accountability and justice. This is another version of "good vs. good"—an expression coined by David Rieff to highlight the divisions between the Darfur activists who demanded military intervention and aid workers concerned about the adverse effects.[70]

Chapter findings

Three insights emerge from this chapter about the implementation of the core R2P norm in the context of Darfur. First, the strategies and policies for implementing R2P were aligned with the discursive context that made the situation meaningful in terms of saving strangers. Against the background of the Darfur narrative, the remedies to save strangers in Darfur emphasized military intervention to provide physical protection to victims, on the one hand, and pressure on and punishment of the perpetrator, on the other. Policymakers reacted accordingly. They spent most of their political capital trying to get peacekeepers deployed and the ICC to take up the matter. This approach came at a cost. It crowded out an alternative strategy centered on peacemaking, for which compromise and collaboration with the Sudanese government would have been needed.

Second, in any situation, the implementation of R2P competes with other policy priorities. The role of norm entrepreneurs was crucial in ensuring that R2P prevailed over other interests related to Darfur. In this regard, the efforts of internal norm entrepreneurs within governments and international organizations, like Kofi Annan, complemented the actions of external norm advocates, like the Save Darfur Coalition.

Third, Darfur showed that translating the R2P norm into concrete policies happens through a difficult and lengthy process of negotiations involving various stakeholders. But there is an inherent danger that the instruments to promote R2P do not match the reality on the ground. This affected the UN-AU peace-keeping force, UNAMID, which was deployed only after the situation in Darfur had evolved considerably. The force also suffered from a misunderstanding of what peacekeepers could realistically achieve in a context like Darfur as well as from the discrepancy between its ambitious mandate and the political will states were willing to muster to save strangers in Darfur.

Notes

1 Interview (CO), Khartoum, November 2010.
2 Interview (AI), Boston, March 2010.
3 Interview (CY), Washington, DC, March 2011.
4 The pictures shown during the exhibit are available from Darfur/Darfur's website: www.darfurdarfur.org/main/ (accessed 8 June 2019).
5 *The Translator* describes the path of Daoud Hari, who was stringer and translator for several international journalists in Darfur, including Nicholas Kristof and Phil Cox, until he was arrested by the Sudanese government and eventually managed to escape. *Tears of the Desert* tells the story of Halima Bashir, a medical doctor from Darfur, who was imprisoned and raped by *janjawid* and subsequently fled Darfur.
6 Quoted in Rebecca Leung, "Witnessing Genocide in Sudan," *CBS News*, 8 October 2004, https://www.cbsnews.com/news/witnessing-genocide-in-sudan-08-10-2004/ (accessed 8 June 2019).

7   Jonathan Foreman, "Endgame in Africa:, *Men's Vogue Magazine*, October 2006.
8   Julie Flint, "Darfur, Saving Itself," *Washington Post*, 3 June 2007.
9   The blog was active from April to September 2009: https://savedarfuraccountabilityproject. wordpress.com/ (accessed 8 June 2019).
10 Sam Dealey, "An Atrocity That Needs No Exaggeration," *New York Times*, 12 August 2007.
11 Interview (AT), Washington, DC, March 2010.
12 Interview with Jerry Fowler, Washington, DC, March 2010. In 2007 and 2008 SDC's revenues decreased to 7.5 and 5 million respectively.
13 Interview (AP), Washington, DC, March 2010.
14 "John Prendergast Peace, Protection & Punishment," 5 January 2008, online video, www.youtube.com/watch?v=oBxOGp74zSc&feature=channel (accessed 8 June 2019), at 1:05–2:01.
15 "John Prendergast: Peace, Protection & Punishment," at 0:49–1:05.
16 Interview (AJ), New York, March 2010.
17 UNSC resolution 1556, 30 July 2004.
18 Quoted in BBC World News, "UK Must 'Deal' with Sudan Crisis," 22 July 2004, http://news.bbc.co.uk/2/hi/uk_news/politics/3917041.stm (accessed 8 June 2019).
19 Fabrice Weissman, "Humanitarian Dilemmas in Darfur," MSF Crash Foundation, 1 July 2008, available from www.msf-crash.org/en/publications/war-and-humanitarianism/ humanitarian-dilemmas-darfur (accessed 8 June 2019).
20 Quoted in Rebecca Hamilton, "Inside Colin Powell's Decision to Declare Genocide in Darfur," *The Atlantic*, 17 August 2011.
21 For details on the creation of the Atrocities Documentation Team, see Bang-Jensen and Frease (2006).
22 Secretary Colin Powell, Interview on National Public Radio with Michele Norris, Khartoum, 30 June 2004, https://2001–2009.state.gov/secretary/former/powell/remarks/ 34053.htm (accessed 8 June 2019).
23 *Documenting Atrocities in Darfur*, State Publication 11182, September 2004, https://2001–2009.state.gov/g/drl/rls/36028.htm (accessed 8 June 2019).
24 Hamilton, "Inside Colin Powell's Decision."
25 "The Crisis in Darfur," Testimony by Secretary Colin Powell before the Senate Foreign Relations Committee, Washington, DC, 9 September 2004, https://2001- 2009.state.gov/secretary/former/powell/remarks/36042.htm (accessed 8 June 2019).
26 See Hamilton, "Inside Colin Powell's Decision."
27 Samantha Power, "Court of First Resort," *New York Times*, 10 February 2005.
28 Human Rights Watch, "U.S. Proposal for a Darfur Tribunal: Not an Effective Option to Ensure Justice," 15 February 2005, www.hrw.org/news/2005/02/15/us-proposal- darfur-tribunal-not-effective-option-ensure-justice (accessed 8 June 2019).
29 Nicholas Kristof, "Why Should We Shield the Killers," *New York Times*, 2 February 2005.
30 For details on the UN sanctions regime regarding Darfur, see the website of Sanctions App, under "Cases and Episodes"/"Sudan II," http://sanctionsapp.com/ (accessed 8 June 2019).
31 Interview with Jendayi Frazer, Washington, DC, March 2010.
32 Interview with Jendayi Frazer, Washington, DC, March 2010.
33 Nicholas Kristof, "Dithering as Others Die," *New York Times*, 26 June 2004.
34 Apart from having operational functions, private security contractors were present in the debate about Darfur, "free-riding" on the R2P discourse to make the case for private security. Doug Brooks, a private security lobbyist, said concerning Darfur:

    What we've seen is the West has largely abrogated its responsibility to put their own people on the ground in places they don't care about. It is willing to author- ize these missions, but it's not willing to put boots on the ground. The private sector can step in. It can fill that gap.

(Quoted in Frank Langfitt, "Private Military Firm Pitches its Services in Darfur," article on the National Public Radio website, 26 May 2006, www.npr.org/templates/story/story.php?storyId=5433902&t=1548682666371 (accessed 8 June 2019))

For a critical analysis of the role of private security contractors in the debate about Darfur, see Leander and van Munster (2007).

35 Interview with lobbyist for private security companies (CX), Washington, DC, March 2011.

36 Hamilton, "Building a Permanent Anti-Genocide Constituency."

37 Jason Zengerle, "Student Aid: Raising Money to Save Darfur," *The Atlantic*, 27 March 2006.

38 Roméo Dallaire, "Looking at Darfur, Seeing Rwanda," *The Toronto Star*, 5 October 2004.

39 For a discussion of AMIS' record in civilian protection, see Williams (2006, 171).

40 Phone interview with EU official (DK), October 2011.

41 Nicholas Kristof, "What Can Be Done about Darfur? Plenty," *New York Times*, 29 November 2005.

42 Interview with Roger Winter, Washington, DC, February 2010.

43 The author obtained this information from an anonymous reviewer during the review process of a paper submitted to the *Journal of Modern African Studies*.

44 Eric Reeves, "Why Abuja Won't Save Darfur," *The New Republic* online, 10 May 2006, http://sudanreeves.org/2006/07/11/why-abuja-wont-save-darfur-from-the-new-republic-may-10-2006/ (accessed 8 June 2019).

45 This section is partly based on a chapter the author wrote for the book *Peacekeeping in Africa*. See Lanz (2014).

46 In fact, UNAMID was the most expensive UN peacekeeping mission for five consecutive budget cycles, even as the resources approved fluctuated from US$1.276 (for the 2007–2008 cycle), 1.5 (2009–2009), 1.599 (2009–2010), 1.808 (2010–2011), 1.689 (2011–2012), to 1.512 billion (2012–2013). Subsequently, UNAMID ceased to be the most expensive UN peacekeeping mission. Data available on the UNDPKO website, https://peacekeeping.un.org/en/how-we-are-funded (accessed 28 January 2019).

47 In addition to supporting the creation of an UN operation in Darfur, France initiated the creation of an EU force across the border from Darfur in eastern Chad as well as in the northeast of the Central African Republic. The force was deployed from March 2008 to March 2009 and consisted of 3,700 soldiers (Lanz 2011). While the EU force did not operate on Darfuri soil, it was primarily conceived as a response to the Darfur conflict. It was strongly promoted by Bernard Kouchner, long-time advocate of humanitarian intervention and leader of the French Save Darfur campaign, after he became foreign minister in Nicolas Sarkozy's government in 2007 (Glaser and Smith 2008, 62–64).

48 Interview (AL), New York, March 2010.

49 Interview with senior UN official (AL), New York, March 2010.

50 Interview (CO), Khartoum, November 2010.

51 Interview (DC), New York, March 2011. For details on the debates about Darfur peacekeeping within the UN Secretariat, see Ben Wallace-Wells, "Darfuristan," *Rolling Stone*, 11 December 2009.

52 The term goes back to an editorial written by Mia Farrow with her son Ronan Farrow: "Genocide Olympics," *Wall Street Journal*, 28 March 2007.

53 For details on the Dream for Darfur campaign, see Ilan Greenberg, "Changing the Rules of the Game," *New York Times Magazine*, 30 March 2008. See also Hamilton (2011, Chapter 10).

54 Interview with Jill Savitt, New York, March 2010.

55   Column Lynch, "A Mission That Was Set Up to Fail," *Foreign Policy* online, 9 April 2014, https://foreignpolicy.com/2014/04/08/a-mission-that-was-set-up-to-fail/ (accessed 8 June 2019).

56   For a discussion of the necessary troop numbers in a civilian protection force in relation to the size of the territory on which it is operating and the number of people it has to protect, see Williams (2006, 176–177).

57   Statement of the Prosecutor of the ICC to the UN Security Council pursuant to UNSCR 1593 (2005), 5 June 2008, www.icc-cpi.int/NR/rdonlyres/71FC0D56–11FC-41B9-BF39–33FC54F2C2A1/223633/ICCOTPST20080605ENG6.pdf (accessed 8 June 2019).

58   Alex de Waal made a similar argument in a blog post: "The ICC vs. Bashir: Debating the Mode of Liability," 9 February 2009, http://africanarguments.org/2009/02/09/the-icc-vs-bashir-debating-the-mode-of-liability/ (accessed 8 June 2019).

59   Luis Moreno Ocampo, "Now End this Darfur Denial," *Guardian*, 15 July 2010.

60   ICC, "ICC Prosecutor Luis Moreno-Ocampo urges arrest of indicted criminals, following release of new Darfur documentary," press release, 6 September 2007, www.icc-cpi.int/Pages/item.aspx?name=icc%20prosecutor%20luis%20moreno_ocampo%20urges%20arrest%20of%20indicted%20criminals_%20following (accessed 8 June 2019).

61   The national NGOs were: the Amal Centre for Rehabilitation of Victims of Violence, the Khartoum Centre for Human Rights Development and Environment and the Sudan Social Development Organisation (SUDO). The 13 international NGOs were: Action Contre la Faim, CARE International, Cooperative Housing Foundation, International Rescue Committee, MSF Holland and MSF France, Mercy Corps, the Norwegian Refugee Council, Oxfam GB, the Planning and Development Collaborative International, Save the Children UK and Save the Children US, and Solidarités (Humanitarian Policy Group 2009, footnote 1).

62   Interview (AG), Khartoum, November 2010. See also Chapter 4.

63   MSF, "MSF Position Regarding the ICC Prosecutor's Case against the President of Sudan," open letter, 29 July 2008, www.msf.org/article/msfs-position-regarding-international-criminal-courts-prosecutors-case-presentation-against (accessed 8 June 2019).

64   MSF, "The Crushing Burden of Rape: Sexual Violence in Darfur," online paper, 8 March 2005, available from www.msf.org/crushing-burden-rape-sexual-violence-darfur (accessed 8 June 2019).

65   Interview with MSF staff (DU), Paris, November 2011 (interview in French, author's translation).

66   MSF, "Second Arrest in Sudan; Dutch Coordinator for MSF in Darfur Held This Morning," 31 May 2005, www.doctorswithoutborders.org/what-we-do/news-stories/news/second-arrest-sudan-dutch-coordinator-msf-darfur-held-morning (accessed 8 June 2019).

67   Christophe Fournier, "Darfur, Punishment or Aid," *New York Times*, 27 March 2009.

68   Indicative of this trend is that in 2010 MSF declared it did not support R2P because the use of force was incompatible with the principles of humanitarian assistance. See Weissman (2010).

69   This is the essence of two internal MSF documents: "Darfur: Aid or Punishment: An Op-Ed Debate" (24 March 2009) and "International Justice and Humanitarian Aid: Elements of the Debate" (27 March 2009).

70   David Rieff: "Good vs. Good," *Los Angeles Times*, 24 June 2007.

References

Akhavan, Payam. 2005. "The Lord's Resistance Army Case: Uganda's Submission of the First State Referral to the International Criminal Court." *American Journal of International Law* 99: 403–421.

Badescu, Cristina G., and Linnea Bergholm. 2009. "The Responsibility to Protect and the Conflict in Darfur: The Big Let-Down." *Security Dialogue* 40: 287–309.

Badescu, Cristina G. 2010. "The African Union." In *The International Politics of Mass Atrocities: The Case of Darfur*, eds. David R. Black and Paul. D. Williams. Milton Park: Routledge. 100–118.

Bang-Jensen, Nina, and Stefanie Frease. 2006. "Creating the ADT: Turning a Good Idea into Reality." In *Genocide in Darfur: Investigating the Atrocities in the Sudan*, eds. Samuel Totten and Eric Markusen. New York: Routledge. 45–57.

Bashir, Halima, and Damien Lewis. 2008. *Tears of the Desert: One Woman's True Story of Surviving the Horrors of Darfur*. London: Hodder & Stoughton.

Bassiouni, Cherif. 2009. "Advancing the Responsibility to Protect through International Criminal Justice." In *Responsibility to Protect: The Global Moral Compact for the 21st Century*, eds. Richard H. Cooper and Juliette Voïnov Kohler. New York: Palgrave Macmillan. 31–42.

Brooks, Sean P. 2008. "Enforcing a Turning Point and Imposing a Deal: An Analysis of the Darfur Abuja Negotiations of 2006." *International Negotiation* 13: 413–440.

Budabin, Alexandra Cosima. 2011. "Genocide Olympics: How Activists Linked China, Darfur & Beijing 2008." In *Sudan Looks East: China, India and the Politics of Asian Alternatives*, eds. Daniel Large and Luke A. Patey. Woodbridge: James Currey. 139–156.

Cayley, Andrew T. 2008. "The Prosecutor's Strategy in Seeking the Arrest of Sudanese President Al Bashir on Charges of Genocide." *Journal of International Criminal Justice* 6: 829–840.

Cheadle, Don, and John Prendergast. 2007. *Not on our Watch: The Mission to End Genocide in Darfur and Beyond*. New York: Hyperion.

Chin, Sally, and Jonathan Morgenstein. 2005. *No Power to Protect: The African Union Mission in Sudan*. Washington, DC: Refugees International. November.

Contessi, Nicola P. 2010. "Multilateralism, Intervention and Norm Contestation: China's Stance on Darfur in the UN Security Council." *Security Dialogue* 41: 323–344.

De Waal, Alex. 2005. "Defining Genocide." *Index on Censorship* 34: 6–13.

De Waal, Alex. 2007. "Darfur's Deadline: The Final Days of the Abuja Peace Process." In *War in Darfur and the Search for Peace*, ed. Alex De Waal. Cambridge, MA: Harvard University Press. 267–283.

De Waal, Alex. 2008. "Darfur, the Court and Khartoum: The Politics of State Non-Cooperation." In *Courting Conflict? Justice, Peace and the ICC in Africa*, eds. Nicholas Waddell and Phil Clark. London: The Royal African Society. 29–35.

De Waal, Alex, Chad Hazlett, Christian Davenport, and Joshua Kennedy. 2010. *Evidence-Based Peacekeeping: Exploring the Epidemiology of Lethal Violence in Darfur*. Cambridge, MA: Harvard Humanitarian Initiative. March.

Duursma, Allard, and Tanja R. Müller. 2019. "The ICC Indictment against Al-Bashir and its Repercussions for Peacekeeping and Humanitarian Operations in Darfur." *Third World Quarterly*: 1–19.

Ekengard, Arvid. 2008. *The African Union Mission in Sudan (AMIS): Experiences and Lessons Learned*. Stockholm: FOI, Swedish Defence Research Agency. August.

Evans, Gareth. 2008. *The Responsibility to Protect: Ending Mass Atrocity Crimes Once and for All*. Washington, DC: Brookings Institution Press.

Fadul, Abdul-Jabbar, and Victor Tanner. 2007. "Darfur after Abuja: A View from the Ground." In *War in Darfur and the Search for Peace*, ed. Alex De Waal. Cambridge, MA: Harvard University Press. 284–313.

Funk, Kevin, and Steven Fake. 2009. *The Scramble for Africa: Darfur-Intervention and the USA*. Montreal: Black Rose Books.

Glaser, Antoine, and Stephen W. Smith. 2008. *Sarko en Afrique*. Paris: Plon.

Hamilton, Rebecca. 2011. *Fighting for Darfur: Public Action and the Struggle to Stop Genocide*. New York: Palgrave Macmillan.

Hamilton, Rebecca, and Chad Hazlett. 2007. "'Not on Our Watch': The Emergence of the American Movement for Darfur." In *War in Darfur and the Search for Peace*, ed. Alex De Waal. Cambridge, MA: Harvard University Press. 337–366.

Hari, Daoud. 2008. *The Translator: A Tribesman's Memoir of Darfur*. New York: Random House.

Human Rights Watch. 2006. *Imperatives for Immediate Change: The African Union Mission in Sudan*. New York: HRW. January.

Humanitarian Policy Group. 2009. *Where to Now? Agency Expulsions in Sudan: Consequences and Next Steps*. London: HPG, Overseas Development Institute. March.

International Criminal Court. 2008. *Situation in Darfur, the Sudan: Public Redacted Version of the Prosecutor's Application under Article 58*. ICC-02/05. 14 July.

International Crisis Group. 2005b. *The AU's Mission in Darfur: Bridging the Gaps*. Africa Briefing No. 28. Brussels: ICG. 6 July.

International Crisis Group. 2006. *To Save Darfur*. Africa Report No. 105. Brussels: ICG. 17 March 2006.

Kagwanja, Peter, and Patrick Mutahi. 2007. *Protection of Civilians in African Peace Missions: The Case of the African Union Mission in Sudan, Darfur*. ISS Paper 139. Pretoria: Institute for Security Studies. May.

Kahn, Clea. 2008. *Conflict, Arms, and Militarization: The Dynamics of Darfur's IDP Camps*. HSBA Working Paper 15. Geneva: Small Arms Survey. September.

Karpman, Stephen. 1968. "Fairy Tales and Script Drama Analysis." *Transactional Analysis Bulletin* 7: 39–43.

Kaufman, Zachary. 2005. "Justice in Jeopardy: Accountability for the Darfur Atrocities." *Criminal Law Forum* 16: 343–360.

Kostas, Stephen A. 2006. "Making the Determination of Genocide in Darfur." In *Genocide in Darfur: Investigating the Atrocities in the Sudan*, eds. Samuel Totten and Eric Markusen. New York: Routledge. 111–126.

L'Abate, Luciano. 2009. "The Drama Triangle: An Attempt to Resurrect a Neglected Pathogenic Model in Family Therapy Theory and Practice." *The American Journal of Family Therapy* 37: 1–11.

Lanz, David. 2011. "EUFOR Chad/CAR: A Regional Solution for a Regional Problem?" In *EUFOR Tchad/RCA Revisited*, eds. Walter Feichtinger and Gerald Hainzl. Vienna: Institut für Friedenssicherung und Konfliktmanagement. 35–58.

Lanz, David. 2014. "The Perils of Peacekeeping as a Tool of RtoP: The Case of Darfur." In *Peacekeeping in Africa: The Evolving Security Architecture*, eds. Marco Wyss and Thierry Tardy. Milton Park: Routledge. 208–225.

Large, Daniel. 2011. "The International Presence in Sudan." In *The Sudan Handbook*, eds. John Ryle, Justin Willis, Suliman Baldo and Madut Jok. Woodbridge: James Currey. 164–176.

Leander, Anna, and Rens van Munster. 2007. "Private Security Contractors in the Debate about Darfur: Reflecting and Reinforcing Neo-Liberal Governmentality." *International Relations* 21: 201–216.

Loeb, Jonathan. 2013. *Talking to the Other Side: Humanitarian Engagement with Armed Non-State Actors in Darfur, Sudan, 2003–2012.* London: Humanitarian Policy Group, Overseas Development Institute. August.

MacKinnon, Michael G. 2010. "The United Nations Security Council." In *The International Politics of Mass Atrocities: The Case of Darfur*, eds. David R. Black and Paul D. Williams. Milton Park: Routledge. 71–99.

Mahony, Chris. 2012. "Emerging Norms of Case Selection at the ICC." Paper presented at the ISA Annual Conference, San Diego, 1–4 April.

Mamdani, Mahmood. 2007. "Blue-Hatting Darfur." *London Review of Books* 29: 18–20.

Mamdani, Mahmood. 2009. *Saviors and Survivors: Darfur, Politics, and the War on Terror.* New York: Pantheon Books.

Mills, Kurt, and Alan Bloomfield. 2018. "African Resistance to the International Criminal Court: Halting the Advance of the Anti-Impunity Norm." *Review of International Studies* 44: 101–127.

Nathan, Laurie. 2007. "The Failure of the Darfur Mediation." *Ethnopolitics* 6: 495–511.

Natsios, Andrew. 2006. "Moving Beyond the Sense of Alarm." In *Genocide in Darfur: Investigating the Atrocities in the Sudan*, eds. Samuel Totten and Eric Markusen. New York: Routledge. 25–42.

Nielsen, Jens, Claudine Prudhon, and Xavier de Radigues. 2011. "Trends in Malnutrition and Mortality in Darfur, Sudan, between 2004 and 2008: A Meta-Analysis of Publicly Available Surveys." *International Journal of Epidemiology* 40: 971–984.

O'Neill, William G., and Violette Cassis. 2005. *Protecting Two Million Internally Displaced: The Successes and Shortcomings of the African Union in Darfur.* Washington, DC, Bern: The Brookings Institution-University of Bern Project on Internal Displacement. November.

Power, Samantha. 2002. *"A Problem from Hell": America and the Age of Genocide.* New York: Harper Collins.

Power, Samantha. 2009. "Foreword." In *Responsibility to Protect: The Global Moral Compact for the 21st Century*, eds. Richard H. Cooper and Juliette Voïnov Kohler. New York: Palgrave Macmillan. vii–xiii.

Prendergast, John. 2007. *The Answer to Darfur: How to Resolve the World's Hottest War.* Washington, DC: Enough Project. March.

Richardson, Courtney. 2011. "Social Influence and Peacekeeping Participation: China and the UN-AU Mission in Darfur (UNAMID), 2004–2007." Paper presented at the ISA Annual Conference, Montreal, 16–19 March.

Risse, Thomas. 1999. "International Norms and Domestic Change: Arguing and Communicative Behavior in the Human Rights Area." *Politics & Society* 27: 529–559.

Savelsberg, Joachim J. 2015. *Representing Mass Violence: Conflicting Responses to Human Rights Violations in Darfur.* Oakland, CA: University of California Press.

Schabas, William. 2010. "The International Criminal Court." In *The International Politics of Mass Atrocities: The Case of Darfur*, eds. David R. Black and Paul D. Williams. Milton Park: Routledge. 134–153.

Scheffer, David. 2008. "Atrocity Crimes Framing the Responsibility to Protect." *Case Western Reserve Journal of International Law* 40: 111–135.

Seymour, Lee J. M. 2014. "Let's Bullshit! Arguing, Bargaining and Dissembling over Darfur." *European Journal of International Relations* 20: 571–595.

Stedjan, Scott, and Colin Thomas-Jensen. 2010. "The United States." In *The International Politics of Mass Atrocities: The Case of Darfur*, eds. David R. Black and Paul D. Williams. Milton Park: Routledge. 157–175.

Steidle, Brian, and Gretchen Steidle Wallace. 2007. *The Devil Came on Horseback: Bearing Witness to the Genocide in Darfur.* New York: Public Affairs.

Strauss, Scott. 2005. "Darfur and the Genocide Debate." *Foreign Affairs* 84.

Tanner, Victor, and Jérôme Tubiana. 2007. *Divided They Fall: The Fragmentation of Darfur's Rebel Groups.* HSBA Working Paper 6. Geneva: Small Arms Survey. July.

Thomas-Jensen, Colin, and Julia Spiegel. 2007. "Activism and Darfur: Slowly Driving Policy Change." *Fordham International Law Journal* 31: 201–216.

United Nations. 2004. *UN Security Council Resolution 1564.* S/RES/1564. 18 September.

United Nations. 2005. *Report of the International Commission of Inquiry on Darfur to the United Nations Secretary-General.* Geneva: United Nations. 25 January.

United Nations. 2007. *UN Security Council Resolution 1769.* S/RES/1769. 31 July.

Weissman, Fabrice. 2009. *Humanitarian Aid and the International Criminal Court: Grounds for Divorce.* Paris: MSF Fondation Crash. July.

Weissman, Fabrice. 2010. "'Not In Our Name': Why Médecins Sans Frontières Does Not Support the 'Responsibility to Protect'." *Criminal Justice Ethics* 29: 194–207.

Williams, Paul D. 2006. "Military Responses to Mass Killing: The African Union Mission in Sudan." *International Peacekeeping* 13: 168–183.

4 Appropriating R2P

The ramifications of saving strangers on the Darfur opposition

> Children began streaming into the camp from all directions, laughing and shouting. Each carried a home-made banner, often little more than a piece of white paper covered in childish writing. "Go on International Criminal Court" read one. "Welcome UN," said another.... The message could be summed up in one simple phrase: "Come and Save Us."
>
> Rob Crilly (2010, 38)[1]

> Ocampo is the only hero in Darfur. He is the only genuine supporter of Darfur!
>
> SLM representative[2]

Exporting the struggle: internationalization as an instrument of opposition politics[3]

Internationalization through media coverage

As outlined in Chapter 2, in post-independence Sudan opposition forces from Darfur were fragmented and failed to mount a unified front against the central government in Khartoum. In the 1990s, the NIF regime absorbed many Darfuri Islamists, while other Darfuris loyal to the Umma Party joined the Sudan Federal Democratic Alliance led by former Darfur governor Ahmed Ibrahim Diraige. In the early 2000s, younger politicians around Abdelwahid al-Nur eclipsed Diraige, starting an armed rebellion with the support of the SPLM.[4] At the same time, Darfuri Islamists, who were largely disaffected by the NIF regime after the ousting of their mentor Hassan al-Turabi, also formed an armed opposition group—the JEM. With the onset of the conflict, the Darfur rebel movements and the armed struggle they were leading came to dominate the Darfur opposition. However, non-military forms of opposition continued to exist within traditional political parties and civil society. What they had in common was an interest to internationalize the conflict and, in particular, to foster the perception of Darfur as a test case for R2P. The rationale for internationalizing the conflict was clear: It served as a strategy to overcome the opposition's structural weaknesses, in particular their internal fragmentation and the vastly superior resources available to those in the center. It was also an attempt to exploit the weaknesses of the enemy. Indeed, in the early 2000s, the Sudanese government engaged in peace negotiations with the SPLM with the aim of rehabilitating itself and normalizing relations with the West (see Chapter 5). Drawing attention to atrocities in Darfur was thus a way for the opposition to thwart these attempts.

The opposition tried to achieve these ends by linking up with international journalists. The media plays an important gatekeeping role in far-away armed conflicts, opening the door to international intervention through its media coverage. The Darfur opposition thus encouraged journalists to visit areas under rebel control. According Rob Crilly, "The Darfur rebels recognized that they could use the international media as a weapon in their war. I found it relatively easy to contact the SLA to travel with them in Jebel Mara, likewise with JEM in North Darfur."[5] These visits were often facilitated by the Darfuri Diaspora in Western countries. On the ground, the journalists were picked up by intermediaries who brought them to rebel-held areas from across the border in Chad or from one of Darfur's main towns. Once they reached these areas, the journalists travelled with rebel contingents for several days or even weeks. One example is the British filmmaker Philip Cox, who was one of the first foreign journalists to visit Darfur in early 2004. His visit was organized by a London-based activist and SLM sympathizer who later also brought Al-Jazeera journalists to Darfur.[6] Cox recalled his visit to Darfur:

> We were driving fucking mad across Darfur.... Finally we got to a place close to Kordofan. We met Minni. I first met his representatives. He spoke eloquent English. We sat together and did a media interview. And then we stayed the night with him and his boys. The next day he was in a convoy of seven vehicles with an array of anti-aircraft guns, machine guns. He had foot soldiers ranging from badly dressed and badly armed to some guys who knew what they were doing. They were very hospitable. We discussed his political aims and chatted in personal terms.[7]

Cox's visit was effective for the Darfur opposition, not only because he gave the rebels a platform to present themselves as responsible actors with serious political aims, but also because he provided the first TV images of the Darfur conflict that were broadcast around the world. He also facilitated the visits of other news teams. Cox said:

> Before I left Darfur I called up BBC and they were very excited. And eventually I sold the material to Channel 4 and CNN, ARD, Scandinavian and Japanese TV. Everyone came in. This was in April, May 2004. And then a lot of people wanted my contacts to get in. For a while there were various news teams. I had no problem putting them in touch with my rebel contacts.[8]

Cox later produced an award-winning and widely broadcast documentary about his time with the SLA.[9]

As Darfur hit the headlines in summer 2004, the rebels also organized visits of international NGOs with journalists embedded in their delegations. Around the same time, John Prendergast and Samantha Power travelled to the rebel-held areas of Darfur. Their accounts, which in essence relayed the opposition's narrative, received a lot of publicity. In a *New York Times* editorial, Prendergast recounted,

> Bodies of young men were lined up in ditches, eerily preserved by the 130-degree desert heat. The story the rebels told us seemed plausible: the dead were civilians who had been marched up a hill and executed by the Arab-led government before its troops abandoned the area the previous month. The rebels assert that there were many other such scenes.[10]

An article by Power in *The New Yorker* included similar gory scenes.[11] Both Prendergast and Power became influential figures in the Darfur advocacy movement.

The closest to a perfect propaganda stunt was a later visit by Bernard-Henri Lévy. His journey to Darfur in March 2007 was paid for by the Save Darfur Coalition and organized by Abdelwahid al-Nur and his supporters in France (Weissman 2010). On the ground, Lévy travelled with Abdelwahid's fighters from the SLA who brought him into Darfur from Chad. Lévy's account of the situation in Darfur was published in different international newspapers.[12] The articles essentially made him a spokesperson of the rebels. He even recommended that the international community arm the rebels to help them win the war in Darfur.[13] While this call did not get traction, Lévy's visit helped galvanize the French advocacy movement and made Darfur a major topic during the French presidential elections in 2007.

Internationalization through activist engagement

Darfur dissidents also engaged with activists from the Save Darfur campaigns in the US, the UK, and France. The campaigns provided a ready-made platform for the opposition that functioned as an intermediary between local actors and international audiences. The campaigns boosted the profile of Darfuri dissidents and gave them instant credibility on what Clifford Bob (2005) called the "market for transnational support." For example, when Suleiman Jamous—who was the SLM's humanitarian coordinator at the time and later a member of JEM living in Slovenia—was held by the government, Ronan Farrow wrote an editorial in the *Wall Street Journal* calling for Jamous' release and comparing him to Nelson Mandela.[14] Likewise, France's Darfur activists courted Abdelwahid al-Nur, allowing him to portray himself as an enlightened leader fighting against a genocidal regime. Bernard-Henri Lévy started a blog for Abdelwahid on his influential online media platform, *La règle du jeu.*[15] The blog included a series of articles in which Abdelwahid relayed his vision and made a number of grandstanding declarations. While they were published in Abdelwahid's name, the articles were drafted by two of his friends in France, including some with minimal input from Abdelwahid himself.[16]

These examples reveal how the Darfur opposition appropriated the campaigns and used them for their own purposes. However, there was mutual interest in collaborating. Linking up with Darfur dissidents was essential for the Darfur activists. It created the impression that the local population supported the campaigns, which in turn conferred legitimacy on the activists. Moreover, Darfuris provided the human faces of the victims that, according to the activists, needed protection. Not surprisingly, therefore, the Darfur activists were keen to collaborate with the Darfuri Diaspora.

Some members of the Diaspora were recruited to work with advocacy groups. For example, Omer Ismail, who left Sudan in 1989 after the NIF took power, has been with the Enough Project since 2007.[17] The Save Darfur Coalition also hired Sudanese staff members, most importantly Amir Osman and Niemat Ahmadi—both of them are political activists who had to flee Sudan to avoid persecution by the Sudanese government. The SDC moreover initiated a gathering of the US-based Diaspora—the Darfuri Leaders Network—in order to coordinate their advocacy and give them a voice in the peace process. After a year and a half, the SDC distanced itself, partly because "the Diaspora members were haggling with each other over their political involvements and affiliations with rebel groups."[18] While the activists expected the Diaspora to play the role of apolitical victims, the latter saw the campaigns as way to further their political aims. The Save Darfur Coalition, in particular, was keen to differentiate itself from the rebels, especially on the question of non-consensual military intervention, which it did not support. This led to frustration among the rebels. According to a SDC representative, "We didn't coordinate with rebel groups, to the contrary. When we met them they were lecturing us [about] why we weren't calling for bombing Sudan."[19] The French activists were less reluctant to associate themselves with rebel movements, even as Jacky Mamou was insisting that Urgence Darfour was "very careful not to be the human rights department of any rebel group."[20] Nonetheless, Abdelwahid al-Nur was very close to the French Darfur activists. He routinely participated in Urgence Darfour meetings, where he was given a prominent platform.[21]

Internationalization through information sharing

Another mechanism that allowed the Darfur opposition to export the cause was information sharing. Local activists would relay information about the conflict to family members and intermediaries in Khartoum. They would then contact international NGOs present on the ground. Suliman Baldo, the head of the ICG office in Khartoum in 2003, explained this process:

> I regularly received information from Darfuris. They showed me photos taken on cell phones of displaced people, of people on the run. These impressions flowed into the first major ICG report ..., "Darfur Raising".

This was the foundational report on which subsequent reports were based. It was published in March 2004, but mostly written at the end of 2003.[22]

Three civil society organizations in Sudan played a particularly important role in receiving information from the field and relaying it abroad. One was the Darfur Information Centre led by Ali Dinar. He was a relative of the last ruler of Darfur, before the British conquered it during the First World War, and an academic in the US with close links to the US-based Darfur advocacy community. A second example was the African Centre for Justice and Peace Studies led by Osman Humeida, a well-known human rights activist in Sudan. He was imprisoned and tortured after the ICC charges against al-Bashir and subsequently fled the country. A third example was the Darfur Relief and Documentation Centre based in Geneva and led by Abdelbagi Jibril. All three organizations routinely published information on their websites about human rights abuses. In addition, they liaised with international human rights NGOs and provided them with information that fed into their reports. Jibril described this process as follows:

> From the beginning, we have played a major role in gathering information for the media or from contacts with people on the ground. To give an accurate description of what is going on. Like other NGOs run by Darfuris, we were trying the help get the information from the field and pass it on to international NGOs. At Amnesty and Human Rights Watch, people were working with us very closely. We get information on the ground and then give it to their people in London and in the U.S. It is very important to feed them with information.[23]

Information was not only given to big NGOs but also to individual activists, like Eric Reeves. His reports on Darfur are detailed and provide information about specific attacks, including the number of people arrested, injured, and killed.[24] Reeves maintains an extensive network of local contacts and closely collaborates with Sudanese exiles, who relay relevant information to him.

Local activists also passed on information via local media outlets. The most important source is Radio Dabanga, which has operated in Darfur since December 2008. It is staffed by local journalists in Darfur and usually operates clandestinely, using the facilities of Radio Netherlands Worldwide to remain beyond the reach of Sudanese authorities. A SLM-affiliated member of the Darfur Diaspora in the UK said,

> Radio Dabanga is one of the main sources of information in Darfur. What happened is that they established a system where [if] a village is under attack they can phone Radio Dabanga and give live information. This is how the communication is handled nowadays.[25]

Radio Dabanga is useful for the Darfur opposition as it regularly publishes critical reports about the government. It also features interviews of opposition leaders and maintains an English website that is often cited by Darfur activists, like Eric Reeves. Another example of an opposition-friendly media outlet is Radio Afia Darfur, which was broadcast from Darfuri refugee camps in eastern Chad until it closed down in March 2018 due to lack of funding.

The rebel movements maintain their own cycles of information that are, at times, congruent with those of the civil society activists. Several rebel movements appointed foreign and information secretaries, usually members of the Diaspora who liaised with international journalists, activists, and government officials. Abdullahi el-Tom, a senior anthropology lecturer at Maynooth University in Ireland, fulfilled this role for JEM. He explains his function as follows:

> I wanted to bring the message to the world. I wanted to connect JEM with the West. Every JEM document that comes in English passes through me. I also give lectures and I go to meetings. And I do interviews. I talk in the radio. I basically represent JEM to the English-speaking world.[26]

El-Tom (2011) also wrote a vivid biography of Khalil Ibrahim, the founder and leader of JEM—Khalil was killed by an SAF airstrike in December 2011.

The Darfur rebels and the perils of fame

Talking the talk of saving strangers

Darfuris have been agents in the transformation of their homeland from a forgotten conflict to a global cause. They helped shape the Darfur narrative, including the notion that the world had a responsibility to protect them. This section focuses on military actors within the Darfur opposition and asks how the international engagement with R2P shaped their discourses and behaviors.

It is common for rebel movements to generate legitimacy by aligning their discourses with well-known international frames. Clapham (1998, 17) aptly captured this dynamic:

> Politicians everywhere use different vocabularies to address different audiences, but the range required of insurgent leaders is particularly great, stretching from the mobilization of indigenous spirituality, on the one hand, to the matching mobilization of Western ideologies of development, democracy or human rights on the other.

In the case of the Darfur rebels, R2P played a central role. One strategy, which SLM members frequently resorted to, was to emphasize the victimhood of the Darfuri population. They did so by associating themselves with other communities that experienced genocide. According to an SLM representative in the Diaspora,

> We gave speeches in schools about genocide. There are lots of Jewish people. For them, history is important. So we came as a real model of

genocide. We also joined the Rwandan activists to speak in schools and in public meetings. Also, we sometimes participate in genocide memorials.[27]

Likewise, in a blog post on Bernard-Henri Lévy's website, Abdelwahid al-Nur expressed gratitude to his French hosts in unequivocal terms:

> In the twentieth century France and Paris, capital of freedom, has welcomed by the thousands, the outlawed, the humiliated, and the soldiers of freedom coming from around the world to take refuge in the land of human rights....
>
> The list is very long. You took in the Armenians at the end of the First World War who were victims of the Turkish genocide. You took in the white Russians who were driven away by communism. You took in the Jews from Central Europe who were fleeing the rise of fascism and anti-Semitism. The German intellectual anti-fascists and the hundreds of thousands of Spanish republicans chased away by Franco took refuge with you.... Now, for the past three years, it is I who benefits from this magnificent tradition and Darfur receives constant support from thousands of French supporters.[28]

The emphasis on victimhood, however, was not without perils. It seemed to undercut the agency of rebel groups. Thus, the Darfur narrative outlined in Chapter 2 does not clearly frame the role of the rebels. Contrary to the public narrative on South Sudan, which cast John Garang as a freedom fighter worthy of international support—an image he skillfully converted into bargaining power—the Darfur rebels were largely absent from news reports.

The rebels also referred to the notion of protecting civilians, which they knew was a more legitimate way of framing an intervention than asking for direct military assistance. NATO's Libya intervention served as a reference point in this regard. According to an SLM member,

> something similar to the NATO intervention in Libya would be good in Darfur. We don't need NATO to take the side of the rebels, they should just protect civilians. We don't want NATO to be a part of the conflict. We are able to deal with the government. We don't ask for that, we only ask for protection.[29]

Similarly, a JEM representative stated:

> The Sudan government used Antonov planes so we asked for a no-fly zone to protect civilians and IDPs.... The international community should also have assisted the armed movements. Not to fight, but to assist in protecting the IDPs from attacks. We asked to be supplied with arms, just to protect through defensive methods. The worst things were the Antanov. Although they are not highly sophisticated, they killed more of the civilians and livestock. Anti-aircraft guns would have deterred the Antanov.[30]

Many rebel representatives used the R2P doctrine to frame their struggle. They had a specific understanding of what R2P meant in the context of Darfur: a legal obligation for the international community to intervene. According to one SLM member, "There is a responsibility to protect in Darfur! By law, the international community should protect civilians."[31] A statement by a JEM official echoed this,

> The responsibility to protect came when Colin Powell and George W. Bush said Darfur was genocide. The law said that if you have recognized genocide you have the responsibility to react. We went along and asked the international community to intervene.[32]

Another SLM member invoked the case of Kosovo, to explain what the implementation of the R2P doctrine in Darfur should have entailed:

> According to the responsibility to protect, we should have a no-fly zone and there should be aerial bombardments against Bashir's airports. Also, the international community should have been protecting civilians from rape and killings and also from the *janjawid* militia. All in all, Darfur should be like the case of Kosovo.... The Kosovo model is that you will have a UN administration in Darfur. The rule of law should be guaranteed by the UN; the same with protection. There should be some sort of local community participation, a lower executive role for the transition period. And then people can choose independence or unity.

Abdullahi el-Tom referred to R2P in connection with the ICC:

> Definitely Darfur is a case for R2P! It is strange to think of al-Bashir as protecting its people. He definitely failed. In the case of dictators attacking their citizens, I agree that the international community can intervene and that it shouldn't bother about sovereignty. I am in support of this way of thinking. In cases of government failure to protect civilians you shouldn't talk about sovereignty. Hence I support the ICC. It is important for humanity.[33]

These statements show how the rebels appropriated R2P: They made the norm their own and deployed it to generate support for their struggle. At the same time, appropriating R2P created new normative reference points and shaped the rebels' expectation that international actors would intervene in Darfur, as they had done in Kosovo or in Libya. When this expectation was not met, general feelings of disappointment and betrayal took root. This becomes clear in the rebels' assessment of the international response to the Darfur conflict. Despite the extensive involvement of international actors and the benefits to the Darfur opposition, the rebels were highly critical. According to El-Tom,

> The international community has been successful in feeding the people. But politically it's a fiasco. They started to make lots of noise. In most instances

the international community is a hindrance. If you want to march on Khartoum they say don't go. The US government and Ban have told us last week that we should seek peaceful change. But Bashir doesn't want to talk![34]

Given these disappointments, it is not surprising that the rebels took out their frustrations on UNAMID, the entity that was supposed to protect civilians. In the eyes of the rebels, the mission had been completely discredited. For example, despite attacks by the government, the rebels at times refused to let UN-AU peacekeepers establish a presence in areas under their control, such as the eastern part of Jebel Marra.[35] According to an UNOCHA official in Khartoum, UNAMID forces would immediately be fired upon if they entered rebel territory.[36] A telling episode in this regard occurred in February 2012 when JEM held 52 UNAMID peacekeepers for two days, accusing them of cooperating with the Sudanese intelligence service.[37]

The rebels were particularly suspicious of African soldiers in the force. One reason for this was Khartoum's insistence on the African character of the peacekeeping mission, which the rebels saw was an attempt to undermine it. Also, African countries were generally less antagonistic toward the Sudanese government than Western states. An SLM representative said in this regard:

UNAMID is a club of dictators. It is an organization that represents a club of dictators. It's the African rulers. UNAMID will never be transparent. It represents the government's will. The Sudan government is a member of the club. They do whatever they want with the mission. I don't trust UNAMID and I don't respect them. They are a group of officers who are collecting good money and salaries. They are expatriates![38]

JEM was similarly dismissive about UNAMID:

When UNAMID was formed it was mostly a joke because it was left for the Sudan government to decide the movement of the troops. And they have to take permission from the Sudan government. They lack helicopters and they lack heavy military equipment. So UNAMID was just designed to be under the influence of the Sudan government. The weaknesses of UNAMID became very clear when it became clear that the mission was unable to protect itself. And there was no peace to protect. Their presence is of no value! And it still isn't of any value.[39]

This statement illustrates the disappointment and the contempt that the rebel movements harbored against UNAMID. Not unlike the activists, they hoped that the mission would be much stronger in confronting the Sudanese government. When faced with the reality, the rebels' hope turned into cynicism, and UNAMID peacekeepers became a symbol for international impotence in Darfur.

Another source of disappointment was NATO's intervention in Libya, which paved the way for the rebels in Benghazi to conquer the country and topple the

Gaddafi regime. The Darfur rebels hoped for a similar scenario in Sudan. Given the international rhetoric around Darfur that evoked genocide on par with Rwanda and the Holocaust, the rebels could not understand why the international community intervened in Libya but not in Darfur. According to Abdullahi el-Tom,

> The Libya intervention just shows the double standards of the international community. We have asked for this. The Libyans didn't go through peaceful change and they were assisted. In Libya, a few thousand people were killed. Compare this to Darfur where half a million, or with a more conservative estimate 250,000 people have been killed! And yet NATO is willing to be a part of the struggle against dictator Gaddafi, but we are advised to be peaceful.[40]

Likewise, a SLM representative related the discrepancy between Libya and Darfur to the R2P doctrine: "In Libya you want to use it but not with us?! R2P is just something that they say, but there is a big difference between what you say and what you do."[41]

Walking the talk? The ramifications of saving strangers[42]

This section formulates a number of propositions that capture how the appropriation of R2P influenced the behavior of rebel groups in Darfur. However, these are not strict causal claims, given that armed rebellions are affected by a multitude of factors, not least the military capabilities of the rebel groups and their adversaries.

Maximalist positions and intransigence

The Darfur narrative seems to have encouraged rebel leaders to adopt maximalist positions. It notably provided them an incentive to make grandstanding demands at the expense of more constructive and realistic propositions for resolving the conflict. The most important rebel leader, Abdelwahid al-Nur, labeled the Sudanese government Islamo-fascist and *génocidaire*. He opened an office in Israel, with whom Sudan entertains no diplomatic relations, and called for regime change on a conservative pro-Israeli online broadcasting platform.[43] Escalating rhetoric is nothing unusual in armed conflicts. However, in other conflicts, rebel groups eventually moderate their stances and seek a compromise with the government. However, the Darfur narrative and the expectation of international salvation, encouraged rebel leaders to adopt a wait-and-see attitude, hoping that international help would be forthcoming in the future.

This attitude is exemplified by the rebels' stance in peace talks. In Abuja, Abdelwahid demanded "a guarantee for implementation like in Bosnia" (quoted in De Waal 2006, 18). According to Alex de Waal (2006), who was present in Abuja as an advisor to the AU mediation team, the fact that the desired NATO intervention was not forthcoming was one of the reasons why Abdelwahid and his followers refused to sign the Darfur Peace Agreement. This position was in sync with the international debate about Darfur at the time: Activists did not pay attention to peace talks but demanded the deployment of a robust peacekeeping mission (see Chapter 3). A Sudanese academic astutely remarked,

> The campaigns gave hope to the movements that they would be supported by the international community. They raised the ceiling of expectations, and it affected their position in peace negotiations insofar as they did not want to settle their dispute. If not, they would have settled in Abuja. Those that didn't accept Abuja expected new rounds of talks.[44]

Some SLM representatives advocated for a more moderate stance: "We tried to convince Abdelwahid to adopt a clear vision; he is always talking about the disarmament of janjawid, about refugees returning back. If this happens, what will you talk about in peace talks!?"[45] However, Abdelwahid remained unshakable. According to one of his former advisors, Abdelwahid's position was motivated by a belief that indicting the Sudanese president would bring regime change.

> He refused to negotiate because he just wanted regime change.... He thinks that the ICC will bring regime change. He thinks the ICC will push people to go out in the street. Because people stand behind the law and because they hate Bashir.[46]

Abdelwahid's intransigence even led his friend Bernard Kouchner to call him "stubborn."[47] In response, Abdelwahid justified his position on Lévy's blog, invoking General de Gaulle for this purpose:

> [My French friends] explained to me how the Maréchal Pétain, in order to avoid military defeat, chose to collaborate with Hitler and deliver the Jews into the hands of the Nazis occupants. They told me how De Gaulle left the country, almost alone, and launched his famous June 18 appeal to the French to refuse defeat and German domination. Of the two, which one won? Who saved France? ... This is why I do not understand why your government is asking me to become the Pétain of Darfur.... Is it surprising that I don't want to surrender to those who have undertaken to exterminate my people? Omar Al-Bashir, wanted by the International Criminal Court, is the criminal.[48]

This statement shows the impact of the international discourse on Darfur. Since Darfur was portrayed as genocide, it would be immoral to make compromises in peace talks. Therefore, intransigence seemed justified. Abdelwahid al-Nur was the most extreme case, but other rebel leaders acted similarly, imposing pre-conditions and making excessive demands during the negotiations. For example, Minni Minawi and the mainstream faction of JEM continuously refused to participate in the Doha peace talks, let alone to recognize the Doha Document for Peace in Darfur (DDPD), which was signed in July 2011 between a minority of the rebel factions and the Sudanese government.

Fragmentation and lack of local engagement

Darfur's status as a global cause célèbre turned it into a prestige object of international diplomacy. As a result, a broad range of international actors—the UN, the AU, the Arab League, the US, European states, Sudan's neighboring countries, and a host of international NGOs—all wanted to contribute to resolving the Darfur conflict. Their aspirations led to a proliferation of often uncoordinated talks, consultations, and workshops that allowed the rebels to shop around for the most promising forum. Peacemaking thus became a lucrative livelihood strategy as the rebels travelled the world, staying in hotels and living off their generous per diems. Delegates in the Abuja talks, which continued on and off for nearly two years, claimed no less than US$150 in daily subsistence allowances (Tieku 2012, 9). According to Flint (2010, 12), "Material benefits, including international travel and hospitality lavished on individual 'rebel' leaders, ... have made the status quo more profitable than peace and the responsibilities of exercising power." The Darfur rebels even earned the nickname "hotel rebels."

The endless talks and the courting of the Darfur insurgents by international actors created several problems. They lowered the barriers of entry for new rebel groups and thus fostered fragmentation and the creation of new factions, often along tribal lines. The establishment of a new group, and therefore the prospect of receiving international recognition and material benefits, was no longer linked to a leader's grassroots support or fighting power. Anybody could be a leader. According to one observer,

> Darfur has become a profitable brand. Any five people making a movement become a force to be reckoned with. It has become impossible to unite these movements, to even deal with them. It's impossible to ignore them and it's also impossible to reach a deal with them.[49]

International connections were instrumental in this process. A UN official who was involved in the re-launch of the peace process after the failure of the Darfur Peace Agreement described how splinter movements operated: "When Eliasson visits them and then pictures are taken with anti-aircraft carriers in the background, the impression is this is an important group. When they are brought to the table, they immediately make demands."[50]

Fragmentation was already a problem during the peace talks in Abuja, because the SLM had split in two, with one faction led by Abdelwahid al-Nur the other by Minni Minawi. After Abuja, fragmentation increased, creating significant obstacles to peace and making serious negotiations impossible with the new multitude of actors whose alliances were constantly shifting (Tanner and Tubiana 2007). Fragmentation also made it easy for the Sudanese government to neutralize the rebel movements by applying the divide-and-conquer tactics it had used during the war against the SPLM. An international journalist, who travelled multiple times to Darfur with the rebels, described these effects as follows:

> Negotiating somewhere in a foreign country with nice hotels, prostitutes, and alcohol made it that the rebels did not feel like returning to Darfur. This creates a caste within the rebel movement, which jet-sets from one conference to another, losing their sense of reality in the process. The less intelligent fighters remain in the field, the more intelligent ones are sent abroad. There, they go into business for themselves and start fighting with each other. Khartoum has consciously fostered this, and the international community has contributed to such factionalization.[51]

In fact, peace talks were convenient venues for the government to dispense patronage money in order to buy the loyalty of individual leaders. Thus they created internal rifts and prevented the emergence of a united front. According to de Waal (2015), such procedures are common in the center-periphery negotiations that characterize Sudan's political marketplace. The bargains concluded this way generally favor the government, which is more experienced and has a lot more resources at its disposal to successfully navigate the marketplace. A statement by an SLM representative about the Darfur peace process reflects this reality: "It is not helpful when a lot of people are brought to the table. They stay five to six months and live together with the regime in the same hotel. The regime uses money for fragmentation."[52]

Another consequence of Darfur's international fame was that rebel leaders were drawn away from the local context. Their extended periods abroad led to a loss of connection with their foot soldiers and the civilian population. This contributed to a rift between movement leaders and their field commanders, with the result that some commanders switched to different factions or were recruited by the government (Flint 2010). The international engagement also meant that the rebel leaders became less capable of organizing resistance at the grassroots level. Hirschman's (1970) classical distinction between different strategies of resistance helps to illustrate to this process: Opposition forces in repressive regimes choose between "voice," staging a protest from within, or "exit," leaving the country altogether. The internationalization of the Darfur conflict and the supposed existence of an external savior created opportunities for "exit," while occasions for "voice" became less attractive. Such developments are dangerous because, as Schlichte (2009) argued, local legitimacy is a necessary condition for armed insurgents to eventually transform into successful political players.

A brief comparison with the SPLM in South Sudan illustrates that the Darfur rebel leaders relied less on their local connections. Unlike the SPLM, the Darfur insurgency did not establish a "guerilla government" (Rolandsen 2005) in the form of a civilian administration in the areas under its control (Branch and Cherian Mampilly 2005). Territorial control has traditionally been the path to internationalization for rebel movements, allowing them to host international NGOs, journalists, and diplomats (Autesserre 2002). The Darfur rebels were not compelled to do this, because Darfur became widely known within only two years of the rebellion's onset. Therefore, they had less of an incentive to establish territorial control and to engage at the local level. In addition, a significant portion of the rebel leaders lived in exile. For example, Abdelwahid al-Nur left Darfur in 2005.

The rebels' international orientation undercut local legitimacy. One indication is that no rebel leader was able to unite all Darfuris as John Garang managed to do in South Sudan. There also seems to be strong resentment against the rebels in Darfur. According to a civil society representative,

> many rebels are even worse than the government. They fight their wars from five-star hotels. They call for justice, the indictment of the president etc. But they are really just a group of warlords and they don't have the support of the people.[53]

Also relevant is the survey by 24 Hours for Darfur, which showed that 48 percent of Darfuri refugees in Chad believe that rebel unity was not achieved because the leaders were self-interested or greedy. This is compared to 32 percent of respondents citing government manipulation and 26 percent citing policy differences as the main reason for disunity (Loeb et al. 2010, 32).

Deterring mass violence

Appropriation also had positive consequences. When armed conflict escalated in Darfur in 2003, it went largely unnoticed. This situation changed drastically, with thousands of international humanitarian workers and peacekeepers establishing a presence on the ground. While it is impossible to ascertain how exactly this affected the belligerents' behavior on the battlefield, it seems plausible that international attention helped to deter extreme violence in Darfur. Chapter 5 delves into the effects of international attention on the government's actions, arguing that mass violence became more costly and thus more difficult for the Sudanese government. The insurgents may have been similarly deterred, despite the serious human rights violations and war crimes they committed. Although the International Commission of Inquiry on Darfur (United Nations 2005) and human rights organizations (e.g., Human Rights Watch 2004) confirmed these abuses, they are in no way commensurate to those perpetrated by the government and its affiliated groups. There is also no indication that the Darfur rebels systematically used mass violence against civilians as part of their war-making effort.

Darfur's international status appears to have played a role in the rebels' reluctance to use mass violence. Compared to the SPLA, the Darfur rebels were more in the spotlight of the international media. While this was generally an asset, it also provided grounds for criticism, potentially jeopardizing the rebels' reputation. For example, they faced criticism when their fighters killed 10 AMIS peacekeepers in September 2007 in Haskanita, South Darfur. This triggered an ICC investigation, which led to charges against three rebel leaders alleged to be responsible. The men voluntarily surrendered to the ICC in June 2010.[54] Before that, both Abdelwahid al-Nur and Khalil Ibrahim had said that they were willing to turn themselves in to the ICC if charges were brought against them.[55]

The ICC seems to have had an impact as well. The filmmaker Philip Cox stated that the rebels "took the ICC very seriously" because "they understood that the ICC could also go after them."[56] Another journalist recounts an episode he observed while traveling with the rebels in Darfur:

> There was talk about a massacre committed by rebels on their own people. The rebels said, "We have to be careful because the ICC now goes against Bashir, but it can also go against us." They had more respect from the ICC than from the UN troops. The ICC scared them. It's possible that when they committed crimes, they thought about how to best hide them. But it's clear to me that the ICC also had a deterrent effect. I was really surprised how often the rebel leaders talked about the ICC. It was often about Bashir, but they knew that the world now looks more closely [at] what they were doing as well.[57]

The international engagement seems also to have influenced the way rebels dealt with disciplinary cases. For example, JEM established courts-martial to judge fighters suspected of misbehavior on the battlefield.[58] Moreover, having being accused of using child soldiers, JEM signed an agreement with UNICEF in July 2010 barring the recruitment of fighters under the age of 18.[59] Likewise, in April 2012, JEM signed a deed of commitment with the NGO Geneva Call, banning the use of anti-personnel mines.[60] Not all of these agreements have been followed through, but they indicate the importance the rebels attached to their good international standing. This implies that the high reputational cost of committing mass violence against civilians made such acts less likely.

The argument that Darfur's international standing had a deterrence effect is contradicted by Kuperman (2009, 281), who claims that "the expectation of benefiting from intervention is what emboldened Darfur's rebels to fight." However, rather than encouraging the rebels to escalate, international engagement seems to have contributed to de-escalation. This is both because the rebels were drawn away from the local battlefield to the international arena and because they feared that the use of excessive violence would discredit them internationally.

Saving strangers and local political opposition

Speaking globally, acting locally: saving strangers at the grassroots level

Having considered the role of the military insurgency, the analysis now turns to the non-armed, civilian opposition. Military and civilian opposition forces do not live in separate spheres, and the following section reveals the similarities between rebels and local activists in the appropriation process. There are, however, differences as well. Civilian opponents from Darfur are more vulnerable to government repression, regardless of whether they are opposition politicians, representatives of national NGOs, lawyers, local intelligentsia, or activists in IDP camps. At the same time, they do not bear arms and may appear less subversive, which should facilitate political accommodation with the government. Against this background, this section considers how the local political opposition engaged with the global discourse on Darfur and how this influenced its behavior.

Darfuri IDP camps are a world away from the air-conditioned offices of the Save Darfur Coalition in Washington, DC, or from the ICC's pressroom in The Hague. Despite this, Darfuris at the grassroots were acutely aware of international discussions about their fate. Similar to the rebels, they contributed to shaping the international discourse on Darfur and, in turn, it shaped their own conceptions of the conflict and ways to resolve it. The notion of R2P was important in this regard. From repeatedly hearing international personalities denounce the crimes in Darfur, compare the situation to Rwanda, and call Omar al-Bashir a war criminal, Darfuris at the grassroots expected external saviors to come. The scene of children in Darfuri IDP camps demonstrating in favor of intervention, as described by Rob Crilly in the epigraph to this chapter, captured this dynamic. As the head of a Khartoum-based NGO explained,

> People hoped that the high cries from the US and Europe would be translated into action. Then we are free! People thought that these *khawajas* mean what they say, they do what they say. They listen to George W. Bush calling Darfur genocide. They think: how many days will it take until US forces come?[61]

Nearly all of the opposition representatives interviewed expressed the hope that international actors would keep their word and provide protection. Many of them expressly talked about R2P. According to an NGO staff, the international community

> should have declared the issue immediately as an international concern and called on the government of Sudan to stop. It should immediately have deployed troops on the ground to defend the people. It should have put pressure on the government to protect its own people.[62]

The head of a Sudanese NGO who regularly works with Darfuris in IDP camps stated,

> R2P is part of my work. I would tell victims that if they receive an international delegation they should speak about R2P. I told them that it is their right to be protected. I told them they have to frame it in this way and not beg for assistance.[63]

As explained in Chapter 3, the international community did react to the Darfur crisis, but the interventions fell short of Darfuris' expectations. The external savior never arrived, causing much disappointment:

> The international community and the UN have issued too many resolutions on Darfur. These resolutions haven't been implemented. This gives the people the impression that the international community is not serious. The international community just arranges meetings, but people in Darfur are fed up with meetings! What is the change? We are still suffering, especially the youth. We are only losing and there is no change.[64]

Likewise, a Darfuri politician said:

> People in Darfur know that the international community knows the details of their sufferings. They met them many times in the camps. They thought that the international community cared about their concerns, that they mean something to them. People in Darfur tell me that they are confused. They listen to many promises, but there are no acts. There has been little or no action to improve protection, justice, and peace.[65]

Some interviewees referred directly to R2P, demonstrating the expectations that the label carries with it. One said, "R2P means nothing! Even in the presence of UNAMID, atrocities continue to happen. Nobody protects the people of Darfur. In the context of the international community, R2P produces no acts."[66]

Similar to the rebels, Darfur's political opposition held the international actors on the ground responsible for what they considered to be the international community's failures. This concerned UNAMID in particular. Many Darfuris thought UN peacekeepers would put a stop to the violence. And after three years of waiting, their expectations were huge when UNAMID was finally deployed. A Sudanese journalist working in Darfur stated:

> People in the camps think that UNAMID is not capable of solving their problems. And so they say to UNAMID that if you are not capable of solving our problem you should get out of Darfur, you rather let us die. In the beginning people expected problems to be solved by UNAMID, they expected to be able to return to their lands, to have peace, to be paid compensation, to have their basic services in health and education met. They expected that the peacekeeping mission would push these things, would help to make peace.[67]

There was a commonplace notion that the UNAMID peacekeepers were incapable of protecting themselves, let alone the people of Darfur. This idea was fed by news of peacekeepers getting killed in ambushes or being captured by *janjawid* militia or rebels. An NGO representative explained that people's disappointment with UNAMID stemmed from confusion about the nature and contributions of a peacekeeping mission.

> Actually people have expectation that these forces will keep the peace. But from their experience they say that UNAMID is weak. Even their cars were attacked, their soldiers were kidnapped. There was a lot of hope when UNAMID was deployed. However, the mission was a choice agreed upon by the government and the international community. This is why there are hybrid forces. People are not aware of what the mandate of UNAMID is. The mission and the mandate were not clear. What are peacekeepers? Why are they so weak, why are they attacked? People did not understand this. People hope that UNAMID can help in their return.[68]

Here lies the heart of the problem of making a peacekeeping force the main instrument to implement R2P: It creates expectations that a peacekeeping mission cannot fulfill, regardless of its staff's determination or how well it is equipped. UNAMID fell into this trap.

In contrast, the ICC resonated strongly with the grassroots Darfuris opposed to those in power. While the Sudanese government had organized demonstrations against the court following the Bashir indictment, many Darfuris were elated. Although the fear of reprisals made it difficult for them to publicly show it, "the Darfuris were very happy about the ICC. They see it as a major step to achieve justice,"[69] as noted by a researcher at an independent Sudanese think tank. According to a Darfuri politician, "The referral was a huge step. It's a breakthrough to tell perpetrators that they don't get away with crimes. The victims are satisfied that their plight receives so much attention, that they are not forgotten."[70] Indeed, many Darfuris saw the indictment as recognition of their suffering and of the injustice that they had experienced.

A survey conducted by 24 Hours for Darfur among Darfuri refugees in Chad also illustrated the grassroots support for the ICC. Over three quarters of respondents had heard of the ICC and, of those, almost all (98 percent) thought that President al-Bashir should be tried in The Hague. Likewise, over 90 percent of Darfuri refugees believed that members of the Sudanese government and the *janjawid* should be held accountable for their crimes (Loeb et al. 2010, 29, 26). However, these results have to be put in context. The survey showed that, apart from justice, Darfuris had other desires as well. Almost all refugees (98 percent) wanted to return home. When asked under what conditions they would return, 43 percent said after the violence stopped. Only 9 percent said they would go home if Omar al-Bashir was arrested (Loeb et al. 2010, 36). These responses may appear contradictory, because a comprehensive settlement is less likely to follow a ceasefire if charges are sought against the head of one party. Although the refugees who had lost their homes would not likely appreciate such tradeoffs, for activists and opposition forces, the ICC was a symbol of justice. The language of accountability has thus become the vocabulary with which grassroots Darfuris express their suffering—particularly in refugee camps and the Diaspora—irrespective of the difficult tradeoffs that peacemaking may require.

Similar to the hopes about peacekeeping, the ICC's involvement raised immense expectations. Many believed that when the international community recognized Omar al-Bashir as a war criminal, they would surely arrest him and his acolytes. However, people's hopes were again disappointed when this did not come to pass. A member of JEM articulated this sentiment,

> The ICC was a dream for the people of Darfur. When it was announced people were jubilant. They were congratulating each other. But we were naïve that Bashir would be arrested. People were disappointed that the international community did nothing. The first time Bashir decided to travel, people were very tense. How could he defy the ICC?![71]

Also telling is a statement by a local activist who initially supported the ICC under great personal risk but grew disillusioned with the court:

> Unfortunately I was one of the people who strongly supported the ICC, and I felt in the beginning that this was the most effective means to stop the perpetrators from committing more atrocities and to bring an end to the conflict..... The result now is frustrating. For me it is disappointing.... It is not the best way to address the issue because it is known from the beginning that it only deals with the big rank of the perpetrators. Because it only targets those people that are in power it will be nothing, it won't be effective. Since you are going to indict the people that are big fish, they are able to defend themselves by simply not responding to request to hand in the perpetrators. So from the beginning it is a very ineffective approach.[72]

Beyond the ICC, this sentiment illustrates how R2P was discursively translated at the local level. As local activists made the saving strangers discourse their own, they gained leverage and gave people a vocabulary to articulate their grievances. However, at the same time, the notion of "responsibility" raised expectations that external protection for victims of mass atrocities would be forthcoming. As Darfur shows, if this is not the case, the result is disappointment or—worse—cynicism and disempowerment.

The impact of the Save Darfur campaigns on local political opposition

This section considers how the appropriation of the R2P discourse influenced opposition politics in Sudan. Similar to the case of the rebels, the findings reveal ambiguous and even paradoxical effects.

Fostering local activism

International exposure mobilized opposition forces in Darfur. It made financial and political support available to local groups, increasing their room for maneuver. Different groups benefited from such support, including Khartoum-based lawyers and national NGOs working in Darfur. These relief and advocacy NGOs belonged to opposition networks even if they did not pursue an explicit anti-government agenda. One example is the Sudan Social Development Organization. Until the government closed it down in 2009, SUDO received funding from different international donors for projects in Darfur. The organization's chairperson Mudawi Ibrahim Adam became internationally known thanks to the Darfur campaigns. The US-based organization Human Rights First gave him a prestigious award and invited him to the US on several occasions for meetings with senior policymakers.[73] Another example is Salih Mahmoud Osman, a human rights lawyer and former Member of Parliament for the Sudanese Communist Party. He was awarded a prize by Human Rights Watch in 2005.[74] In 2007, he received the Sakharov Prize from the European Parliament, whose previous recipients included Nelson Mandela and Aung San Suu Kyi.[75]

The outbreak of the Darfur conflict led to the emergence of many local community-based organizations. Although they officially worked on social welfare issues at the grassroots level, they often had a clandestine advocacy component and even founded a joint advocacy platform—the Human Rights and Advocacy Network for Democracy—which links grassroots relief work and higher-level advocacy at the national level and in the Diaspora.[76] These activists played an important role in the above-mentioned transfer of information from the local to the international level. Community-based organizations have benefited from the international engagement in Darfur, partly because international exposure provides local activists with a level of protection. They also collaborated with international humanitarian NGOs and received funding for their contribution to the relief operation in Darfur.

Local opposition also manifested itself in everyday grassroots resistance against the government. The primary venues for such resistance were IDP camps, in which a large proportion of Darfuris have been living since the outbreak of the conflict in 2003. Camp leaders often articulate radical political demands, which are in line with those of the rebel movements.[77] The same is true for youth, which a Darfuri activist described as "a generation of anger" (quoted in Amnesty International 2008, 15). International engagement played a role, as the presence of humanitarian organizations meant that the livelihoods of camp residents were not dependent on the government. Moreover, as Darfur became famous, many international dignitaries travelled to the IDP camps in Darfur. This gave the camp sheiks a platform to articulate political demands that was safe from government repression. Also relevant was access in camps to media sources beyond the government's control, most importantly by radio. Through BBC Arabic and later Radio Dabanga, Darfuris in the camps were exposed to the international discourse about Darfur, which fueled local opposition against the government.

Justice politicized and opposition divided

Another effect of the international intervention in Darfur is that it politicized certain activities, such as justice, human rights, and gender. Since these issues were part of the Darfur narrative, which portrayed the government as the perpetrator of genocide, activists and NGOs working in these fields were suspected of subversive aims. The Sudanese government promptly used this as a pretext to step up repression. As a result, the space for advocacy and civil society activism diminished. The ICC's actions against al-Bashir brought this starkly to the fore. When the indictment was announced, the government closed down three national NGOs that had been active in reporting human rights violations in Darfur. One activist recalled the government's reaction:

> They were very strong. Civil society wasn't able to defend the indictment. The government launched a campaign against civil society. Now there aren't any local organizations documenting crimes being committed. They expelled the most effective groups, SUDO, the Amal Centre, the Khartoum Center, and also 13 international NGOs. These were the most effective organizations. There are other organizations that are still operating, but they just do awareness raising, not monitoring and reporting of crimes.
>
> The campaign started even before the indictment of Bashir.... The government enforced all the bad provisions in Sudanese law against human rights organizations. They harassed human rights defenders and journalists. The head of security, Salah Gosh, said in the newspaper that he will amputate the hands and legs of all those who support the ICC.... They created an environment of fear.[78]

After the government's move, the senior staff of the organizations concerned went into hiding, and some eventually fled Sudan. This meant that Sudanese civil society not only lost its most capable organizations, but also some of the most committed and well-connected human rights activists. The indictment also had repercussions for those remaining in Sudan. Activities related to justice, human rights, and gender were automatically linked to the ICC, and the government made clear that this red line was not to be crossed. Several local activists confirmed this. One of them said, "For civil society it has become impossible to work on justice issues, which adds to an already difficult environment with a lot of suspicions and surveillance. The government stepped up the repression."[79] A Sudanese academic confirmed this assessment, "The work for human rights and justice advocates has become more difficult. They cannot do anything and they always have to take into account negative consequences."[80] The repercussions also affected relief organizations in Darfur. Some Sudanese NGOs found a way around this by working on specific every-day human rights issues and by involving government actors in their programs. However, their leeway was limited.[81]

Many of those who were opposed to the government were forced to leave the country. They continued their struggle in a more militant fashion from abroad. Those who stayed in Sudan faced a tricky dilemma. To maintain their credibility, they needed to speak truth to power regarding the government, but at the same time, they had to differentiate themselves from the campaigns' discourse. As opinions polarized, the space for non-violent opposition within the system shrunk. Therefore, in Hirschman's (1970) terms, the saving strangers discourse, which aims to stigmatize the perpetrator of atrocities, tended to reinforce the exit option at the expense of voice and protest.

This had serious consequences for opposition politics. If opposition forces decided to side with the government against outside intrusion, they would risk being seen as co-opted. This was the case with the opposition parties—the Umma Party, the Democratic Unionist Party, and to some extent the Sudanese Communist Party—that criticized the ICC indictment.[82] However, most civil society representatives had no alternative but to accept their limitations in the polarized debate between government apologists and the dissidents demanding international intervention. Disillusionment followed, in particular among Khartoum-based Darfuri intellectuals. Working as university professors, think tank researchers, and journalists, they could have been bridge-builders between Darfur and elites in the center. Indeed, many of them were involved in the Heidelberg process, an informal dialogue track that produced a detailed plan to address the root causes of violence in Darfur.[83] One participant called it "a good attempt to find a way out of the crisis, because the people in Darfur are currently taken hostage by the government and the rebels."[84] However, the Heidelberg Outcome Document was not taken up by the government or the rebels. Another disillusioned participant said in this regard, "The government doesn't give an opportunity for dialogue, they just intervene. We as intellectuals were emptied of our substance!"[85]

Another consequence of the high-pitched discourse on Darfur was the rift it caused between the opposition forces opting for voice within the existing system of governance in Sudan—Darfuri intellectuals, opposition parties, and civil society in Khartoum—and those opting for exit from the system—political activists operating clandestinely, rebel movements, and most of the Diaspora. The latter appropriated the saving strangers discourse, while the former tried to emancipate themselves from it. This caused tensions. One indication is the widely held critical attitude that many civil society representatives in Khartoum, including those that opposed the government, exhibited vis-à-vis the Save Darfur campaigns in the West. One NGO worker said,

> The mobilization was not meant to help the people of Darfur, but to bring the government down.... I dislike hypocrisy. I don't support the government, but I totally disagree with using guns and bullets. There is an international hypocrisy behind the campaigns, a hidden agenda.[86]

A Darfuri academic echoed this,

> It is difficult to find out what the motives were in Darfur. The Save Darfur Coalition collected 40 million. That's a lot of money. People in Darfur are dying so why are you taking on their cause, taking money for this, and spending money on newspaper ads? Why don't you take the money and give it to the Darfuris?[87]

This is not meant to suggest that Darfur's civil society opposed the Save Darfur campaigns. On the contrary, many dissidents supported them. The campaigns did, however, create a rift in Sudan's political opposition, pitting mainstream groups against the rebels and Diaspora dissidents who were calling for armed uprising and regime change.

Where are the Arabs?

The Darfur opposition's appropriation of the saving strangers discourse had another unintended consequence: it excluded Darfuri Arabs. The narrative portrayed the conflict as an ethnic war by Arabs against Africans. The main culprit was the Sudanese government, with its henchmen, the *janjawid*, recruited from the Arab tribes of Darfur. As shown in Chapter 2, the press coverage on Darfur did not make clear the social context from which the militia emerged, nor did it acknowledge the fact that the majority of Arab tribes were not involved in the counter-insurgency campaign. Instead, the *janjawid* were portrayed as the projection of evil and as part of a conspiracy by Arabs to eradicate Africans. According to a Darfuri academic, "This has driven a wedge between the tribes in Darfur! I have never heard of African tribes before 2003. This is a completely new concept. The genocide narrative has brought a polarization of Darfuri society."[88]

It is important to mention that racial polarization existed before the conflict. Its origins go back to British colonial rule, successive post-independence governments, and, in particular, the divide-and-conquer efforts of the NCP regime. Therefore, the Darfur narrative did not create the Arab vs. African frame, but it did help to perpetuate it. The narrative's most serious consequence is that it minimized the likelihood of reconciliation between Arab and non-Arab tribes, let alone the establishment of a common political front.

The Darfur narrative cemented the view among non-Arabs that Arabs were their tormentors, and most importantly, it alienated Arab tribes from the opposition. Interviews with Darfuri Arabs revealed how strong their feeling was of being unfairly treated, even of being victimized by the dominant version of the conflict:

> People are saying that the Arabs are burning and looting, that they have no morals. They accuse the Arabs of rape, although they fail to produce proof. And did the rebels not rape? There may have been some cases of rape during the war, but it was on both sides.[89]

The word "*janjawid*" was particularly sensitive, as it carried a special stigma:

> The Arabs will be very angry if you mention this word! They don't like it. Before the war, this word referred to people that you cannot control. The rebels use this word to hurt the Arabs. It hurt the Arabs a lot! ... The others used it very effectively. The rebels made a bad name of the Arabs with it.[90]

The Arabs' alienation also stemmed from the Darfuri opposition's support of international involvement in Darfur. They did not trust international actors: "The international community is biased. It's obvious! There are no schools and clinics, and there is no employment with NGOs. This pushes the nomads to be with the government."[91] A research project about the Northern Rizeigat Abbala, carried out by the Feinstein International Center, confirmed the precarious socio-economic situation of Darfuri Arabs (Young et al. 2009). In addition, an international humanitarian worker pointed out that the Arabs' feeling of neglect was not baseless either:

> The problem was the portrayal of the Abbala as Janjaweed. It made it difficult for people working in conflict to engage with them. They were portrayed as the next step of the axis of evil. Many NGOs, when they drove through Nomadic land, they never stopped. They didn't understand that the system was not that simple, that the Abbala received guns, that they received the status from the government that they had long before been denied.[92]

Many Darfuri Arabs were wary of international involvement, in particular the deployment of UN peacekeepers that the Darfur opposition was vehemently demanding:

> The Arabs were against the UN coming to Sudan with a Chapter VII mandate. They fear that they will punish only the Arabs. This was their experience with the international community. They fear that UNAMID will build courts and put Arabs in prison.[93]

The opposition's appropriation of the international discourse on Darfur, which the Arabs believed stigmatized them, is one factor that undermined an all-Darfur opposition alliance. A Darfuri civil society leader explained the obstacles that would need to be overcome for such an alliance to be feasible:

> The tragedy of Darfur is that a broad-based alliance between Arabs and Africans has never been realized. The argument of Arabs vs. Africans is silly! ... We need to replace the racial agenda with a civic one in Darfur. It is time for the Africans to realize that they cannot rely on the international community. Nor should Arabs bank on the government.... Tactically and morally, it does not make sense to coalesce with the government. The Africans were deceived and counted on the international community to alleviate their suffering. Also, they have to realize that only a minority of Arabs have committed crimes. There should be a moral vision to create a common Darfur front similar to how the southerners united.[94]

However, the requirement to overcome the racial agenda, not rely on the international community, and acknowledge that not all Arabs are perpetrators goes against the logic of the international discourse on Darfur that opposition forces made their own. It is, therefore, easy to understand why the Darfur opposition has remained fragmented.

In sum, the appropriation of the core R2P norm had a profound effect on the Darfuri political opposition. It has provided them with a vocabulary to articulate their grievances and to attract international support for their causes. It has also fostered local political activism. At the same time, it has politicized justice and human rights work, complicated relations between opposition forces inside the country and in exile, and deepened the rift between Arabs and non-Arabs in Darfur.

Chapter findings

Three findings derive from this chapter's analysis of the Darfur opposition's engagement with the core R2P norm. First, the concept that best captures the opposition's engagement with the saving strangers discourse is appropriation. They used R2P as a strategic tool to exert pressure on the government. Appropriation also meant that the Darfur opposition changed its outlook on the world, including its understanding of the conflict and its remedies. In particular, R2P fostered an expectation among Darfuris that the international community would intervene in Darfur and resolve the conflict on their behalf. When help was not forthcoming, the hopes of many Darfuris turned into disillusionment and cynicism.

Second, the Darfur case contradicts the moral-hazard literature (e.g., Kuperman 2008), which predicts that rebels will step up a war in order to attract an international military intervention. Internationalization did not lead the rebels to step up fighting in Darfur. If anything, it led to more restraint from mass violence because the rebels did not want to jeopardize their reputation. More problematic was the tendency to adopt intransigent and maximalist positions in peace talks, as the rebels were counting on an international intervention in the future.

Third, framing Darfur as an R2P case also had an impact on the political opposition. It provided local groups with political and financial support. On a more negative note, the international discourse politicized human rights and justice activities and thus made individuals and organizations working in these areas vulnerable to government repression. The R2P discourse also weakened "voice" as an opposition strategy, as opposed to "exit," for which Darfur's status as a global cause had created many opportunities. This caused a rift between opponents operating within the system and those outside the country who had adopted an anti-government agenda in line with the international campaigns.

Notes

1 Rob Crilly is a freelance journalist writing for UK newspapers, who covered Darfur for five years. The quote is an excerpt from his book *Saving Darfur: Everybody's Favourite African War* (2010). It recounts what Crilly's experienced on one of his trips to an IDP camp in Darfur.

2 Interview (DT), Cardiff, November 2011.
3 This section is partly based on an article published in the *Journal of Modern African Studies*. See Gabrielsen and Lanz (2013).
4 In an interview with the author (London, April 2011), Diraige stated that he opposed armed rebellion, fearing the it would lead to brutal retaliation from the government. However, in late 2006, he joined the rebellion as head of the National Redemption Front, an amalgam of Darfur rebels, which disintegrated a few months after its formation.
5 Phone interview with Rob Crilly, December 2011.
6 Interview with SLM member (DE), London, April 2011.
7 Interview with Philip Cox, London, November 2011.
8 Interview with Philip Cox, London, November 2011. ARD is a publicly funded TV channel in Germany.
9 Cox' film was called *Sudan: The Darfur War*, www.nativevoicefilms.com/the-films/native-voice-films-director-philip-cox-and-his-sudanese-guide-dawd-abute-were-the-first-filmmakers-smuggle-themselves-into-the-troubled-state-of-darfur/ (accessed 8 June 2019).
10 John Prendergast, "Sudan's Ravines of Death," *New York Times*, 15 July 2004.
11 Samantha Power, "Dying in Darfur," *The New Yorker*, 30 August 2004.
12 Lévy published articles about his trip to Darfur in *Le Monde* (France), *Corriere della Sera* (Italy), *El Mundo* (Spain), the *Frankfurter Allgemeine Zeitung* (Germany), *Haaretz* (Israel), the *National Post* (Canada), *The New Republic* (US), and *The Financial Times* (UK).
13 See e.g., Bernard-Henri Lévy, "Dangerous Thinking," *Financial Times*, 4 May 2007.
14 Ronan Farrow, "Darfur's Forgotten Rebel," *The Wall Street Journal*, 21 June 2007.
15 The collection of articles in Abdelwahid's blog is available at https://laregledujeu.org/contributeur/abdelwahid-al-nour/ (accessed 8 June 2019).
16 Interview with Darfur activist (DW), Paris, November 2011 (interview in French, author's translation).
17 Information available from the staff website of the Enough Project, https://enoughproject.org/about/our-team (accessed 8 June 2019).
18 Interview with SDC staff member (AU), Washington, DC, March 2010.
19 Interview with former SDC staff member (CW), Washington, DC, March 2011.
20 Interview with Jacky Mamou, Paris, November 2011 (interview in French, author's translation).
21 The author is indebted to Maria Gabrielsen Jumbert for drawing his attention to this point.
22 Interview with Suliman Baldo, New York, March 2011.
23 Interview with Abdelbagi Jibril, Geneva, November 2011.
24 On his website, Eric Reeves maintains an archive with thousands of Darfur-related articles: http://sudanreeves.org/archive/ (accessed 8 June 2019).
25 Interview with SLM member (DF), London, April 2011.
26 Interview with Abdullahi el-Tom, Maynooth, November 2011.
27 Interview with SLM member (DR), London, November 2011.
28 Abdelwahid al-Nour, "Merci aux amis français," blog post, 24 April 2010, https://laregledujeu.org/2010/04/24/1332/merci-aux-amis-francais/ (accessed 8 June 2019; article in French, English translation from earlier version of the blog).
29 Interview with SLM member (DE), London, April 2011.
30 Interview with JEM representative (DO), London, November 2011.
31 Interview with SLM member (DE), London, April 2011.
32 Interview with JEM representative (DO), London, November 2011.
33 Interview with Abdullahi el-Tom, Maynooth, November 2011.
34 Interview with Abdullahi el-Tom, Maynooth, November 2011.
35 Interview with UNAMID official (BF), Khartoum, October 2010.
36 Interview with UNOCHA official (BU), Khartoum, November 2010.

37 Reuters, "Rebels Say Holding 52 Peacekeepers in Sudan's Darfur," 20 February 2012, www.reuters.com/article/us-sudan-darfur/rebels-say-holding-52-peacekeepers-in-sudans-darfur-idUSTRE81J0T620120220 (accessed 8 June 2019).

38 Interview with SLM member (DT), location in the UK, November 2011.

39 Interview with JEM representative (DO), London, November 2011.

40 Interview with Abdullahi el-Tom, Maynooth, November 2011.

41 Interview with SLM member (DR), London, November 2011.

42 This section is based on an article the author wrote with Maria Gabrielsen Jumbert. See Gabrielsen and Lanz (2013).

43 DemoCast, "'Global Jihad Fueling Genocide in Darfur, Fuels Muslim Conquest vs Israel', Sudan Opposition Leader," www.youtube.com/watch?v=OOUYmZDC2mM&feature=youtube_gdata (video accessed 8 June 2019).

44 Interview with Sudanese academic (BA), Khartoum, October 2010.

45 Interview with SLM member (DF), London, April 2011.

46 Interview with SLM member (DR), London, November 2011.

47 The original quote in French is: "Personne ne comprend son entêtement et son isolement croissant constitue un obstacle." See Bernard Kouchner, "Oui, on peut être militant et ministre," *Libération*, 24 March 2010.

48 Abdelwahid al-Nour, "Merci aux amis français," blog post, 22 April 2010, https://laregledujeu.org/2010/04/17/1260/oui-je-m%e2%80%99%c2%abentete%c2%bb-contre-les-genocideurs-du-darfour/ (accessed 8 June 2019; article in French, English translation from earlier version of the blog).

49 Interview with Sudanese academic (DH), Cambridge, April 2011.

50 Interview with UN official (CO), Khartoum, November 2011.

51 Interview with international journalist (DL), Zurich, November 2011 (interview in German, author's translation).

52 Interview with SLM member (DE), London, April 2011.

53 Interview with member of Sudanese civil society (BN), Khartoum, November 2010.

54 Al-Jazeera, "Darfur Rebels Surrender to ICC," 16 June 2010, www.aljazeera.com/news/africa/2010/06/2010616151942988526.html (accessed 8 June 2019). However, none of the three Darfur rebel leaders, against whom the prosecutor pressed charged, has had to stand for trial at the ICC. The pre-trial chamber did not confirm charges against Idriss Abu Garda; the ICC discontinued proceedings against Mohamed Jerbo Jamus following his passing in 2013; and Abdallah Banda, against whom the ICC confirmed charges in 2014, failed to appear for trial, despite the fact that he appeared voluntarily during the pre-trial stage. See ICC website on ongoing cases: www.icc-cpi.int/cases (accessed 8 June 2019).

55 Sudan Tribune, "Darfur Rebels Vow Full ICC Cooperation ahead of Ruling on Bashir Case," 2 March 2009, www.sudantribune.com/spip.php?article30331 (accessed 8 June 2019).

56 Interview with Phil Cox, London, November 2011.

57 Interview with international journalist (DL), Zurich, November 2011 (interview in German, author's translation).

58 Interview with Abdullahi el-Tom, Maynooth, November 2011.

59 UN News Centre, "UNICEF Signs Child Protection Pact with Key Rebel Group in Darfur," 21 July 2010, https://news.un.org/en/story/2010/07/345432-unicef-signs-child-protection-pact-key-rebel-group-darfur#.UEm2MLLiZSQ (accessed 8 June 2019).

60 Geneva Call, "Sudan: the Justice and Equality Movement Pledges against Anti-Personnel Mines," online communiqué, 24 April 2012, www.genevacall.org/sudan-justice-equality-movement-pledges-anti-personnel-mines/ (accessed 8 June 2019).

61 Interview with the head of a Sudanese NGO (CM), Khartoum, November 2010. *Khawaja* is an expression used in Sudan to designate white Europeans and North Americans.

62 Interview with staff of Sudanese NGO (DQ), London, November 2011.
63 Interview with the head of a Sudanese NGO (CM), Khartoum, November 2010.
64 Interview with staff of a Sudanese NGO (CJ), Khartoum, November 2010.
65 Interview with Darfuri politician (CP), Khartoum, November 2010.
66 Interview with Darfuri politician (CP), Khartoum, November 2010.
67 Interview with Sudanese journalist (CF), Khartoum, November 2010.
68 Interview with Darfuri NGO staff (CJ), Khartoum, November 2010.
69 Interview with researcher at a Sudanese think tank (AZ), Khartoum, October 2010.
70 Interview with Darfuri politician (CP), Khartoum, November 2010.
71 Interview with JEM representative (DO), London, November 2011.
72 Interview with Sudanese activist (DQ), London, November 2011.
73 Interview with Human Rights First staff (AD), Washington, DC, February 2010.
74 Human Rights Watch, "Human Rights Watch Honors Sudanese Activist," online announcement, 27 October 2005, www.hrw.org/news/2005/10/26/human-rights-watch-honors-sudanese-activist (accessed 8 June 2019).
75 European Parliament, "Sakharov Prize 2007 Awarded to Salih Mahmoud Osman, who Calls for World to Intervene in Darfur," online press release, 11 December 2007, www.europarl.europa.eu/sides/getDoc.do?type=IM-PRESS&reference=20071 211IPR14773&format=XML&language=EN (accessed 9 June 2019).
76 Interview with Suliman Baldo, New York, March 2011.
77 This is based on the author's own experience working with UNMIS on a project to identify the political dynamics of IDP camps in Darfur.
78 Interview with Sudanese activist (DQ), London, November 2011.
79 Interview with Sudanese activist (AZ), Khartoum, October 2011.
80 Interview with Sudanese academic (BS), Khartoum, November 2010.
81 Interview with Sudanese NGO worker (CJ), Khartoum, November 2010.
82 Sudan Tribune, "Sudan Political Parties Positions' on ICC Move against Bashir," 4 March 2009, www.sudantribune.com/spip.php?article30092 (accessed 8 June 2019).
83 The Heidelberg Darfur Dialogue was facilitated by the Max Planck Institute for Comparative Public Law and International Law in Heidelberg and the Peace Research Institute at the University of Khartoum. The outcome document, which was launched in May 2010, is available online at www.operationspaix.net/DATA/DOCUMENT/4752~v~ Heidelberg_Darfur_Dialogue_Outcome_Document_Containing_Draft_Proposals_for_ Consideration_in_a_Future_Darfur_Peace_Agreement.pdf (accessed 8 June 2019).
84 Interview with Darfuri intellectual (BK), Khartoum, October 2010.
85 Interview with Sudanese intellectual (AZ), Khartoum, October 2010.
86 Interview with Sudanese NGO worker (BN), Khartoum, November 2010.
87 Interview with Darfuri academic (BL), Khartoum, November 2010.
88 Interview with Darfuri academic (BL), November 2010.
89 Interview with Darfuri Arab researcher (BX), Khartoum, November 2010.
90 Interview with Darfuri Arab researcher (BX), Khartoum, November 2010.
91 Interview with Darfuri Arab researcher (BX), Khartoum, November 2010.
92 Interview with international humanitarian worker (CH), Khartoum, November 2010.
93 Interview with Darfuri Arab researcher (BX), Khartoum, November 2010.
94 Interview with Sudanese civil society leader (CK), Khartoum, November 2010.

References

Amnesty International. 2008. *Displaced in Darfur: A Generation of Anger.* AFR 54/001/2008. London: AI. January 2008.
Autesserre, Severine. 2002. "United States 'Humanitarian Diplomacy' in South Sudan." *Journal of Humanitarian Assistance.*

Bob, Clifford. 2005. *The Marketing of Rebellion: Insurgents, Media, and International Activism*. New York: Cambridge University Press.

Branch, Adam, and Zachariah Cherian Mampilly. 2005. "Winning the War, But Losing the Peace? The Dilemma of SPLM/A Civil Administration and the Tasks Ahead." *Journal of Modern African Studies* 43: 1–20.

Clapham, Christopher. 1998. *African Guerillas*. Oxford: James Currey.

Crilly, Rob. 2010. *Saving Darfur: Everyone's Favourite African War*. London: Reportage Press.

De Waal, Alex. 2006. "I Will not Sign." *London Review of Books* 28: 17–20.

De Waal, Alex. 2015. *The Real Politics of the Horn of Africa: Money, War and the Business of Power*. Cambridge: Polity Press.

El-Tom, Abdullahi Osman. 2011. *Darfur, JEM and the Khalil Ibrahim Story*. Trenton, NJ: Red Sea Press.

Flint, Julie. 2010. *Rhetoric and Reality: The Failure to Resolve the Darfur Conflict*. HSBA Working Paper 19. Geneva: Small Arms Survey. January.

Gabrielsen Jumbert, Maria, and David Lanz. 2013. "Globalised Rebellion: the Darfur Insurgents and the World." *Journal of Modern African Studies* 51: 193–217.

Hirschman, Albert O. 1970. *Exit, Voice, and Loyalty: Responses to Decline in Firms, Organizations, and States*. Cambridge, MA: Harvard University Press.

Human Rights Watch. 2004. *Darfur Destroyed: Ethnic Cleansing by Government and Militia Forces in Western Sudan*. New York: HRW. May.

Kuperman, Alan J. 2008. "Mitigating the Moral Hazard of Humanitarian Intervention: Lessons from Economics." *Global Governance* 14: 219–240.

Kuperman, Alan J. 2009. "Darfur: Strategic Victimhood Strikes Again?" *Genocide Studies and Prevention* 4: 281–303.

Loeb, Jonathan, Benjamin Naimark-Rowse et al. 2010. *Darfurian Voices: Documenting Darfurian Refugees' Views on Issues of Peace, Justice, and Reconciliation*. New York: 24 Hours for Darfur.

Rolandsen, Øystein H. 2005. *Guerrilla Government: Political Changes in the Southern Sudan During the 1990s*. Uppsala: Nordic Africa Institute.

Schlichte, Klaus. 2009. *In the Shadow of Violence the Politics of Armed Groups*. Frankfurt a. M.: Campus-Verlag.

Tanner, Victor, and Jérôme Tubiana. 2007. *Divided They Fall: The Fragmentation of Darfur's Rebel Groups*. HSBA Working Paper 6. Geneva: Small Arms Survey. July.

Tieku, Thomas Kwasi. 2012. *How Perks for Delegates Can Influence Peace Process Outcomes*. CIGI Africa Initiative Discussion Paper No. 2. Waterloo, ON: Center for International Governance Innovation. April.

United Nations. 2005. *Report of the International Commission of Inquiry on Darfur to the United Nations Secretary-General*. Geneva: United Nations. 25 January.

Weissman, Fabrice. 2010. "'Urgence Darfour': Les artifices d'une rhétorique néoconservatrice." In *Médias et islamisme*, ed. Olfa Lamloum. Beyrouth: Presses de l'Ifpo. 113–132.

Young, Helen, Abdul Monium Osman, Ahmed Malik Abusin, Michael Asher, and Omer Egemi. 2009. *Livelihoods, Power and Choice: The Vulnerability of the Northern Rizaygat, Darfur, Sudan*. Medford, MA: Feinstein International Centre. January.

5 Defying R2P

Sudanese government reactions to the international push to save strangers in Darfur

When the camel's nose enters the tent, the rest of the camel cannot be far behind.
Bedouin proverb

The noise is mostly coming from America. Facts about Sudan are bent by activist groups. Have you seen the student-teacher material on Darfur that they prepared? This is breeding a new generation of Sudan haters. The roots go really deep. We are the new Serbs!
Sudanese government consultant[1]

The logic and trajectory of the NCP regime in Sudan

Islamist ascension in Sudan

In order to understand the context of the Sudanese government's response to the rebellion in Darfur and later to the international push to save strangers, it is important to take a close look at the NCP regime, which was in power when Darfur became a global cause. In post-independence Sudan, Islamists initially played a marginal role. This changed in 1964 when Hassan al-Turabi assumed the leadership of Sudan's Islamist movement. When Jaafar Nimeiry came to power in 1969, al-Turabi was initially hostile towards the government but, in 1977, joined the regime as attorney general (Berridge 2017, Chapter 2). The Islamists' ascension to the government was crucial. Al-Turabi "adopted a comprehensive strategy to transform the Islamist movement into a political force capable of assuming power in its own right" (Sidahmed 2011, 95). One element was to place fellow Islamists in strategic positions within the army and civil service. Another strategy was to establish Islamist banks and place key people in the business sector (De Waal and Abdel Salam 2004, 81). Al-Turabi also sought to increase his influence in civil society: "a drive to increase membership tenfold was launched, coupled with complete decentralization within the movement to make the organization more efficient and resistant to crackdowns. Decentralization was enhanced by setting up numerous autonomous satellite organizations and loosely affiliated groups" (El-Affendi 1991, 115).

In an attempt to neutralize the growing influence of Islamists, Nimeiry imposed in 1983 the September Laws, which instituted the Sharia. Al-Turabi was not involved in the decision, but "it came as a blessing to the Islamists" since it "provided a justification for their alliance with Nimeiry's regime, its corrupt character notwithstanding" (Sidahmed 2011, 95). Also fortunate for the Islamists was their expulsion from the government a few weeks before Nimeiry was deposed in a popular uprising in April 1985. This "enabled the [Islamist] movement to make a come-back to the political scene despite its rather long association with the defunct regime" (Sidahmed 2011, 95). For this purpose, al-Turabi rebranded his movement National Islamic Front. NIF deliberately exploited resentment against the Sudanese government's collusion with Western powers, in particular the US and Israel. This resonated beyond Islamist milieux, partly because of an affair in early 1985 in which Sudanese government officials collaborated with the CIA and the Mossad to fly several thousand Ethiopian Falasha Jews from refugee camps in Sudan to Israel (Karadawi 1991). At the time, Sudan had emerged as one of the US' most important Cold War allies in Sub-Saharan Africa, even though Nimeiry had initially aligned himself with the Soviet Union.[2]

Al-Turabi's Islamists were staunch opponents of Sadiq al-Mahdi, who acted as prime minister following the Umma Party's victory in the 1986 elections. In June 1989, a group of mid-ranking soldiers staged a coup under the leadership of Brigadier Omar al-Bashir and deposed al-Mahdi's government. The coup leaders played a game of deception, imprisoning al-Turabi to assuage fears of an Islamist takeover. However, it quickly became clear that al-Turabi was, in fact, the mastermind of the coup and that NIF had usurped power. The Islamists were in control of the Sudanese government and moved decisively to consolidate their rule. For this purpose, al-Turabi and his followers embarked on a campaign to purge the Sudanese state and society of dissidents. Spearheaded by its intelligence service, NIF "emasculated Khartoum's political life, sweeping through the Three Towns[3] and the provincial urban centers and arresting human-rights activists, intellectuals, and university professors, as well as professionals, particularly doctors, lawyers, and journalists" (Collins 2008, 189).

Becoming a pariah

Al-Turabi embarked on an ambitious state-building project, which included a U-turn in foreign relations (Verhoeven 2015). During the first Gulf War (1990–1991), Sudan exposed itself for the first time as one of the only countries in the world that supported Saddam Hussein. Al-Turabi then announced the creation of the Popular Arab and Islamic Congress and welcomed Islamists from all over the world, including Osama bin Laden.[4] Sudan's role in promoting fundamentalist Islamist groups registered when it became clear that Sudanese diplomats in the US assisted the terrorists of the Egyptian *jama'at al-islamiyya* (Islamic Group), who had planted a bomb in New York's World Trade Center on 26 February 1993. The US government subsequently accused Sudan of supporting terrorist organizations, such as Hamas, Hezbollah, and the Egyptian groups Islamic Jihad and *jama'at al-islamiyya*, and added Sudan to the list of states sponsoring terrorism (Collins 2008, 199). Sudan definitely became a pariah in 1995. On 26 June, *jama'at al-islamiyya* terrorists made a failed assassination attempt on Egyptian president Hosni Mubarak in Addis Ababa. The Ethiopian government soon confirmed that the assassins were aided by the NIF regime in Khartoum, which had provided false passports and weapons (Collins 2008, 215–216). As a result, many Arab and African states turned away from Sudan, and in 1996, the UN Security Council imposed sanctions.

The US exhibited particular hostility towards the NIF regime in Khartoum after Bill Clinton took office in January 1993. Its ill will was a consequence of Sudan's support for terrorist groups that were targeting the US, but it was also influenced by Sudan's north–south civil war. Indeed, NIF had stepped up the war against the SPLA. Not unlike the Darfur conflict, NIF relied on a combination of regular armed forces, paramilitary units, and tribally organized militias, which committed countless atrocity crimes, especially in communities suspected of supporting the rebellion. The violence was particularly gruesome in the northern Sudanese communities that bordered southern Sudan (African Rights 1995). As a result, two anti-Khartoum constituencies formed in the US. One revolved around members of Congress Frank Wolf, Sam Brownback, and Donald Payne, who showed an early interest in Sudan. The other was based at the State Department. Along with Secretary of State Madeleine Albright, it included Albright's Assistant Secretary for African Affairs, Susan Rice, Rice's advisor John Prendergast, and USAID consultant Gayle Smith. Since these actors played an important role in the internationalization of the Darfur conflict after 2004, it is not surprising that the Sudanese government experienced a sense of déjà vu.

President Clinton expanded the sanctions against the NIF regime in 1997, prohibiting most trade between the US and Sudan. The only export exception was humanitarian aid. In addition, several members of Congress and officials from the State Department regularly met John Garang and travelled to SPLA-held territories in southern Sudan. In December 1997, Secretary of State Albright met the SPLM leader and other opposition figures in Uganda and effectively called for regime change in Sudan. She said, "This meeting is a demonstration of support for a regime that will not let Khartoum become a viper's nest for terrorist activities" (Quoted in De Waal 2004, 220). After Al-Qaida bombed the US embassies in Kenya and Tanzania in August 1998, the US government retaliated and launched a cruise missile strike against the Al-Shifa pharmaceutical company in North Khartoum on the grounds that it was producing chemical weapons—a claim that was probably inaccurate.[5]

Another important element of Sudan's relations with the West pertained to humanitarian aid. The main framework for delivering aid in Sudan was Operation Lifeline Sudan (OLS), which had been set up as a tripartite agreement in April 1989 between the Sudanese government, the SPLM, and the UN. As such, OLS represented the cutting edge of aid operations. As Large (2011, 170) wrote, "OLS was the world's first humanitarian programme to assist civilians on both sides of an ongoing war within a sovereign state." OLS developed into a massive operation, which cost several hundred million US dollars per year (Burr and

Collins 1995). Some OLS projects directly supported Khartoum's development objectives (Large 2011, 171). However, it was the SPLM that drew the biggest benefit from OLS. The tripartite structure of OLS and the collaboration between the SPLA and UN officials conferred legitimacy on the rebel movement and allowed it to establish quasi-state structures (Rolandsen 2005). Moreover, many humanitarians working in the SPLA-held areas became SPLM sympathizers and helped to popularize its struggle.[6] More tangibly, SPLA soldiers diverted food aid and used it to finance their operations. In short, humanitarian aid became a strategic tool in Sudan's civil war, creating an increasing perception on the part of the government that aid was being used against them.

Un-becoming a pariah

After the assassination attempt on Hosni Mubarak, Sudan was not only isolated internationally but became encircled by hostile neighbors, such as Egypt, Eritrea, Ethiopia, and Uganda. The dangers of al-Turabi's foreign policy had become apparent, with two consequences on the NIF regime. First, it led to a pragmatic foreign policy turn that included Osama bin Laden's expulsion in 1996. Second, backlash from the Mubarak assassination attempt meant that al-Turabi was no longer inviolable within the regime, opening an internal rift between civilian Islamist cadres loyal to al-Turabi and the military leadership around al-Bashir. This rift was the main parameter of Sudanese politics in the years to follow. In 1998, the government legalized political parties. As a result, the National Islamic Front gave way to the National Congress Party, with al-Turabi as its secretary general. Things seemed to go in al-Turabi's favor, but in 1999 he over-reached by proposing the direct election of state governors as well as the creation of a prime minister post—measures that "would have reduced the President to little more than a figurehead" (De Waal and Abdel Salam 2004, 107). Al-Bashir reacted by declaring a state of emergency and dissolving the National Assembly in December 1999. In May 2000, it became clear that the rift within the Sudanese Islamist movement was irreversible. Al-Turabi was disposed and put under house arrest. He was, however, allowed to form his own opposition party, the Popular Congress Party (PCP).

The split between al-Turabi and al-Bashir created vulnerabilities in the NCP regime. It undermined the legitimacy of the Islamist project by exposing the primary interest of the NIF cadres—retaining power (De Waal and Abdel Salam 2004, 108–109). It also deprived the NCP regime of grassroots support and narrowed its power basis. Some of al-Turabi's followers switched over to the al-Bashir camp, most importantly Ali Osman Taha. But many left the government, in particular Islamist cadres from Sudan's peripheries, above all Darfur. Their discontent at Al-Turabi's ousting was compounded by their disappointment that the Sudanese Islamist movement could not overcome the racism toward and marginalization of the peripheries, issues they had joined the movement to rectify. Resulting from these dynamics was both the publication of the Black Book and the foundation of JEM, as described in Chapter 2. Given the regime's precariousness, al-Bashir and his acolytes decided to perform another foreign policy U-turn in the hopes of shedding their pariah image.

To do so, the NCP knew that it had to end the war in the south. In addition, a stalemate was arising in the military confrontation between Khartoum and the SPLM. Also relevant was that in 1999, after many years of exploration, Sudan began to export oil for the first time. But as the ongoing war prevented the full exploitation of its oil fields, an agreement with the SPLM was needed to boost oil production and create revenues for the government.[7] Finally, in 2001, the September 11 terrorist attacks changed the international context. Having hosted Osama bin Laden, Khartoum was vulnerable vis-à-vis the US. But as it possessed valuable information about bin Laden's terrorist network, it was a potentially interesting partner for Washington in its war on terror. Therefore, George W. Bush signaled that the US was willing to normalize relations with the Sudanese government, but on the condition of peace with the SPLM.

Peace talks started in earnest in 2002 in Kenya under the auspices of the Intergovernmental Authority on Development, an East African regional organization (H. F. Johnson 2011). In January 2005, Taha and Garang signed the Comprehensive Peace Agreement, which officially ended Africa's longest and one of its bloodiest civil wars. The CPA foresaw a six-year transitional period, at the end of which South Sudan would hold an independence referendum. During the transitional period, the NCP and the SPLM would share power at the national level as well as revenues from the oil fields in the south. Despite the dominance of NCP pragmatists that favored a settlement with the SPLM, the CPA represented a significant risk. The peace talks were exclusive, with opposition parties and civil society groups left out and regime hardliners sidelined (Young 2005). This meant that those within the NCP who negotiated the agreement were going to be held accountable if the peace process did not deliver what was promised—namely, a normalization of relations with the US and the end of Sudan's pariah status. What is more, the NCP negotiators interpreted the US position in a simplistic fashion: The key to normalization was signing an agreement with the SPLM. Other issues, such as Darfur, or a more general commitment to human rights and democracy were not part of the arrangement.[8]

Counter discourses on Darfur

Public discourse in Sudan

To understand the Sudanese government's reaction, it is important to shed light on public discourse in Sudan, in particular how Khartoum positioned itself in relation to the notion of Darfur as a test case for saving strangers. To this end, the analysis presented draws on Sudanese media reports and interviews conducted in Sudan, making it possible to examine the early phase of the Darfur conflict and develop a broad view of public discourses in the country. During this period, the media in Sudan was primarily a repository of discourses emanating from the government, which controlled it to ensure a presentation of information that best suits its interests. In this sense, Chalk (2009) is right that the media served as a propaganda tool used by the NCP to promote distorted versions of the Darfur conflict. Radio, television, and the two national news agencies—the Sudan News Agency (SUNA) and the Sudanese Media Centre (SMC)—were fully in the government's hands until Omar al-Bashir's ousting in 2019. The NCP also had tight links with the many newspapers owned by businessmen affiliated with the regime. However, beyond propaganda, discourses in official media reports reveal the worldviews and normative convictions of the regime as well. Media reports also reflected a certain diversity in Sudanese public discourse. According to Deckert (2012, 16), government control

> does not mean that the majority of papers are absolutely conformist in their editorial lines. On the contrary: Many of them represent the in-house opposition of the NCP, which hosts quite a broad range of differing interests in the absence of a proper opposition. Hence, the Sudanese press is fairly diverse even though it reflects a somewhat narrow spectrum of elitist opinion.

To analyze the Sudanese media coverage of Darfur, the media service BBC Monitoring was used, which includes a broad range of sources in Sudan, such as radio, TV, news agencies, and newspapers.[9] In total, 349 media reports were analyzed that dealt with Darfur and were published in Sudan between January 2003 and September 2004. This interval was chosen because it spans the beginning of the rebellion (early 2003), the government's counterinsurgency campaign (late 2003 and early 2004), the internationalization of Darfur in the context of the tenth anniversary of the Rwanda genocide (spring 2004), and the emergence of Darfur as a cause célèbre in Western public opinion (summer 2004).

Initial denial and information control

At the outset of the Darfur rebellion in early 2003, when the rebels were procuring weapons and carrying out their first attacks against government installations, reports were infrequent in the Sudanese press. This demonstrates that the Khartoum establishment underestimated the situation in Darfur. Telling in this regard is the reporting about Darfur in the *Al-Sahafa* newspaper, which was more candid about the deteriorating security situation than anything published after April 2003. In an article published on 26 January 2003, *Al-Sahafa* quoted a Darfuri parliamentarian, Hashim Abbas, regarding armed attacks in North Darfur,

> Hashim said the situation in Darfur had completely broken down and there was no trace of state control or authority. He said the talk about restoration of security in the region was just nonsense. He appealed to the international and civil society organizations to immediately and urgently intervene since the government had failed to resolve the problem.[10]

The Sudanese government practiced pre-censorship at the time. If the report slipped past the censors, it is because Darfur had not yet manifested as a major issue. When reports of violent incidents multiplied, the government opted to deny them. For example, on 26 February 2003, when the rebels overran the Golo district headquarters, the government-controlled media was quick to say that everything was under control. Sudan TV quoted the governor of North Sudan saying that "the armed forces were carrying on with their routine duties of providing security to the lives of the citizens and their properties, and were in totally control of Golo locality."[11]

The situation changed after the 25 April 2003 attack by SLA and JEM forces on the airport in El-Fasher. As mentioned in Chapter 2, the attack was a success for the rebels as it decimated the Sudanese air force. It also elevated Darfur to a pressing national security issue, prompting a debate within the government about how to react. In the days following the El-Fasher attack, there were multiple media reports. The newspaper *Akhir Lahza*, which was affiliated with the PCP at the time, published a statement by JEM on its website.[12] Likewise, *Al-Sahafa* printed the communiqué of an opposition meeting in Eritrea, which "blamed the government for spreading destruction and devastation" in Darfur.[13] However, independent media reports subsided when the security cabal—a group that favored heavy-handed military responses—took control over the Darfur file. Alongside its counterinsurgency efforts, the government established strict control over the information about Darfur that was published in the Sudanese media.

The government also increasingly moved to propagate a narrative that relayed its version of events. One way it did so was by holding outside actors responsible for the violence in Darfur. As President al-Bashir said, "what is happening in Darfur is being backed by foreign forces and the aim of which is to destabilize security and stability, entrench the rebellion and destabilize the social fabric in Darfur."[14] The Darfur rebels were also blamed for the violence, although their role was generally downplayed. For example, SUNA reported a debate in Sudan's Parliament in May 2003:

> The assembly has denounced the assaults which are being staged against the tribes by the outlaws and armed robbery gangs, and called on the state to adopt all means to protect the citizens. The National Assembly indicated that these outlaw gangs do not represent any tribe in Darfur.[15]

The role of the government was often portrayed as that of an uninvolved third party trying to protect its citizens from harm—a particularly cynical depiction, given that the government was running a brutal counterinsurgency campaign at the time that involved mass atrocities. For example, the foreign minister, Mustafa Osman Ismail, said that "the government will live up to its role for keeping security and boosting the political stability in Darfur states."[16] The Sudanese press also gave the impression that the government was actively providing assistance to victims, even though it was in fact impeding the work of humanitarian organizations. As President al-Bashir said on Sudan TV, "We also want the people of Darfur to feel that Sudan is supporting them. That is why we requested all the states to send convoys [of assistance] to Darfur."[17] When the situation in Darfur deteriorated in early 2004, media reports multiplied and the government increased its attempts to show that efforts to quash the rebellion had been successful. To this effect, President al-Bashir made several statements on Sudan TV. On January 6, he avowed that "our priority is to direct all resources, energies and capabilities to hit the rebellion."[18] On 1 February, he doubled down, saying

> the great responsibility, which we accepted to carry out and of which we are responsible on the judgment day had forced us to resolutely combat terrorism and armed robbery in Darfur in order to stop blood-shed of innocent people and to safeguard security of the citizens.[19]

While the Sudanese government generally suppressed critical voices, it did not enjoy full control of what came out in the press. There were cases of articles that, while not openly critical, indirectly subverted the official narrative. For example, an October 2003 article in the newspaper *Al-Khartoum* cited an NCP official, who "strongly denied the government was supporting the Janjaweed [Arab] militias"[20]—thereby indirectly acknowledging that militias were indeed operating in Darfur. Likewise, an *Al-Sahafa* article, in which the SAF denied that the rebels had cut off the roads to Darfur's provincial capitals,[21] could be read to imply that a major rebel offensive had taken place. According to a Sudanese academic, the public was accustomed to government censorship and astute at picking up such references.[22] This suggests that there was a wider debate about Darfur within the Khartoum establishment. Nevertheless, the government narrative was dominant even though it contradicted what was actually happening in Darfur. This changed after March 2004 when Darfur became a fully fledged issue in the international sphere.

Futile attempts to relieve pressure

Mukesh Kapila's statement of March 2004, in which he compared the situation in Darfur to the Rwanda genocide, marked the beginning of a new phase in Sudanese public discourse. The government narrative was soon eclipsed by discussions about Darfur in international forums, to which the Sudanese media had to respond. Instead of being able to put forward its own account, the government was forced to stem the tide of criticism that suddenly washed over it. In this context, the Sudanese media functioned as a pressure relief valve, as the government tried to neutralize the accusations of international actors—most importantly claims that it was committing atrocities against its own citizens in Darfur.

After Mukesh Kapila's statement, the Sudanese media featured a series of relatively clumsy ripostes and denials from the government. According to the Ministry of Humanitarian Affairs, "Kapila deviated from the virtues which a resident representative should have, that is, neutrality, and transcended to open political work." Moreover, "the situation in Darfur, following the call by the president of the republic, has notably witnessed a lot of stability and a number of tens of thousands of refugees and displaced have returned."[23] Ten days later, President al-Bashir said that Kapila's statement was "far from reality."[24] Likewise, in reaction to ethnic cleansing allegations, SUNA quoted Sudan's ambassador to India who pointed out

> that Darfur had suffered from a prolonged drought for the last decade and owing to meagre resources, there has been an emergence of armed bandits.... He explained that the Sudanese government has made it clear to the UN secretary-general not to take at face value the reports of NGOs providing such baseless information with respect to the situations in Darfur.[25]

After George W. Bush's and Kofi Annan's speeches in Geneva on 7 April 2004 (see Chapter 2), Khartoum's response became more sophisticated. SUNA featured the following report:

> A statement issued by the Ministry of Foreign Affairs Thursday [8 April] explained that as the government appreciates the concern of the UN secretary-general and the international community with the issue of Darfur [western Sudan], it affirms that it has spared no efforts in taking the necessary measures in pursuit of a lasting comprehensive solution for the issue of Darfur.
>
> In this respect, the statement explained that the government established a consultation mechanism, made up of the concerned ministries, humanitarian aid organizations, representatives of EU and donors, in order to get acquainted with the situations and to guarantee the flow of humanitarian assistance to the needy people.
>
> Moreover, the president of the republic has set up a ministerial committee comprising ministers of foreign affairs, justice, defence, interior and humanitarian affairs, to work for the achievement of security and stability, repatriation of the displaced people and collection of arms from all persons and groups other than the regular forces, including Janjawid militia, bringing to justice outlaw groups as well as supervising delivery of assistance to the needy people.[26]

The difference between these statements may seem puzzling as they range from antagonism and denial to constructive engagement. The inconsistency in them partly reflects the disunity within the Sudanese government and the power struggles between different actors linked to different power bases and ideologies. However, in line with the spiral model, it is typical for states that seek to relieve the pressure generated by international norms campaigns to vacillate between denial and repression, on the one hand, and tactical concessions, on the other. Therefore, the Sudanese media reported on measures taken by the government to respond to international demands, such as establishing an Arab League committee to investigate the situation in Darfur,[27] easing restrictions for humanitarian organizations,[28] and issuing a presidential order to arrest *janjawid* militia.[29]

At the same time, however, the government-affiliated media cried foul over the international pressure. For example, foreign minister Ismail said that "the campaigns launched by some circles to destroy the image of Sudan will never cease."[30] Moreover, at a press conference, President al-Bashir "reiterated that claims by the Western media that the government was waging an ethnic-cleansing campaign in Darfur were fabrications and lies that had no basis in truth."[31]

As before, the newspapers striving for editorial independence were prevented from freely reporting about Darfur. However, there were a few instances of critical reporting. For example, *Al-Sahafa* quoted an MSF representative who said that

> the displaced were in appalling conditions and there was an urgent need for water and food [and] that many organizations operating in the region could not deliver aid: "We lose 20 children a day and receive 500 others who are sick."[32]

In sum, during the phase that followed Kapila's genocide analogy, international discussions about Darfur dominated in the Sudanese media. The government lost control of the narrative and tried to use the media to relieve pressure, although it vacillated over how best to do this—either by displaying its willingness to cooperate or by pushing back against foreign intrusion.

In defiance of saving strangers

A third stage in Sudanese public discourse about Darfur began in July 2004 when Tony Blair talked about a possible military engagement in Sudan. Blair backtracked on it a few days later,[33] but it nonetheless caused a storm in Sudan, as Colin Powell's genocide determination did a few weeks later. The Sudanese government reacted by adopting an increasingly defiant stance. For example, after Blair's statement, President al-Bashir "called for the need to unify national ranks and foil attempts by foreign quarters which are trying to sow discord."[34] The Sudanese foreign minister linked Blair's statement to the situation in Iraq, which was rapidly deteriorating at the time. He said, "the existence of any foreign forces in Darfur will be regarded by the citizens as occupation troops, and soon resistance work will begin, such as the situation in Iraq."[35] Another consequence was that the NCP began to move away from denying the factual accuracy of Western media reports, but instead attacked the legitimacy of the message and the messenger. The Sudanese government devised counter-discourses aimed at defying the notion that the international community ought to intervene to protect civilians in Darfur. The following sections consider three sets of counter-discourses in detail.

Saving strangers as a double standard

The first counter-discourse criticized the double standard behind the claim that external intervention was needed to protect civilians in Darfur. Accordingly, while Western NGOs and governments decried the situation in Darfur and held the government accountable for it, violations elsewhere were ignored or tolerated. This discourse does not oppose the core R2P norm per se but questions its legitimacy because the way the norm is translated into practice violates the basic principles of fairness and consistency. While the double standard critique is generally applicable, it usually took an anti-American and anti-Israeli undertone in Sudan.

A statement by the Islamist intellectual Hassan Makki exemplifies the double standard discourse: "Theoretically I agree with the idea of conditional sovereignty and protection of civilians. But when I look at Guantanamo, Abu Ghraib, Gaza, the bombing of Iraq it doesn't make sense to me."[36] A Sudanese government official similarly claimed,

> I myself believe in the responsibility to protect. Many believe in this. But what we don't like are the double standards. In the world now, if you don't respect human rights you should not have sovereignty. But what about Israel, Palestine, Iraq? The same standards should be applied anywhere.[37]

This argument resonated beyond government circles. A Sudanese NGO worker said, "In my mind, if you look at what is happening in Gaza, Afghanistan, Iraq, even Libya, there isn't much protection. The issue of protecting civilians is not genuine.... The Americans are bombing civilians all the time."[38] Khartoum tapped into these sentiments, which were widely shared in Sudan and beyond. In response to Colin Powell's genocide determination on 9 September 2004, SUNA published the following strongly worded Ministry of Foreign Affairs statement:

> It will be interesting to hear what Mr Powell would say about all the civilians who have been killed by the US nuclear bombings of Hiroshima and Nagasaki, and about the annihilation of millions of people in Vietnam and Somalia by the American war machine. If he is really keen on historical accounts, then what will he say about the mass killing of tens of thousands of civilians in Iraq and Afghanistan, which is still taking place.
>
> The Sudanese government has opened the country's border; it welcomed droves international observers, as well as thousands of NGOs representatives, UN agencies representatives, foreign media reporters and human rights activists in order to see for themselves the real situation in Darfur. Will the USA open Abu-Ghurayb gates to human rights activists to see for themselves how Iraqi prisoners are being tortured with no clothes on and how they are being molested?[39]

This statement illustrates how counter-discourses operate. They do not address the accusation per se, in this case the claim that genocide was occurring in Darfur, but attack the legitimacy of the message and those emitting it, in this case the US government.

The double standard discourse was particularly present in the government's response to the ICC indictment of Omar al-Bashir. This is not surprising since the jurisdiction of the Court is not universally accepted, and the al-Bashir indictment was supported by the US, which itself has not ratified the Rome Statute. The Sudanese regime proved savvy in exploiting this. As a scholar affiliated with the NCP stated:

> The issue of the ICC is complex. We should arrive at some theory of international justice. States are not isolated. But at present the methods, mechanisms, and structures of international justice are not widely accepted as leading to real justice. Some Western powers are opposed to the ICC. Satirically enough they are the ones that are pressuring the Sudan case! My objection stems from such double standards.[40]

Other proponents of the regime were more aggressive in their opposition to the ICC, although they also cited double standards. A journalist working for a pro-government newspaper claimed,

> They did not indict any criminal in Darfur, but instead they went after our president. What about the presidents of the US, UK, France? All the Western governments have committed crimes in Afghanistan and Iraq.... Where was the ICC when all of this happened?[41]

Saving strangers vs. national sovereignty

A second counter-discourse was that international intervention to save strangers in Darfur constituted a violation of Sudan's national sovereignty. Echoing the pluralist critique of humanitarian intervention, several Sudanese observers thus insisted that the government's actions in Darfur were legitimate because they aimed to defend the integrity of the state. One NCP representative stated, "The government felt that it was its right to maintain security. The notion of sovereignty was very present here: the government considered it its right to act against those who breach the peace."[42] A Sudanese academic summed up the government's position, "Bashir says that I am responsible for the security of the state. If there are factions against me, I have a right to fight these rebels. In the history this is what governments have done!"[43] Implicit in these statements is the critique that international R2P obligations hinder governments from effectively quelling insurgency and, thus, foster disorder. Another critique echoed the global discussion about intervention (see Chapter 1), claiming that R2P was a smokescreen for a big-power agenda to marginalize the Global South. As one academic affiliated with the NCP argued:

> The government was skeptical about the position of Western powers on the Darfur issue.... The aim of these countries is to extract more concessions vis-à-vis the country's sovereignty. In reaction, the government took on a

position of political independence. It affirmed that it will resist the campaigns. Basically the government was defying the international community on Darfur.[44]

The sovereignty discourse resonated in Sudan. This is in part because historically Sudan had to defend its independence against outside rulers—the Mahdi uprising in 1885 being the most important example. Therefore, the government tried to use the national sovereignty counter-discourse to engender a rally-round-the-flag effect. The NCP secretary general, Ibrahim Ahmed Omar, said that "Western circles were targeting Sudan because of its wealth, values and humanity, an issue which calls on all Sudanese people to wake up and face this challenge." The NCP was thus "striving to hold consultations with all political parties to foil the [media] attacks which are being made by the Western quarters."[45]

The NCP played the national sovereignty card most frequently in connection with the ICC indictment of President al-Bashir. Many in the Sudanese political elite, including those in opposition parties, saw it as violation of national sovereignty. This statement by a prominent Sudanese academic is telling in this regard, "I wish the president was out tomorrow, but I don't like what the ICC did."[46] Likewise, a Darfuri academic said, "It is a grave thing to have a president indicted. The Sudanese, even the staunchest enemies of Bashir, don't accept the indictment. It is a question of national dignity."[47] Similarly, a civil society leader, who was a fierce opponent of the NCP regime, stated about the indictment, "My personal attitude is that the president is a national symbol and an attack against him is an attack against the nation."[48]

Saving strangers as conspiracy

A final counter-discourse portrayed the Saving Strangers Norm as the latest manifestation of a conspiracy to subjugate Sudan, to rein in the regime, and to bring it back into the Western sphere of influence. One popular notion in Islamist circles was that the international push to save strangers in Darfur aimed to denigrate Islam. Telling in this regard is the position of Hassan Makki (1989), who described Islam's broad appeal in Sudan and in Africa as a whole, which led the West to vilify Islam in an attempt to curtail its expansion. With regards to Darfur, Makki said in an interview:

> In 1898, the Mahdiya state was destroyed. In the books about Sudan you find Gordon represented as the good, while the people who killed him, the Mahdi, were described as evil. It is the same story with slavery. And the slavery campaigns are similar to the stories about Darfur today. There is an aggression on the part of the U.S. and the international community against Sudan. If you read the Western media and literature about Sudan, Darfur, the *janjawid*, the killing of innocent people, a picture of an evil society emerges that needs to be handled. This leads to sanctions and boycott.[49]

In this view, the Save Darfur campaigns served to curb Islam and the Sudanese government promoting it, and they aimed to punish the NCP regime for moving Sudan outside the orbit of Western influence. According to Makki, "our leadership talked openly about what the U.S. has done and how they have harmed us. We attack them. We talk back in a way that the U.S. does not like and that makes them want to retaliate."[50] A number of government-affiliated observers also drew a parallel between the Darfur campaigns and the campaigns on South Sudan in the 1990s. According to a government consultant,

> The activists never relinquished the belief in regime change. Darfur is really a continuation of South Sudan campaigning. The language is the same. It ties in with the exceptionalism of Sudan. It paints Sudan as the only country that has discrimination along racial and geographic lines. The economic issues are neglected.... The people who campaigned on the South were active on Darfur. These people have not been to Sudan in many years and are influenced by political exiles and Diaspora.[51]

Following this logic, the timing of the Darfur campaigns was deliberate. While the pretext was saving strangers, the real reason was to continue the pressure on Khartoum following the CPA in the hope of normalizing relations with the West: "When the CPA was signed the activists thought that the Sudanese government would escape so they needed a campaign to bring them back."[52]

Another formulation of the conspiracy discourse related to the global level and the way humanitarian arguments have been used to justify military interventions globally. In particular, the 2003 US-led war in Iraq was on many people's minds. According to Makki, "The calls for intervention in Darfur were reminiscent of what was happening in Iraq, especially the slogans of mass destruction, the myth of rape, robbery, genocide, *janjawid*, and human rights violations."[53] It appears the Sudanese government was indeed concerned about becoming the target of the next regime change intervention after Iraq, with saving strangers in Darfur as its pretext. As one Darfuri affiliated with the NCP regime said, "The shadow of what happened in Iraq loomed over Sudan."[54]

Repercussions of the Darfur campaigns on the Sudanese government

Pressure induces change

Given these discourses, how did the Sudanese government react to the construction of Darfur as a test case for saving strangers? The initial reaction was denial and repression but, after March 2004, denial was no longer an option. In conjunction with defiance discourses, the NCP took action in an attempt to neutralize international pressure. In Europe, it recruited right-wing lobbyist David Hoile who, through the European-Sudanese Public Affairs Council, attempted to influence public debates in favor of Khartoum. However, Hoile's efforts were largely unsuccessful, apart from the sympathetic verdict of the British Advertising Standards Authority mentioned in Chapter 3. Similarly ineffectual were the government's public diplomacy efforts. For example, the Sudanese embassy in Washington, DC, organized a fact-finding mission to Darfur to try to counteract the dominant narrative in the media. As a Sudanese diplomat confirmed, almost everyone invited—congressional staffers, journalists, NGO workers—declined to take part.[55]

Given the government's inability to neutralize international pressure on Darfur, which continued to mount in the summer of 2004, the Sudanese government was forced to accommodate the campaigns to some degree. The government's change of behavior manifested itself in five areas, which the following sections consider in turn.

Humanitarian aid

Perhaps the most significant change in the government's policy towards Darfur concerned humanitarian aid. The numbers speak for themselves. As mentioned in Chapter 3, the amount of humanitarian workers jumped from a few hundred in April 2004 to over 10,000 one year later. This rise was clearly correlated with the emergence of Darfur as a global cause. Aid was a central component in the saving strangers discourse, and the restrictions the Sudanese government had imposed in this area had contributed to its vilification in the Western media. To ease the pain, the government was obliged to open Darfur to humanitarian organizations. Instrumental in this regard was the liberalization of the visa and permit regime, which had previously crippled humanitarian operations. Process-tracing is revealing in this context: The Sudanese government changed its policy in May 2004, precisely when the Darfur issue started to gain traction in the Western media. On 21 May 2004, SUNA announced, that

> the government [had] decided [on a] suspension of the procedures concerning permits for travel to Darfur for a period of three months, indicating that [for] entry visas, informing the Ministry of Humanitarian Affairs [of] the name of the concerned person and the visit's programme are enough [to] work in Darfur.[56]

The push to open Darfur to humanitarian organizations came from the NCP cadres around Ali Osman Taha, who were negotiating the CPA in Kenya at the time. As an NCP negotiator said, after Darfur hit the news, "our call to Khartoum was to allow humanitarian organizations [to Darfur], saying we should be flexible."[57]

The concurrent visits of Colin Powell and Kofi Annan in June and July 2004—trips that were motivated by Darfur's framing as a test case for saving strangers—played an important role in the further facilitation of humanitarian access. Both statesmen explicitly demanded that Khartoum lift all aid delivery restrictions. Powell included this demand in a list of actions he expected from the Sudanese government to rectify the situation in Darfur.[58] Annan, in turn, negotiated a joint communiqué, in which the government committed to "implementing a 'moratorium on restrictions' for all humanitarian work in Darfur," including the "suspension of visa restrictions for all humanitarian workers and permitting freedom of movement for aid workers throughout Darfur."[59]

A Sudanese academic confirmed the impact of the Powell–Annan visit: "They got an agreement from the government to allow access to Darfur for humanitarian organizations. Before, it was difficult to go to the region. After that, it became much easier."[60] While many restrictions remained, a report by the Humanitarian Policy Group described the period from May 2004 to the end of 2006 as the "golden age of access" (Loeb 2013, 9). Likewise, an MSF worker explained that liberalization resulted in a multiplication of the number of permits issued by the Sudanese government. This allowed humanitarian organizations to establish a new presence or expand their existing operation in Darfur. It also made it possible for humanitarian organizations to deliver aid in areas that had previously been inaccessible.[61]

Peacekeeping

Another area in which the government made concessions was international peacekeeping. The deployment of an international protection force in Darfur was a key demand of the activists. At the outset, the Sudanese government categorically rejected an international peacekeeping presence. For example, after Kofi Annan's April 2004 speech at the UN Commission on Human Rights, foreign minister Mustafa Osman Ismail said that Sudan "does not need any foreign military assistance in Darfur."[62] However, as the pressure for international protection forces continued to mount, Khartoum was forced to relent. Only a few weeks later, Khartoum was willing to accept African Union observers to monitor the N'Djamena Humanitarian Ceasefire Agreement in Darfur.[63] This paved the way for the deployment of the first AMIS observers in early June 2004 (Appiah-Mensah 2005, 8).

The policy adopted by the government at the time was summarized by NCP secretary general, Ibrahim Ahmed Omar, who in *Al-Anba* newspaper rejected the deployment of a foreign army in Darfur of any size or under any pretext, adding "What is acceptable to us is the deployment of observers charged with monitoring the implementation of the cease-fire agreement."[64] However, Khartoum was again forced to abandon this position. It first had to accept the deployment of a few hundred troops responsible for protecting the unarmed AMIS observers. Then, the Sudanese government was confronted with increasingly louder calls for more forceful international intervention to protect civilians in Darfur, which it initially opposed. Interior minister Abdel Raheem Muhammad Hussein, for example, stated that "his country 'will absolutely not accept the presence of any foreign troops' on its territory, even if they are African or Arab."[65] Despite this statement, the Sudanese government agreed to the transformation of AMIS into a full-fledged peacekeeping force a few weeks later.[66]

The establishment of a UN peacekeeping force followed the same pattern. The Sudanese government was fiercely opposed to the transformation of AMIS into a Chapter VII UN peacekeeping mission and did everything in its power to prevent it. President al-Bashir, for example, said

> Sudan holds to the idea that the African peacekeepers in Darfur should remain one which is effectively African.... Sudan does not want to become a field in which weakness of the African Union in safeguarding ... its own peace would be displayed. It also does not want to become a field in which international [political] scores are settled. It does not ... want to become an inlet for the forces of the international hegemony.[67]

However, as described in Chapter 3, Sudan ultimately had to acquiesce to the deployment of a joint UN-AU peacekeeping force equipped with a robust Chapter VII mandate. The situation surrounding international peacekeeping followed a pattern similar to the one surrounding humanitarian aid. As international pressure intensified, the government's cost-benefit analysis began to change, and it ultimately had to yield to international demands.

Peace talks

A further dynamic pertained to peace talks. After the Darfur conflict became a global cause, Khartoum almost continuously engaged in some form of peace negotiations with representatives of the Darfur rebel movements.[68] In applying the core R2P norm to Darfur, peace talks can be understood in two ways. First, the internationalization of Darfur reflected negatively on the Sudanese government and generated international pressure. Insofar as the Darfur rebels contributed to making Darfur a test case for saving strangers, their bargaining power increased, and the Sudanese government could no longer ignore them. A Sudanese academic accurately captured this dynamic, "The government recognized that there is a real problem. At first, they said that the rebels had no reason to fight and that they were bandits. Then they accepted to negotiate with them."[69]

Second, engaging in peace talks was seen as a way to neutralize international demands to protect civilians. In that regard, the timing of peace talks is striking. There appears to be a direct correlation between the government's willingness to engage in peace talks and worldwide attention to Darfur. Thus, the N'Djamena Humanitarian Ceasefire Agreement was concluded in April 2004, only a few days after news of Darfur broke out in the international media. The AU-led talks in Addis Ababa and Abuja started in the summer of 2004 when pressure intensified. The Darfur Peace Agreement was concluded in May 2006, shortly after the big "Save Darfur" rally was held in Washington. The talks in Doha were stepped up in spring 2010 when the government faced criticism over its handling of the elections in Darfur.

The peace talks in Abuja in the spring of 2006 are particularly telling. The Darfur campaigns had built momentum in the US, and serious discussions were ongoing about some form of military intervention. As Jendayi Frazer recounts:

> The establishment of a no-fly zone was a real possibility. There were discussions including lawyers, security experts, the State Department, and our Chargé in Khartoum at the time, Cameron Hume, to fine-tune this option. This was when the peace talks in Abuja were at a critical moment. At this moment, the Sudan government signaled that it was willing to sign. And it looked like the rebels would sign too. Zoellick therefore made a case not to use the military option.[70]

The dynamic at play seems similar to the one that resulted in the government's acquiescence over humanitarian aid and the deployment of international peacekeepers. Thus, the government accommodated some of the international community's demands in order to deflect pressure and avoid more forceful measures. Tactical concessions also served to divide international actors between those willing to accept marginal changes and those advocating to keep up the pressure.

Cooperation on anti-terrorism

The Darfur campaigns also affected the Sudanese government's cooperation with the US in its war on terror. Pre-dating the Darfur conflict, its cooperation had been part of a broader strategy to normalize relations with the West, in particular the US. (Stedjan and Thomas-Jensen 2010, 164). However, Darfur prompted the NCP to step up cooperation and become a valued partner for the CIA in the war on terror. It appears that the Sudanese government detained Al-Qaida affiliates or handed them over to CIA-affiliated Arab intelligence agencies for interrogation by US officials. The Sudanese government also provided evidence about a number of suspected terrorists, many of whom had passed through Sudan in the 1990s. Some of these measures were apparently agreed in April 2005 by the then intelligence chief Salah Gosh, who the CIA flew to Washington, DC in an executive jet.[71] At around the same time, the government agreed to the construction of a new US embassy compound on the outskirts of Khartoum, "which will supposedly house the biggest CIA listening post outside of America."[72]

This reveals the same pattern that was behind Khartoum's concessions on aid and peacekeeping: tactical concessions to defuse tensions. More specifically, by making the CIA its ally, Khartoum wanted to prevent the US government from unifying internally against Sudan. This turned out to be successful as evidenced by Jendayi Frazer who confirmed the CIA was a significant stakeholder in deliberations within the Bush administration about Sudan.[73] That Khartoum had—as far as the US government was concerned—"a rather clean record" on the counterterrorism side, was one factor in preventing a more robust intervention.[74]

Violence reduction

The Darfur campaigns also had repercussions on the situation in Darfur itself. In this context, it is particularly difficult to draw causal inferences. Armed conflict is manifestly influenced by a multitude of factors, in particular the ups and downs on the battlefield. However, it seems plausible that the internationalization of the Darfur crisis through saving strangers campaigns contributed to reducing the most brutal form of violence in Darfur. There are numbers to corroborate this argument. As described in Chapter 2, the Darfur conflict was at its most violent between mid-2003 and mid-2004. After this time, the intensity of the violence and mortality rates began to diminish. One reason for this was the growing presence of humanitarian organizations (Degomme and Guha-Sapir 2010).

Beyond this, the diminishing violence also reflected a change in the behavior of the Sudanese government, which was influenced by the international outcry over Darfur. With the activation of the R2P norm and the eyes of the world focused on Darfur, the cost of mass violence rose to the point that it exceeded the counterinsurgency benefits. Some efforts were then made by Khartoum to rein in the militias. According to a Sudanese academic, after becoming a cause célèbre, "the government started to deal seriously with Darfur. Before, the *jan-jawid* were acting freely, attacking villages. When the international community spoke out about accountability, the government started to control the militia."[75] Likewise, a Darfuri aid worker said, "The violence was lessened. There were no attacks like those in February 2004. But there was human insecurity. There were individual killings, even inside the cities."[76] Moreover, with thousands of aid workers flocking to Darfur, foreign dignitaries and journalists going in and out, and peacekeepers being deployed, it was more difficult to conceal crimes. Considering these factors, it seems plausible that the government took measures to reduce the use of mass violence in Darfur, even while it continued its counterinsurgency campaign.

Domestic politics also played a role in this process. The NCP regime came under pressure from opposition forces, in particular the Umma Party and al-Turabi's PCP, over its handling of the Darfur conflict. Darfuris in Khartoum, including some in the regime, were also displeased. The NCP did not want to hear these voices, but the international outcry made them impossible to ignore. One consequence was that, on 8 May 2004, President al-Bashir established a national fact-finding committee "to investigate human rights facts in Darfur."[77] The committee was led by former Chief Justice of the Sudanese Supreme Court Dafallah al-Haj Yousef and staffed with a number of Sudanese lawyers. The committee issued its final report on 20 January 2005, concluding that "serious human rights violations took place," in which "all parties to the conflict were involved to varying degrees, thus leading to human suffering of the people of Darfur, causing internal displacement and people taking refuge in neighboring Chad."[78] Nonetheless, "What had happened in Darfur despite its graveness did not constitute a genocide crime" and "those killed on all sides did not exceed a few thousand persons."[79] This verdict echoed the regime's narrative and made clear that the committee was not independent. However, several people acknow-ledged that al-Haj Yousef was not a government figurehead and took his work seriously. One of his rapporteurs explained, "The committee had a mission from the President to assess what was going on in Darfur. We went there with govern-ment helicopters to the camps, especially in Nyala and El-Geneina. As a rappor-teur I wanted to see all places."[80]

Evidently, the presence of national and international investigators, human-itarian workers, and peacekeepers did not stop the government from committing acts of violence, including direct attacks against civilians. However, the signi-ficant reduction in violent deaths after mid-2004 demonstrates the likelihood that the increase in eyes and ears in Darfur and the international outrage sparked when the core R2P norm was activated did deter the use of extreme violence by the government and its affiliates.

Plus ça change, plus c'est la même chose[81]

These developments raise the question of whether the government went beyond tactical concessions. Did it accept the norms that underpin the saving strangers concept and make fundamental changes in governing its western periphery? The answer is clearly negative. During the period when Darfur was a global cause, Sudan remained an authoritarian state, with political power concentrated in Khartoum and the NCP largely in control of state institutions. The "war of visions" described by the Sudanese scholar and former foreign minister Francis Deng (1995) continued, as Sudan's rulers tried to impose their conception of Arab-Islamist identity on populations in the peripheral regions. The continued marginalization of the periphery meant that the root causes of civil war in Sudan remained unchanged (D.H. Johnson 2011). In Darfur, the government continued to exercise its authority through a mix of repression, violence, alliances with local leaders, and a patronage scheme that rewarded loyalty. The government's policy was heavily influenced by the security services and, as Chapter 6 shows, repression increased after 2011 when the attention of the international com-munity waned. Clearly, Khartoum's behavior in Darfur did not reflect a new-found commitment to the norms of protecting civilians and international human rights that underpinned the Darfur activist campaigns.

The question must be raised as to why this did not happen. Undeniably, the international response to the Darfur conflict did not generate sufficient coercive power to force Khartoum to change its behavior. However, had the Sudanese government cooperated on Darfur, this would have been consistent with its intention after September 11 to normalize relations with the West, which was the motivation behind signing the Comprehensive Peace Agreement in the first place. Why would Khartoum make such painful and far-reaching concessions, most importantly agreeing to a referendum on the independence of South Sudan, and then deprive itself of the rewards? The answer to Khartoum's intransigence seemed, at least partly, related to three dynamics that were triggered by the acti-vation of the core R2P norm and the emergence of the Darfur campaigns.

Compromising the compromisers

The first dynamic affected the situation inside the NCP regime. As de Waal (2007) explained, despite its authoritarian disposition, the Sudanese state was inherently instable, with different power centers competing with each other. During the NCP regime, there was a schism between the pragmatists and the hardliners. The pragmatists believed the Sudanese state could be transformed and Sudan's international image rehabilitated, while the hardliners were skeptical about international engagement, favored maintaining the status quo, and promoted the use of force to suppress discontent. For example, the pragmatists around Vice President Ali Osman Taha were the driving force behind Khartoum's engagement in peace talks, arguing that a compromise with the SPLM would be rewarded by the US and European countries through a lifting of sanctions and boost in trade relations. The struggle between pragmatists and hardliners had important ramifications for Darfur. IDF and Assal (2010, 33) described the NCP's internal dynamics after the UN Security Council referred the situation in Darfur to the ICC in March 2005, two months after the CPA was signed:

> Taha's group advocated for a different policy in dealing with the conflict in Darfur and called for a lenient approach to international society. For the pragmatists, the aim was to ensure that their great achievement in Naivasha should not be sabotaged by a counter-productive policy in Darfur. But by this stage the balance of power was clearly in favour of the hardliners. In addition to the discontent caused by the new political and military order of the CPA, the security apparatus and the military maintained the upper hand on the management of the situation in Darfur.

One consequence was that an NCP hardliner, Majzoub al-Khalifa, assumed responsibility for the Darfur file and represented Khartoum in the peace talks with the Darfur rebels. Al-Khalifa reported directly to President al-Bashir. He personified the uncompromising attitude that was predominant within the NCP at the time of the Abuja talks:

> For al-Bashir and for all the hardliners, another Naivasha scenario was out of the question. There would be no more substantial political and military concessions for the rebels, no more concessions to international society and no more pre-eminent role for Taha.
>
> (IDF and Assal 2010, 33)

After al-Khalifa's sudden death in a car accident in June 2007, the strongman of the NCP security establishment at the time, Nafie Ali Nafie, took control of the Darfur file. This meant that the government continued to view Darfur through a security lens, and security actors—in particular the intelligence services— continued to have an important presence on the ground, preventing fundamental changes that would be consistent with R2P.

Why did the hardliners prevail over the pragmatists on Darfur? The main reason is because the rewards promised by the CPA's international guarantors failed to materialize. An NCP member expressed the disappointment, saying,

> In 2005 there was an era of optimism after the CPA was signed, hopes for starting a new chapter in the relationship between Sudan and the West. Khartoum hoped to see sanctions lifted, its name on the list of states sponsoring terrorism removed etc. But nothing has materialized.[82]

Among those who negotiated the CPA, there was a sense of betrayal: "I heard it myself in a meeting in Nairobi ... Colin Powell said 'sign this agreement and every problem between our governments will be resolved, including the sanctions and the terrorism list.'"[83] While US officials deny having made such promises, it is clear that in early 2005, the US and European governments had absolutely no appetite for normalizing relations with Khartoum. The reason for this was Darfur. As the campaigns that denounced the Sudanese government for slaughtering civilians were gaining momentum, sanctions were expanded rather than lifted.

Pariah indeed

The second dynamic was related to the self-image of the NCP regime. It had initially identified itself as a revolutionary actor, promoting Islamic extremism. Its stance was decisively anti-Western, and particularly anti-American. As a result, Sudan became an international pariah. Sudanese Islamists used their pariah image to gain political support, both internally and abroad, claiming it was a consequence of speaking truth to Western powers. Following the September 11 terrorist attacks, the NCP sought to shed its image and to normalize relations with the West. However, with the international outcry over the government's role in Darfur, Khartoum was again a pariah. Khartoum therefore reverted to portraying itself as the victim of a conspiracy, seeking the support of the public as well as states in Africa and the Arab world to defend itself. One element of this strategy was to remain intransigent in the face of the Western intervention in Darfur.

Khartoum used its pariahdom as a political strategy in connection with the ICC. When Omar al-Bashir was indicted, the Sudanese government launched an angry campaign against the court, denouncing it as a political instrument of Western powers. Several interlocutors opined that the indictment only increased the popularity of al-Bashir and the NCP regime in Sudan. According to a Sudanese academic,

> The ICC was absolutely useful. The government portrayed itself as the victim of an attack from the outside. Every Sudanese felt like this was an insult. This is the sitting president, why don't they wait until he is gone? As a sitting president, you have the right to declare war. The indictment gave legitimacy to the president.[84]

Opposition parties even opposed the indictment, with the exception of the PCP. The NCP also used the ICC indictment as a campaign tool during the national elections in April 2010. Many campaign posters depicted al-Bashir as a leader who courageously defied the big powers in the West. In the end, al-Bashir won 68 percent of the votes.[85]

The NCP also used the fallout over the ICC indictment to generate support abroad—initially with some success. As one Sudanese pundit argued, "The indictment elevated Bashir's standing in the region: neither African nor Arab countries want a precedent of this type. Nobody wants it."[86] Sudan was successful in rallying support from the African Union. It sponsored resolutions critical of the ICC in July 2009 and again in October 2013, when the AU summit unanimously agreed that no sitting African head of state should be tried in international court (Mills and Bloomfield 2018). This shows that Sudan managed to conjure some international support for defying the West. At the same time, many foreign dignitaries shunned Sudan or, when that was not possible, avoided meeting al-Bashir, even though he was head of state. Likewise, the initial support the indictment had generated began to dissipate from domestic political opinion, culminating in the ousting of Omar al-Bashir in April 2019.

Pariah status gave Khartoum an excuse to revert to well-known patterns, like using grandstanding rhetoric and spreading conspiracy theories about international assistance in Darfur. In this context, the mechanisms borne out of the international response to the Darfur conflict became the poster children for Western interventionism—something that needed to be curtailed. The pariah label also meant that the cost of continued obstructionism was low. If the state's reputation was already tarnished, international criticism over another episode of non-cooperation would not make much difference. The Sudanese government's decision to expel humanitarian groups after the Bashir indictment can be seen in this light.

The camel's nose

The third dynamic related to Sudan's deep mistrust of liberal internationalist projects, which it saw as a smokescreen for regime change similar to US Sudan policy in the 1990s and the 2003 war in Iraq. In this context, the idea of giving in to international demands on Darfur was seen as treading down a slippery slope that would lead to more interventions and, ultimately, a full-fledged invasion. Many people in Khartoum thought the Darfur campaigns were the latest plot in the conspiracy against Sudan. In this context, humanitarian workers and peacekeepers were suspected, as al-Bashir said, of being an "inlet for the forces of the international hegemony."[87] Therefore, their presence had to be circumscribed to prevent the proverbial camel's nose from entering the Sudanese tent.

With respect to humanitarian organizations, an NCP member who belonged to the pragmatist camp stated:

> The humanitarian community is suspect. Only a few are altruistic. This is an industry, a business, and aid organizations are flexing with the muscles of

their home governments. The foot soldiers are all genuine. They are ideal-
istic, young doctors who are willing to endure circumstances that many of
their Sudanese counterparts would not. I don't want to criticize them. But
aid organizations are not apolitical. They cannot look impartially at the government of Sudan.... Many of these organizations inform the policies of
their home countries. The UN listens and the media places a high premium
on their reports. Also, I have no doubt that the way they choose their local
staff is 100% political. You would be amazed at how many liberal, anti-
Islamic people are employed by aid groups.[88]

This statement exemplifies the deep mistrust that the Sudanese government harbored against humanitarian aid. This was exacerbated by the conflation of aid
and advocacy in the Darfur campaigns. A government representative cites the
example of Brian Steidle, the US defense contractor turned activist:

He came to this country with a humanitarian visa! The government can't
oppose purely humanitarian assistance. But under the umbrella of humanitarian assistance a lot of things are going on. There is a fear that people are
using humanitarian umbrella for their agenda. ... Yes, there were restrictions for humanitarian organizations, but there are reasons for this as well.[89]

The government evidently wanted to avoid eyes and ears on its war in Darfur.
However, Khartoum's resistance also reflected a belief that many humanitarian
organizations were enemy forces seeking to undermine Sudan's national sovereignty. This way of thinking was ingrained in the psyche of the NCP regime.

Peacekeeping also raised red flags in Khartoum. As mentioned above, the
Sudanese government was strongly opposed to the deployment of international
peacekeepers in Darfur and only accepted UN forces after intense pressure.
Fueling Khartoum's defiance and, later, the systematic obstruction of
UNAMID's operations was the fear that peacekeepers would eventually be the
forerunner of a more forceful NATO-led intervention. In this context, the portrayal of UN peacekeeping as an instrument of saving strangers seems to have
enhanced such fears and heightened the perception of peacekeeping as a strategic tool of the West. A scholar affiliated with the NCP stated,

The fear was that, like in Iraq, international troops will force their agenda.
The example that is often mentioned in this regard is that of Lumumba in
the DRC, who was removed from power partly as a result of UN intervention. So there was a sense that international forces foster regime change.[90]

A UN official confirmed that regime change was one of the main concerns in the
Sudanese government's position on peacekeepers, saying

Why is the Sudanese government so opposed to UN peacekeeping? It's the
5th column issue. From 2001 to 2003, the Sudanese thought that they would

be next on the list as regime change efforts were coming from the West. Therefore the notion of deploying anything with bayonets on their territory raised red flags.[91]

To be sure, there are other reasons why Sudan opposed a strong peace-keeping force in Darfur. For one, it did not want evidence of its crimes to be brought to light. However, neither AMIS nor UNAMID attempted to collect such evidence, and UNAMID's cautious approach during its first years should have dissipated any fears that it was the vanguard of regime change. Another consideration is that, while Khartoum fiercely resisted peacekeepers in Darfur, it gave the green light for another mission, UNMIS, which also had a Chapter VII mandate to protect civilians. This illustrates a pertinent point: Peacekeepers and aid workers were not sufficiently subversive to explain Khartoum's strong resistance to their presence in Darfur. Instead, Khartoum feared they were part of a hidden regime change agenda, for which the saving strangers discourse was the façade.

Chapter findings

Three main insights emerge from this chapter. First, as is the case with other international norms, domestic political structures in Sudan acted as filters and affected the way the core R2P norm was translated into practice. In particular, the Sudanese government's reaction to the Darfur campaigns was influenced by the competition between different factions within the NCP regime. The campaigns strengthened regime hardliners against moderates, who had negotiated a peace agreement with the SPLM but were now unable to reap the benefits in terms of normalizing relations with West. This meant that beyond tactical concessions Khartoum was unwilling to change the way it governed Darfur.

Second, the reception of the Saving Strangers Norm was filtered by the worldviews and normative beliefs held by elites within the government. Given their ideology and negative experience with Western humanitarianism in the 1990s, Sudanese Islamists interpreted the Darfur campaigns as the façade of regime change and never accepted as legitimate the notion that the international community had a responsibility to protect people in Darfur. This reinforced the government's approach of making tactical concessions to defuse international pressure over Darfur, but to stymie deeper changes.

Third, the government mounted a number of counter-discourses to neutralize the accusations leveled against it via the Darfur narrative. Counter-discourses are a form of norm defiance. They call into question the legitimacy of an existing discourse and the people promoting it. They also challenge the discourse by expressing alternative worldviews and normative commitments. In this context, the NCP regime described R2P as a smokescreen for imperial intervention in contravention of the principle of sovereignty. This discourse had some resonance in connection with the ICC, but it failed in preventing the deployment of international peacekeepers.

Notes

1 Interview (BB), Khartoum, October 2010.
2 For a rich account of US–Sudan relation in the 1970s, see Korn (1993).
3 The Three Towns refer to the Khartoum metropolis at the convergence of the Blue and the White Nile, with Khartoum in the south, Bahri (also called North Khartoum) in the north, and Omdurman in the north-west.
4 For background of Osama bin Laden's connections to Sudan, see Randal (2005).
5 See James Risen, "To Bomb Sudan Plant, or Not: A Year Later, Debate Rankle," *New York Times*, 27 October 1999.
6 The most famous example is a British aid worker, the late Emma McCune, who married Riek Machar—SPLA commander, and later vice president of South Sudan and leader of the SPLM-In Opposition faction. *Emma's War*, a book written by Deborah Scroggins about McCune's experiences in South Sudan, became an international bestseller.
7 Interview with Safwat Fanous, Khartoum, November 2010.
8 This position was clearly articulated in an interview with an NCP negotiator at the CPA talks, Khartoum, December 2010.
9 The analysis includes reports from the following media sources and affiliations during the analysis period (2002–2004): Sudan TV (short for Sudan National Broadcasting Cooperation, government-controlled), Radio Omdurman Sudan (government-controlled), the news agencies SUNA (led by Sudan's Ministry of Information) and SMC (led by National Intelligence and Security Services), and the newspapers *Akhir Lahza* (initially close to PCP, then linked to National Intelligence and Security Services), *Al-Anba* (government-owned, later defunct), *Al-Khartoum* (pro-government, later defunct), *Akhbar Al-Youm* (pro-government), *Al-Ra'y al-Amm* (generally pro-government, represents the Khartoum establishment), *Alwan* (Islamist paper linked to PCP opposition), *Al-Sahafa* (semi-independent), *Al-Ayyam* (independent), and *Khartoum Monitor* (pro-SPLM, later defunct). For a complete list and assessment of Sudanese newspapers, see Elgizouli (2012).
10 *Al-Sahafa*, "Twenty-four Killed in Cattle Raid in Western Sudanese state," 26 January 2003 (retrieved from and translated by BBC Monitoring).
11 Sudan TV, "Sudan: Official Refutes Reports on Rebels' Occupation of Locality in West," 27 February 2003 (retrieved from and translated by BBC Monitoring).
12 *Akhir Lahza*, "Sudanese Rebels in the West Call on Chad to Keep Off Darfur Conflict," 26 April 2003 (retrieved from and translated by BBC Monitoring).
13 *Al-Sahafa*, "Sudan: Opposition Alliance Concludes Meeting in Eritrea, Issues Communique," 27 April 2003 (retrieved from and translated by BBC Monitoring).
14 Sudan TV, "Sudan: 'Our Priority' Is to 'Hit the Rebellion' in Darfur—Al-Bashir," 4 January 2004 (retrieved from and translated by BBC Monitoring).
15 SUNA, "Sudan: National Assembly Condemns Recent 'Aggression on Al-Fashir Town'," 6 May 2003 (retrieved from BBC Monitoring, original in English).
16 SUNA, "Sudanese Foreign Minister Hopes for Early Cease-fire," 18 June 2003 (retrieved from BBC Monitoring, original in English).
17 Sudan TV, "Our Priority Is to Hit the Rebellion."
18 Sudan TV, "Our Priority Is to Hit the Rebellion."
19 Sudan TV, "Sudan: Government to Combat Terrorism, Blood-shed in Darfur—Al-Bashir," 1 February 2004 (retrieved from and translated by BBC Monitoring).
20 *Al-Khartoum*, *(Corr)* "Sudan: Government Condemns Rebel Attack in Western Region," 7 October 2003 (retrieved from and translated by BBC Monitoring).
21 *Al-Sahafa*, "Government Denies."
22 Interview with Sudanese academic (BA), Khartoum, October 2010.
23 Radio Omdurman Sudan, "Sudan: Mission of UN Coordinator Terminated Following 'Fabricated' Information," 20 March 2004 (retrieved from and translated by BBC Monitoring).

24 Radio Omdurman Sudan, "Sudanese President in Talks with UN Envoy over Darfur, Peace Talks," 30 March 2004 (retrieved from and translated by BBC Monitoring).

25 SUNA, "Sudanese Envoy to India Refutes Ethnic Cleansing Claims by US Paper," 8 April 2004 (retrieved from BBC Monitoring, original in English).

26 SUNA, "Sudan Issues Statement on Annan's Call for Intervention," 8 April 2004 (retrieved from BBC Monitoring, original in English).

27 Radio Omdurman Sudan, "Sudanese Foreign Minister Says US Criticism over Darfur 'Unjustified'," 23 April 2004 (retrieved from and translated by BBC Monitoring).

28 E.g., SUNA, "Sudan Adopts New Measures for Delivery of Humanitarian Aid," 21 May 2004 (retrieved from BBC Monitoring, original in English).

29 SMC, "Sudan: President Al-Bashir Orders 'Arrest of Janjawid Militias'," 19 June 2004 (retrieved from and translated by BBC Monitoring).

30 Sudan TV, "Campaigns by Some Circles against Sudan Will Never Cease—Official," 24 April 2004 (retrieved from and translated by BBC Monitoring).

31 Sudan TV, "Sudan's Al-Bashir Says Claims of Ethnic Cleansing in Darfur 'Lies'," 23 June 2004 (retrieved from and translated by BBC Monitoring).

32 *Al-Sahafa*, "Aid Agencies Warn of Humanitarian Crisis in Western Sudan," 10 April 2004 (retrieved from and translated by BBC Monitoring).

33 *Guardian*, "Sudan Warns Blair against Sending Troops," 22 July 2004.

34 Radio Omdurman Sudan, "Sudan: President Al-Bashir Says Foreign Quarters Trying to sow Discord," 22 July 2004 (retrieved from and translated by BBC Monitoring).

35 SUNA, "Sudanese Foreign Minister Criticizes US, British Stands over Darfur Crisis," 22 July 2004 (retrieved from BBC Monitoring, original in English).

36 Interview with Hassan Makki, Khartoum, November 2010.

37 Interview (CQ), Khartoum, December 2010.

38 Interview (DJ), Bern, October 2011.

39 SUNA, "Sudan Criticizes Powell 'Dangerous' Remarks on Darfur," 13 September 2004 (retrieved from and translated by BBC Monitoring).

40 Interview (BB), Khartoum, October 2010.

41 Interview (BJ), Khartoum, October 2010 (interview in Arabic, interpretation into English by author's research assistant).

42 Interview (CS), Khartoum, December 2010.

43 Interview (CL), Khartoum, November 2010.

44 Interview (BP), Khartoum, November 2010.

45 Radio Omdurman Sudan, "Sudanese Official Says Western Quarters Targeting Sudan because of its Wealth," 24 July 2004 (retrieved from and translated by BBC Monitoring).

46 Interview (BG), Khartoum, October 2010.

47 Interview (BL), Khartoum, November 2010.

48 Interview (CC), Khartoum, November 2010.

49 Interview with Hassan Makki, Khartoum, November 2010.

50 Interview with Hassan Makki, Khartoum, November 2010.

51 Interview (BB), Khartoum, October 2010.

52 Interview (BB), Khartoum, October 2010.

53 Interview with Hassan Makki, Khartoum, November 2010.

54 Interview (BW), Khartoum, November 2010.

55 Interview with Sudanese diplomat (CT), Khartoum, 2 December 2010.

56 SUNA, "Sudan adopts new measures."

57 Interview (CS), Khartoum, December 2010.

58 Colin Powell, "Sudanese Promises Are not Enough for Darfur: I Gave the Khartoum Government a List of Actions to Take in Darfur," *Guardian*, 20 July 2004.

59 Joint Communiqué between the Government of Sudan and the United Nations on the occasion of the visit of the Secretary-General to Sudan, 29 June–3 July 2004, p. 3, www.un.org/news/dh/sudan/sudan_communique.pdf (accessed 8 November 2014).

60 Interview (BS), Khartoum, November 2010.

61 Interview with MSF worker (DU), Paris, November 2011 (interview in French, author's translation).

62 Sudan TV, "Sudan 'Does Not Need' Foreign Military Assistance in Darfur—Foreign Minister," 7 April 2004 (retrieved from and translated by BBC Monitoring).

63 *Al-Ra'y al-Amm*, "African Union to Deploy Monitors in Western Sudan Next Week," 15 April 2004 (retrieved from and translated by BBC Monitoring).

64 *Al-Anba*, "Sudan: Ruling Rejects Deployment of Foreign Army in Darfur," 14 June 2004 (retrieved from and translated by BBC Monitoring).

65 *Al-Sharq al-Awsat*, "Sudanese Interior Minister Says Foreign Troops not Accepted in Darfur," 6 August 2004 (retrieved from and translated by BBC Monitoring). [*Al-Sharq al-Awsat* is a London-based newspaper in Arabic.]

66 *Al-Sahafa*, "Sudan 'Agreed' to Increase AU Forces to 4,300 Officers, 250 Observers in Darfur," 1 October 2004 (retrieved from and translated by BBC Monitoring).

67 Sudan TV, "Sudanese Leader Reiterates Objection to International Peacekeepers," 26 November 2006 (retrieved from and translated by BBC Monitoring).

68 The Small Arms Survey provides a chronology of the Darfur peace process from 2006 to 2014: www.smallarmssurveysudan.org/de/archive/sudan/darfur/darfur-peace-process-chronology.html (accessed 8 June 2019).

69 Interview (BS), Khartoum, November 2010.

70 Interview with Jendayi Frazer, Washington, DC, March 2010.

71 Ken Silverstein, "Official Pariah Sudan Valuable to America's War on Terror," *Los Angeles Times*, 29 April 2005.

72 *The Economist*, "Glittering Towers in a War Zone," 7 December 2006.

73 Interview with Jendayi Frazer, Washington, DC, March 2010.

74 Interview with Jendayi Frazer, Washington, DC, March 2010.

75 Interview (BS), Khartoum, November 2010.

76 Interview (CJ), Khartoum, November 2010.

77 SMC, "Sudan: Committee to Investigate Human Rights Situation in Darfur Formed," 9 May 2004 (retrieved from and translated by BBC Monitoring).

78 Quoted in Agence France-Press, "Sudan Committee Acknowledges Rights Abuses in Darfur but Rejects Genocide," 20 January 2005, available from http://reliefweb.int/report/sudan/sudan-committee-acknowledges-rights-abuse-darfur-rejects-genocide (accessed 8 November 2014).

79 Quoted in Agence France-Press, "Sudan Committee Acknowledges Rights Abuses."

80 Interview (CP), Khartoum, October 2010.

81 French proverb meaning "the more things change, the more they stay the same."

82 Interview (BP), Khartoum, November 2010.

83 Interview (CS), Khartoum, December 2010.

84 Interview (BY), Khartoum, November 2010.

85 Jeffrey Gettleman, "Bashir Wins Elections as Sudan Edges Toward Split," *New York Times*, 26 April 2010.

86 Interview (BD), Khartoum, October 2010.

87 Sudan TV, "Sudanese leader reiterates objection to international peacekeepers."

88 Interview (CS), Khartoum, December 2010.

89 Interview (CT), Khartoum, December 2010.

90 Interview (BE), Khartoum, October 2010.

91 Interview (DC), New York, March 2011.

References

African Rights. 1995. *Facing Genocide: The Nuba of Sudan*. London: African Rights. July.

Appiah-Mensah, Seth. 2005. "AU's Critical Assignment in Darfur: Challenges and Constraints." *African Security Review* 14: 7–21.

Berridge, Willow J. 2017. *Hasan al-Turabi: Islamist Politics and Democracy in Sudan.* Cambridge: Cambridge University Press.

Burr, Millard, and Robert O. Collins. 1995. *Requiem for the Sudan: War, Drought, and Disaster Relief on the Nile.* Boulder, CO: Westview.

Chalk, Frank, and Danielle Kelton. 2009. "Mass-Atrocity Crimes in Darfur and the Response of Government of Sudan Media to International Pressure." In *The World and Darfur: International Response to Crimes against Humanity in Western Sudan*, ed. Amanda F. Grzyb. Montreal: McGill-Queen's University Press. 112–151.

Collins, Robert O. 2008. *A History of Modern Sudan.* New York: Cambridge University Press.

De Waal, Alex. 2004. "The Politics of Destabilisation in the Horn, 1989–2001." In *Islamism and its Enemies in the Horn of Africa*, ed. Alex De Waal. Bloomington, IN: Indiana University Press. 182–230.

De Waal, Alex. 2007. "Sudan: The Turbulent State." In *War in Darfur and the Search for Peace*, ed. Alex De Waal. Cambridge, MA: Global Equity Initiative. 1–38.

De Waal, Alex, and A. H. Abdel Salam. 2004. "Islamism, State Power, and *Jihad* in Sudan." In *Islamism and its Enemies in the Horn of Africa*, ed. Alex De Waal. Bloomington, IN: Indiana University Press. 71–113.

Deckert, Roman. 2012. "The Current State of the Sudanese Press." In *The Sudanese Press after Separation*, ed. Anja Wollenberg. Berlin: Media in Cooperation and Transition. 16–18.

Degomme, Olivier, and Debarati Guha-Sapir. 2010. "Patterns of Mortality Rates in Darfur Conflict." *The Lancet* 375: 294–300.

Deng, Francis Mading. 1995. *War of Visions: Conflict of Identities in the Sudan.* Washington, DC: Brookings Institution Press.

El-Affendi, Abdelwahab 1991. *Turabi's Revolution: Islam and Power in Sudan.* London: Grey Seal.

Elgizouli, Magdi. 2012. "An Overview of the Sudanese Print Media 2012." In *The Sudanese Press after Separation—Contested Identities of Journalism*, ed. Anja Wollenberg. Berlin: Media in Cooperation and Transition. 34–39.

IDF, and Munzoul Assal. 2010. "The National Congress Party and the Darfurian Armed Groups." In *The International Politics of Mass Atrocities: The Case of Darfur*, eds. David R. Black and Paul D. Williams. Milton Park: Routledge. 27–48.

Johnson, Douglas H. 2011. *The Root Causes of Sudan's Civil Wars: Peace or Truce.* Woodbridge: James Currey.

Johnson, Hilde F. 2011. *Waging Peace in Sudan: The Inside Story of the Negotiations That Ended Africa's Longest Civil War.* Eastbourne: Sussex Academic Press.

Karadawi, Ahmed. 1991. "The Smuggling of the Ethiopian Falasha to Israel through Sudan." *African Affairs* 90: 23–49.

Korn, David A. 1993. *Assassination in Khartoum.* Bloomington, IN: Indiana University Press.

Large, Daniel. 2011. "The International Presence in Sudan." In *The Sudan Handbook*, eds. John Ryle, Justin Willis, Suliman Baldo and Madut Jok. Woodbridge: James Currey. 164–176.

Loeb, Jonathan. 2013. *Talking to the Other Side: Humanitarian Engagement with Armed Non-State Actors in Darfur, Sudan, 2003–2012.* London: Humanitarian Policy Group, Overseas Development Institute. August.

Makki, Hassan M. A. 1989. *Sudan: The Christian Design.* London: Islamic Foundation.

Mills, Kurt, and Alan Bloomfield. 2018. "African Resistance to the International Criminal Court: Halting the Advance of the Anti-Impunity Norm." *Review of International Studies* 44: 101–127.

Randal, Jonathan C. 2005. *Osama: The Making of a Terrorist.* New York: I.B. Tauris.

Rolandsen, Øystein H. 2005. *Guerrilla Government: Political Changes in the Southern Sudan During the 1990s.* Uppsala: Nordic Africa Institute.

Sidahmed, Abdel Salam. 2011. "Islamism and the State." In *The Sudan Handbook*, eds. John Ryle, Justin Willis, Suliman Baldo and Madut Jok. Woodbridge: James Currey. 94–107.

Stedjan, Scott, and Colin Thomas-Jensen. 2010. "The United States." In *The International Politics of Mass Atrocities: The Case of Darfur*, eds. David R. Black and Paul D. Williams. Milton Park: Routledge. 157–175.

Verhoeven, Harry. 2015. *Water, Civilisation and Power in Sudan: The Political Economy of Military-Islamist State Building.* Cambridge: Cambridge University Press.

Young, John. 2005. "Sudan: A Flawed Peace Process Leading to a Flawed Peace." *Review of African Political Economy* 32: 99–113.

6 Deactivating R2P

The deconstruction of Darfur as a case for saving strangers

The security situation in Darfur has remained relatively stable.

United Nations (2018a)

The change in the narrative is appalling and disgraceful.

Eric Reeves (Sudan activist)[1]

In general, the trust in the international community is diminishing. There is a feeling that Darfur is a forgotten place, that it's not important.

Aid worker from North Darfur[2]

Darfur's slide back into a forgotten conflict

Developments since 2011

At the time of writing, violent conflict in Darfur was still ongoing, even though Sudan's long-time ruler, Omar al-Bashir, was ousted from power in April 2019. With the root causes of the conflict unaddressed, insecurity and poverty remain high. Despite this, the conflict, and Darfuri society as a whole, has profoundly changed since the beginning of the war more than 16 years ago. As explained in Chapter 2, the most violent period of the conflict occurred between 2003 and 2004, during which the Sudanese government and affiliated militias—the *janjawid*—conducted a brutal counterinsurgency campaign. Atrocities against civilians particularly targeted the non-Arab groups presumed to support the rebels. Violence in Darfur did not end through a political settlement. Instead, the situation developed into a low-intensity, but highly protracted, conflict that is characterized by complex battlefield dynamics, fragmented rebel groups, the proliferation of tribal militias, widespread insecurity, and spurts of extreme violence.

The year 2011 marked a turning point in the evolving conflict context, making developments since that time particularly relevant. In July, South Sudan declared its independence and seceded from the rest of the country, after a referendum held six months before. This process absorbed domestic and international political attention and led to a reconfiguration of the Sudanese polity. Although the NCP had comfortably won the elections in 2010 and solidified its rule, including in Darfur, losing Sudan's south created vulnerabilities for the NCP regime and changed the international context. The Arab Spring also created turbulence across the region, particularly in neighboring Libya and Egypt, where long-standing regimes were toppled. Protests also took place in Sudan, but government repression limited their momentum.

Considering these changes, how has the situation in Darfur evolved since 2011? Five developments can be highlighted. The first concerns intercommunal conflict, which makes up a significant proportion of the violence in Darfur. Spurred into action by the easy access to small arms (Small Arms Survey 2016), tribal militias are the main actors. Their emergence reflects the breakdown of public order in Darfur, the conflict over land (Abdul-Jalil and Unruh 2013), and the government's extensive use of proxy militia in its counterinsurgency and periphery-governance efforts. Thus, violence has become one of the main currencies in Darfur's political marketplace, allowing armed groups to stake their claims and auction off their loyalties to the highest bidder (De Waal 2015, Chapter 4). Since 2011, intercommunal violence has manifested itself in many ways. One way sees different non-Arab groups pitted against each other—often government-supported militias from smaller groups set against larger communities, especially the Zaghawa (Gramizzi and Tubiana 2012). Violence between non-Arab groups results from infighting between rebel factions as well as disputes over land, pasture, and other resources (International Crisis Group 2015, 6–10). Arab militias also continue to attack civilian populations from non-Arab tribes (Small Arms Survey 2017).

A second development since 2011 was the Sudanese government's growing assertiveness on the battlefield, as it stepped up efforts to eradicate the rebellion in Darfur. As in the past, these operations involved the Sudanese army as well as proxy militias, especially the Rapid Support Forces (RSF)—a paramilitary force created in 2013. Following a fall out with former *janjawid* leader Musa Hilal, and the rise of Hilal's rival, Mohamed Hamdan "Hemeti" Dagolo, the Sudanese government assembled the RSF from the same *janjawid* militias in North Darfur that had fought alongside it in the beginning of the conflict (Small Arms Survey 2017). The government deployed the RSF to do its dirty work, including in Darfur, where it carried out several offensives against the rebels and committed atrocity crimes targeting civilians (Baldo 2017b). The main hub of these campaigns was Jebel Marra, a mountainous region in the center of Darfur inhabited by the Fur and a traditional stronghold of the rebels, especially Abdelwahid al-Nur's faction. The largest campaign took place in early 2016 when the government recaptured different Jebel Marra territories from the SLA rebels (United Nations 2016, paras 3–10). Overall, since 2011, the government has been successful in marginalizing the rebels on the battlefield.

The third development concerns the three main Darfur rebel movements, which united in November 2011, and founded the Sudan Revolutionary Front (SRF) together with the SPLM-North. This group posed a significant threat to the government, especially in South Kordofan, where it launched coordinated attacks in 2012 and 2013 (McCutchen 2014). However, the SRF failed to become a significant player in the Darfur arena. Forming a coalition was insufficient to overcome the differences between the movements, and they continued to splinter. At the same time, opportunities for external patronage diminished with the Sudan-Chad rapprochement in 2010, which saw both countries end their proxy war, including Chad's withdrawal of support for the Darfur insurgency (Tubiana 2011). However, the Darfur rebels found new opportunities for external support in Libya and South Sudan, where they were still present at the end of 2018 (United Nations 2019). By early 2019, Minni Minawi had the largest presence in Libya, as his rebels were fighting with General Haftar's forces. JEM had some forces in Libya too, but was mostly based in South Sudan.[3] Fighters loyal to Abdelwahid al-Nur were the only rebel group with a military presence in Darfur. They were concentrated in Jebel Marra, where they conducted hit-and-run operations against the government (United Nations 2019, paras 48–49). Overall, however, the threat posed to the government by the Darfur rebels has weakened since 2011.

The fourth development pertains to the political process. In 2011, the government signed the Doha Document for Peace in Darfur with the Liberation and Justice Movement (LJM)—a new rebel group made up of splinter factions that were patched together by external backers. However, while the government did implement elements of the agreement, for example, creating a regional authority for Darfur, it was not serious about sharing power or wealth with the opposition. The LJM's political and military influence was too limited for the DDPD to be effective (International Crisis Group 2014). In addition, after 2011, international mediators tried to bring the SRF into the political process. Talks facilitated by Germany in 2015 produced a declaration, in which the Sudanese opposition— including the SRF—agreed to join a government-initiated national dialogue process.[4] However, subsequent AU-mediated negotiations failed to secure a seat at the table for the SRF (Saeid 2017). As a result, the political process remained stalled since 2011.

The fifth development concerns the situation on the ground. Since generalized warfare ended in Darfur, some areas have enjoyed relative stability, and some displaced people have been able to return home. However, displacement levels remain high: 2.7 million Darfuris were still internally displaced in 2018,[5] alongside the 340,000 Darfuri refugees living in eastern Chad.[6] Urbanization partly explains this dynamic: People have adapted their livelihood strategies to the camps, which have effectively become cities. Another reason is widespread poverty, as the conflict, compounded by ecological changes caused by drought and desertification, has destroyed the livelihoods of farming and nomadic communities in Darfur (Buchanan-Smith and Bromwich 2016). As a result, 3.1 million Darfuris—roughly 40 percent of the population—were dependent on humanitarian assistance in 2018.[7] Despite these factors, the main cause of high levels of displacement remains insecurity and violence in many areas of Darfur. In fact, displacement continues because of intercommunal violence and military offensives by the government and its affiliated militias. For example, the large government offensive in Jebel Marra in early 2016 forced 160,000 to 195,000 people to leave their homes (United Nations 2017, para 78).

As human rights organizations have documented, these attacks regularly involved atrocity crimes including sexual and gender-based violence (e.g., Human Rights Watch 2015a, 2015b; Amnesty International 2016).[8]

In sum, the nature of the violence, the battlefield dynamics, and the configuration of belligerent groups have changed, but the situation in Darfur remains volatile. The possibility of escalation is real, given the history of extreme violence, the presence of paramilitary forces similar to the ones responsible for mass atrocities in 2003 and 2004, and instability in Khartoum since Omar al-Bashir's ousting in April 2019. These indicators show that Darfur remains a case that continues to merit the close attention of those who promote R2P.

Deactivating R2P as the main interpretive frame

Previous chapters showed that Darfur's transformation into a global cause was enabled by a simple and morally compelling narrative, with the idea of saving strangers at its core. The narrative translated the core R2P norm into practice and shaped the international response to the conflict. To explain this process, previous chapters examined public perceptions of Darfur in the media. Chapter 2 thus analyzed editorials published between 2003 and 2005 in major newspapers in North America and Western Europe. However, this was not feasible for the period 2011 to 2018, as the number of editorials published about Darfur was insufficient for robust analysis. Therefore, to assess changing views about Darfur from 2011 to 2018, a broader selection of newspaper articles was drawn upon, in addition to editorials.[9]

Three main findings can be drawn from the media coverage of Darfur after 2011. One is that the media resonance to the Darfur conflict drastically decreased. In 2011 and 2012, Darfur occasionally appeared in the media, partly owing to the secession of South Sudan and the escalation of the conflict in South Kordofan and Blue Nile—two areas on the southern periphery of the Sudanese state that border the newly independent South Sudan. Afterwards, Darfur largely disappeared from the news—a trend that has increased in recent years. Just 10 years ago Darfur generated massive coverage, making it a household name; therefore, its absence from coverage is striking. Illustrative of the decline in media resonance is Figure 6.1, which depicts the number of editorials[10] about the Darfur conflict published each year from 2003 to 2018 in the *New York Times* and the *Washington Post*.

Statistics of online searches confirm a similar trend. Figure 6.2 shows how frequently Google users searched for "Darfur," relative to the site's total search volume per quarter between 2004 and 2018.[11] It illustrates that public interest in Darfur picked up in the second half of 2004, reached a high between 2006 and 2008, began to diminish in 2009, continued to decrease and, from 2012, waned almost completely. These statistics demonstrate that, in the international media, Darfur has become a forgotten conflict.

Beyond numbers, a second finding is the way the articles between 2011 and 2018 communicated the situation in Darfur to the public. The narrative about

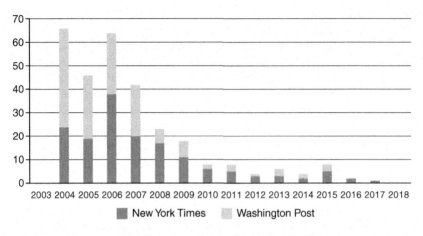

Figure 6.1 Number of editorials about the Darfur conflict, 2003–2018

Darfur was no longer coherent, with a clear portrayal of who the perpetrators and the victims were or what could be done to remedy the situation. Reporting about Darfur became disparate, covering different aspects of the conflict, offering different opinions, and providing different interpretive frames. In addition, few articles were written about Darfur alone. Most reports mentioned Darfur in reference to other issues, like South Sudan's secession, the war in Syria, or the ICC. In addition, personal stories of Darfuri suffering, which were very common when Darfur was a cause célèbre, largely disappeared. Instead, media reports about Darfur referred to the military situation or the posture of Omar al-Bashir, but Darfuris themselves—the strangers in need of saving—were rarely featured.

A third finding is that references to saving strangers in Darfur also decreased. When R2P references did appear, they were articulated in three frames. The first

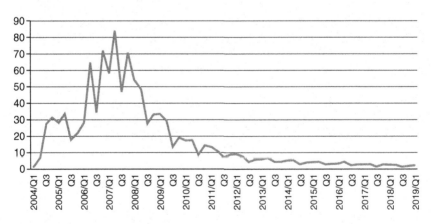

Figure 6.2 Google search trends for the term "Darfur", per quarter 2004–2019

frame subsumed R2P in Darfur into other causes. This meant that when Darfur was mentioned as a case of saving strangers, it was not used in its own right but rather to make sense of another situation—similar to the way the Rwanda genocide was invoked to mobilize action on Darfur (see Chapter 2). For example, journalists used Darfur to describe the escalating conflict in South Kordofan's Nuba Mountains. As Nicholas Kristof wrote in 2012,

> Bombings, ground attacks and sexual violence—part of Sudan's scorched-earth counterinsurgency strategy—have driven hundreds of thousands of people from their homes in South Kordofan … [T]he brutality here feels like an echo of what Sudan did in Darfur, only now it is the Nubans who are targets.[12]

An article in *The Times* likewise warned that violence in the Nuba Mountains "threatens Africa with the spectre of another Darfur."[13] Journalists also invoked Darfur in connection with Syria. In 2013, expressing discontent over the US government's inaction in Syria, Fred Hiatt reminded Susan Rice, John Kerry, and Barack Obama of their position on Darfur:

> All three had condemned the Bush administration for allowing people to starve in Darfur, Sudan, and passionately demanded action. Today, an equivalent humanitarian catastrophe is unfolding in Syria. … Yet, the Obama administration, while providing aid for the refugees, has done virtually nothing for people inside.[14]

A 2016 *Washington Post* editorial said about South Sudanese refugees crossing the border into the Darfur, "Today's hungry are migrating to yesterday's killing fields in hopes of survival."[15] These articles reiterated the R2P frame, but consigned mass atrocities in Darfur to history. Contrary to the facts on the ground, they implied that the need to save strangers in Darfur was long past.

The second frame reproduced the initial R2P narrative, talking about ongoing mass atrocities in Darfur and the need to protect civilians. However, such articles were few and far between. They also differed from the original narrative in that they largely abstained from offering remedies. For example, in 2013, Nicholas Kristof wrote two editorials about Darfur "to shine a bit more light on the continuing slaughter in Darfur."[16] However, he acknowledged that, aside from speaking out, "there are no magic wands to end the horrors of Darfur."[17] Authors who reproduced the original frame often spoke about Darfur as "forgotten"[18] or "forsaken,"[19] trying to reinvigorate activism on the issue. However, these labels unintentionally also confirmed that Darfur was a cause of the past.

The third frame suggested that the situation in Darfur had evolved and that R2P was no longer a primary concern. In 2012, Jeffrey Gettleman visited Darfur and wrote about returning IDPs:

> More than 100,000 people in Darfur have left the sprawling camps where they had taken refuge for nearly a decade and headed home to their villages

over the past year, the biggest return of displaced people since the war began in 2003 and a sign that one of the world's infamous conflicts may have decisively cooled.

He further cited a UN official saying, "It's amazing.... The people are coming together. It reminds me of Lebanon after the civil war."[20] While the article mentioned that fighting continued in some areas, the frame that stuck was that Darfur has moved on from the dark times of war and atrocities. Likewise, in 2014, the *Washington Post* featured an interview with Omar al-Bashir, in which he said that peace in Darfur was "getting wider and wider and deeper and deeper." As result, there was no need for international peacekeepers. Concerning Darfuris in IDP camps, al-Bashir opined, "To them, it is an easy life ... They would rather stay in these camps than go back to work."[21] While the article also cited views critical of al-Bashir, it is nonetheless noteworthy that he received a platform in a mainstream US news outlet.

The conclusion that can be drawn is that the Darfur narrative has largely unraveled. Moral clarity about the conflict has disappeared, the clear stigmatization of the perpetrators has been lost, and the voices of the victims have been silenced. The need for action to protect civilians in Darfur has been over taken by other priorities. Compounded by the drastic decrease in media coverage, R2P has been largely deactivated as the main interpretive frame for the Darfur conflict. Thus, since 2011, the activation process that began in 2004 has been reversed.

An episode with clear relevance for R2P confirms this assessment. In September 2016, Amnesty International published a report accusing the Sudanese army of using chemical weapons in its counterinsurgency campaign in Jebel Marra. The report presented photographic evidence and interview data to back up the claim (Amnesty International 2016). In addition to being prohibited by the Chemical Weapons Convention, which Sudan has ratified, the use of chemical weapons in warfare is an atrocity crime. Nonetheless, the international reaction was very tame. When the report was released, some newspapers picked it up.[22] However, newspapers failed to follow up on the story, for example, by pressing policymakers on the measures Amnesty International recommended: for the Sudanese government to grant UNAMID access to Jebel Marra or for an investigation by the Organization for the Prohibition of Chemical Weapons. No action materialized.

Making sense of Darfur's backsliding

Two common explanations

How can we make sense of Darfur's transformation from a global cause to a forgotten conflict? Two explanations were common in political debates. The first was that the situation in Darfur improved and the interventions to address the situation were no longer needed. This explanation is implicit in the above-mentioned accounts of the return of displaced persons. It is also an argument put forward by UN and AU officials to justify the drawing down of UNAMID.[23]

The situation in Darfur has indeed improved as compared to the initial phase of conflict escalation in 2003 and 2004, which saw widespread atrocities and a high number of civilian fatalities. However, despite the improved security and humanitarian situation, Darfur is not at peace. Armed violence is ongoing, and atrocity crimes still occur. As Figure 6.2 above shows, Darfur was at the height of its fame from 2006 to 2008, when the Save Darfur campaign was at its most powerful. At that time, the most violent phase of the conflict had ended, humanitarian access had significantly improved, and war fatalities were much reduced. The situation worsened from 2013 to 2016, when the government was conducting large-scale military offensives and re-establishing ties with Arab militias from North Darfur. Data from the Armed Conflict Location & Event Data Project (ACLED) (Raleigh et al. 2010) confirms this. Figure 6.3 shows that the number of conflict events increased in late 2012. Particularly between 2013 and 2016, the level of violence in Darfur reached higher levels than in any other period after 2005.[24] This leads to a paradoxical conclusion: Violence in Darfur was *lower* when the conflict was a cause célèbre and *higher* when it became a forgotten conflict. Developments on the ground in Darfur, therefore, were not behind the fluctuation in international engagement.

A second explanation holds that Darfur became a forgotten conflict because of shifting interests among the countries that had been pushing for a strong response in line with R2P. As a result, Darfur became less of a priority. Observers commonly invoked these arguments when explaining the US government's decision to lift sanctions on Sudan in October 2017: Khartoum was a reliable partner in counterterrorism, it had helped manage the conflict in South Sudan, and it had distanced itself from Iran.[25] These interests trumped concerns over Darfur, pushing it to the back seat.

The explanation is plausible, but nonetheless falls short. When Darfur was a global cause, there were other foreign policy interests in Sudan as well, and some of them competed with Darfur. As explained in Chapter 5, public interest in Darfur had prevented Western countries from normalizing relations with Khartoum,

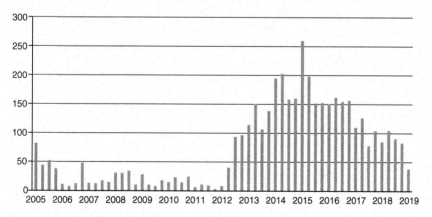

Figure 6.3 ACLED conflict events (battles and violence vs. civilians) in Darfur, 2005–2019

making them renege on the key promise that led Khartoum to sign the CPA in January 2005. Temin (2018, 38) showed that because of Darfur, the US did not fully focus on CPA implementation. Beyond the CPA, normalizing relations with Khartoum after 2005 would have helped Western countries to ensure full cooperation on counterterrorism, to curb migration, and to limit the influence of other powers, foremost China. However, these interests were put on the back burner because of a discursive context that made saving strangers in Darfur the top priority. Only when saving strangers stopped being the dominant interpretative frame did other interests begin to prevail. Therefore, shifting priorities were not the *cause*, but the *consequence* of Darfur's slide back into a forgotten conflict.

Backsliding can be understood by drawing on the same framework used to make sense of why Darfur initially became a cause célèbre. Darfur became famous after 2004 because of a compelling narrative, with the R2P norm at its core. The narrative provided a comprehensive account of mass atrocities that was easy to understand. It gained traction because of a conducive political context and because activists, decision makers, and representatives of the opposition actively promoted it. As the following section shows, these factors have been absent since 2011, which helps understand Darfur's deconstruction as a case for saving strangers.

Narrative unraveled

A narrative that successfully commands public attention and triggers a meaningful response to prevent mass atrocities has four features, as laid out in Chapter 1: It should be complete, simple, coherent, and emerge in a conducive political context. The story around Darfur fit all of these requirements. However, an analysis of media reports about Darfur since 2011 show that this was no longer the case.

First, media accounts were no longer complete in how they attributed the cause and treatment of the Darfur issue. Darfur was no longer portrayed as a genocide committed by Arabs against Africans that had to be stopped by international peacekeepers. Many articles only tangentially covered the situation in Darfur. Those that went deeper often mentioned new conflict dynamics, like intertribal conflict. For example, Michael Meyer wrote in the *New York Times* in 2013, "A decade after the fighting that some called a genocide, that conflict has entered a new chapter. Today, nomadic Arab tribes that once fought chiefly against black-skinned farmers have turned on one another."[26] In 2015, an article in *Die Welt* referred to Darfur as a "war about water," as nomads and sedentary farmers competed about scarce resources.[27] Ambiguity also crept in about solutions to the conflict. After the deployment of UNAMID, peacekeeping in Darfur was no longer an abstract concept. There was an actual mission on the ground that could be judged. Most articles about UNAMID were critical. For example, a 2014 article in the *Washington Post* cited Ibrahim Muhammed, a Darfuri who had fled to South Sudan,

The UN peacekeepers have not been able to stop the violence in Darfur, and so I came here.... But in South Sudan now, the situation is similar to Darfur. It's tribe against tribe. The peacekeepers won't be able to stop the attacks.[28]

Second, the simplicity of the narrative, with its images of good and evil, and clear victim and perpetrator roles, has been weakened. The government was no longer an unambiguous force of evil. Journalists still mostly painted the Sudanese government, and Omar al-Bashir in particular, in a negative light. However, they also talked about the need to engage with Khartoum and to make compromises with the government. This shift happened around the 2011 referendum on South Sudan's independence. International observers were concerned that secession could lead to war and recognized the need to engage with Khartoum and secure its cooperation. US president Barack Obama said as much in an editorial published during the referendum, "Today, I am repeating my offer to Sudan's leaders—if you fulfill your obligations and choose peace, there is a path to normal relations with the United States."[29] An article published a few days later in the *Süddeutsche Zeitung* made the same point, "The struggle in Sudan is continuing, and it is now important that Khartoum is not falling even more deeply into isolation. If the North recognizes Juba's independence and preserves peace with the South, Khartoum needs to be compensated."[30] Rather than a regime of *génocidaires*, Khartoum became a potential partner.

The victims were largely absent from media reports about Darfur since 2011. The few articles that still personified their suffering and gave a voice to the people in need of protection no longer exclusively qualified them as Africans. For example, in an editorial about the prevalence of rape in Darfur, Nicholas Kristof told the story of a woman from the Salamat, an Arab tribe in Darfur that had been attacked by a government-affiliated militia group.[31] Another aspect that complicated the narrative had to do with the Darfur rebels. Their media presence was never very strong, but after 2011, they were almost completely absent. The few reports that followed now portrayed them in a negative light, for example, referring to Minni Minawi as an "armchair war lord"[32] or mentioning that Colonel Gaddafi hired JEM fighters as mercenaries in the war in Libya in 2011.[33] In sum, the simple and easy-to-understand frames that initially underpinned the narrative, pitting good against evil and perpetrators against victims, were no longer present.

Third, the coherence of Darfur's public image also suffered, as competing accounts challenged the initial narrative, for example, articles that stated peace was taking hold or that IDPs were returning. So too did reports that criticized international intervention in Darfur as ineffectual or for even doing harm. As mentioned, UNAMID received much of this criticism. Media reports also highlighted problematic aspects of the ICC. For example, about al-Bashir's indictment, the *Guardian* argued in 2014, "An unintended consequence is that 70-year old Bashir is determined to cling on to power at all costs."[34] Darfur activists were also attacked. For example, Nesrine Malik wrote that simplistic Western narratives about war in Sudan have prevented viable political solutions. The Darfur conflict was sold by activists and the media as genocide perpetrated by an ethnically domineering Arab majority—a crude and harmful view that isolated and entrenched the government in the North while eliminating the possibility of international mediation.[35]

In short, the saviors of Darfur as set out in the original narrative became open to doubt. Without a narrative everyone could agree on, Darfur became a controversial case that was open to debate.

Fourth, a factor that helped to amplify the Darfur issue in 2004 was the narrative's synchronicity with existing interpretive frames and political interests. In 2011, perceptions of the Arab world—and of Sudan in particular—changed. This change contributed to the unravelling of the Darfur narrative, which was based on the notion that international intervention to stop a government committing mass atrocities against its citizens could lead to progressive change—the core idea behind R2P. This idea was a central motivation behind the coalition led by France, the UK, and the US, which intervened in Libya against the Gaddafi regime (see Chapter 1). Irrespective of whether the intervention had merit, it failed to bring stability to the country. Stories about continued fighting, fragmented political authority, and refugee flows from Libya were very present in Western media.

Continuing war and insecurity in Libya affected the willingness to support causes like Darfur. According to a Sudan expert, "The Arab Spring is the point of change. We are today more careful to support regime change with flying colors. In Libya, the outcome was horrible, and this changed our view of Darfur too."[36] As the fallout from the Arab Spring became apparent, people stopped believing that Western intervention could bring progressive change to countries in the Arab world. Conversely, the willingness to tolerate the repressive practices of autocratic governments increased. This was particularly the case after 2014 when influxes of refugees prompted European governments to step up cooperation with countries of origin and transit—many of them authoritarian regimes (Koch et al. 2018). Given these attitudes, the Darfur narrative lost its traction. It no longer seemed to matter that the Sudanese government was a perpetrator of violence that had to be stopped through international intervention. Instead, it began to be seen as a partner.

Losing the champions

A key factor that made Darfur a cause célèbre and pushed for an R2P-inspired response, was the work of activists. "Save Darfur" became a rallying cry that gave rise to a large-scale social movement in North America and, to a lesser degree, in Europe (Lanz 2011). In addition to the narrative unravelling, the waning of this movement is a key element to understand why Darfur fell from grace.

While a few individuals and organizations in the US, France, and the UK continue to campaign for Darfur today, they have limited resources and no longer
benefit from prominent media coverage or grassroots mobilization. In France, the
advocacy movement was less institutionalized than in the US and relied more on
individuals—primarily the public intellectuals around Bernard-Henri Lévy and
Bernard Kouchner. As of early 2019, the Collectif Urgence Darfour still exists,
and its members continue to protest with the Darfuri Diaspora in France, but
overall its activities remain limited.[37] Likewise, Lévy's blog, *La règle du jeu*,
occasionally publishes articles about Darfur. But even there, Darfur was largely
overshadowed by other causes, like Syria or Libya where Lévy in 2011 prominently advocated for military intervention.[38] In the UK, the Protect Darfur Campaign no longer exists. Members of the Diaspora are still active within the Darfur
Union. Likewise, the NGO Waging Peace regularly draws attention to the ongoing
conflict in Darfur and the need to protect civilians. But its primary mission is to
support Sudanese refugees in the UK, doing so with only two permanent staff.[39]
Overall, there is no longer a significant advocacy push on Darfur in the UK.

The US had the largest and most influential advocacy movement, with the
Save Darfur Coalition at its core. By 2019, the movement has largely disappeared. Only a few campaigners remain. One is the Enough Project led by
John Prendergast, who continues to advocate for atrocity prevention in Darfur.
However, the Enough Project's new focus on other African conflicts—in particular South Sudan—has reduced its Darfur engagement.[40] The other is Eric
Reeves, the private activist who has campaigned on Sudan since 1999. Unaf-
fected by the decreasing popularity of the Darfur issue, he has maintained a
network of informants in Sudan and the Diaspora, and regularly posts on his
website about abuses committed by the Sudanese government. Because of these
efforts, the save Darfur discourse has not completely disappeared from US
public opinion. However, the main advocacy outlets no longer exist. In 2010, the
Save Darfur Coalition and the Genocide Intervention Network[41] merged into
United to End Genocide. But in 2016, that organization too closed shop. Having
lost confidence, its funders, like Humanity United, decided to pull out.[42]

Apart from the changing zeitgeist, the reasons that the US Darfur advocacy
movement met its demise were endemic to it. One reason was that, in the run-up
to South Sudan's secession, the activists primarily concerned with South Sudan
re-focused their efforts on north–south issues. This fragmented the movement
and exposed its "wide but not deep" nature, as it attracted many people who
were new to atrocity prevention, in particular students, who did not stay engaged
long-term.[43] The second reason concerned Barack Obama's election as US president. Obama was himself active in the Darfur campaign[44] and, when he took
office in 2009, many Darfur activists joined his administration. They included
prominent figures, like Samantha Power, Susan Rice, and Gayle Smith, but also
experts, like Colin Thomas-Jensen and Sean Brooks from the Enough Project
and SDC, who became State Department advisers. With their people on the
inside, "the movement started being less critical.... The mistake was that the
activists thought Obama would solve all problems. They thought if we have

access to the president, we don't need to protest anymore."[45] This diluted the campaign's messages. The third reason was strategic disagreements. Some wanted to broaden the movement into the permanent anti-genocide constituency Samantha Power had been promoting (see Chapter 2). Others wanted to maintain an exclusive focus on Sudan. The disagreement came to the fore when SDC and GI-Net negotiated their merger into United to End Genocide, but it failed to be resolved.[46]

With the decline of the advocacy movement, R2P in Darfur lost its champion. Decision makers were no longer pressured into paying attention, and journalists were no longer pestered into writing about Darfur. Local activists from Darfur lost an important platform to disseminate information. The movement's influence was also weakened by inconsistencies in the campaigns, in particular, their sensationalist tendencies. At a time when violence in Darfur was sharply decreasing and when relief organizations ran the world's largest humanitarian operation, activists still claimed that a genocide of the most horrific proportions was unfolding. As Julie Flint remarked, the activists were at times "reading from an outdated script."[47] This created tensions and led to criticism from those who knew the reality on the ground. It also prompted journalists in search of a good story to divert from the script. Jeffrey Gettleman's article on the return of IDPs is a case in point as it contradicted the narrative being promoted by the activists. Rob Crilly, a freelance journalist who covered Darfur for UK-based newspapers, deliberately wrote articles that differed from the dominant narrative.[48] The public's moral outrage also proved impossible to sustain over so many years. There was a feeling of "compassion fatigue" that was compounded by disillusionment over UNAMID's ineffectiveness, proving wrong the activists' claim that a robust peacekeeping force would save Darfur.

Khartoum's push

Local actors in Sudan also contributed to Darfur's unravelling as a pressing case for saving strangers. After 2011, Khartoum adopted three strategies to accelerate this process. The first relied on counter-discourses that delegitimized international intervention in Darfur. To this end, Khartoum claimed violations of national sovereignty and cast itself as the victim of a neo-colonial conspiracy (see Chapter 5).

Khartoum's second strategy aimed to cut off the oxygen supply to the Darfur narrative by restricting the eyes and ears on the ground, in particular humanitarian organizations. Although they did not have an explicit reporting mandate, they were nonetheless important sources of information in the early phases of the conflict. As described in Chapter 3, the government expelled many humanitarian organizations after the ICC's indictment of Omar al-Bashir in March 2009. Some returned, but the government permanently restricted activities related to protection, human rights, and gender-based violence. It also restricted access, especially to the Jebel Marra areas under rebel control. According to Loeb (2013, 31),

By 2012, there was less humanitarian access to areas outside of Government of Sudan control than at any time since access opened up in May 2004. Throughout 2012, with very few exceptions, INGOs and UN agencies provided no assistance in areas controlled by the rebel movements.

The government also barred UNAMID from accessing certain areas in Darfur to prevent it from investigating alleged violations or from deploying preemptively.[49] This undermined the mission's civilian protection efforts (Duursma 2019). The government also prevented human rights organizations from carrying out investigations in Darfur, especially in Jebel Marra. According to Jonathan Loeb, the lead researcher of the Amnesty International report that alleged the use of chemical weapons by the Sudanese government, "nobody could go to Jebel Marra. That was the hard truth of the situation. Access was absolutely blocked."[50] This forced Amnesty International to conduct remote research and to rely on evidence collected by undercover local informants. Finally, access restrictions affected the journalists who wanted to travel independently throughout Darfur. The consequences for those trying to get in without government permission were severe. In 2016, Philip Cox—the first filmmaker to enter Darfur in 2004—attempted to visit Jebel Marra over a clandestine route from Chad. He and his interpreter, Daoud Hari, were arrested, tortured, and kept in a high-security prison in Khartoum for several weeks.[51] In sum, because of the tightening of access restrictions, less information about the violence in Darfur came to light.

The third strategy that Khartoum employed was to position itself as the partner of Western countries. The Sudanese government thus adapted its behavior to create the impression of compliance with Western demands and entice further cooperation. For example, Khartoum signed a peace agreement—the DDPD—in July 2011, the same month that South Sudan declared its independence. It did so to avoid fighting on too many fronts, as tensions in Abyei, South Kordofan, and Blue Nile were mounting. At the same, it wanted to capitalize on the praise it received for its role in ensuring the peaceful separation of the South, thereby maneuvering itself out of the pariah image caused by Darfur and moving toward normalization of relations with the West (International Crisis Group 2014). Another example was the war in Libya, in which Sudan had backed the rebels in Benghazi. In Syria too, the NCP regime had disavowed Bashar al-Assad in 2011, thus siding with the Gulf countries and the West. In 2014, Sudan pivoted away from Iran, again finding itself on the same side as Western countries. Khartoum also provided troops to support the Saudi Arabia-led coalition in the war in Yemen. These actions had broad motivations, but one deliberate effect was softening the West's confrontational stance against Khartoum. It thus contributed to unravelling the Darfur narrative that portrayed the Sudanese government as a force of evil.

In sum, as Darfur transformed from a global cause to a forgotten conflict, R2P was deactivated as its main interpretive lens. Three factors contributed. The narrative, which had effectively communicated to the public why they should care about Darfur, became diluted and eventually unraveled. The activists, who were the champions of saving strangers in Darfur, lost their influence. Finally, the Sudanese government, by combining sticks and carrots, employed its agency to successfully push Darfur into the background.

Consequences of Darfur's backsliding

Re-articulating political interests in Sudan

When Darfur became a cause célèbre, the international discourse created a context that obliged policymakers to take action in response to mass atrocities. Policy-makers prioritized Darfur, and it eventually prevailed over other foreign policy interests in Sudan, like normalizing relations with Khartoum or CPA implementa-tion. Darfur's slide back into international oblivion reversed this process. Darfur as a whole and the need to protect Darfuris from atrocities were moved to the back burner, paving the way for other interests in Sudan to take precedence. This process had far-reaching consequences. To illustrate them, this section focuses on two actors, the US and the EU, showing how they re-articulated their political interests in Sudan after 2011, gradually crowding out R2P in Darfur.

Lifting US sanctions

After taking office in 2009, President Obama appointed a special envoy for Sudan, Scott Gration, and announced a new Sudan strategy based on three objectives: ending atrocities in Darfur, ensuring the implementation of the CPA, and countering terrorism.[52] According to a member of Gration's team, "Darfur was the top priority for the US in the beginning."[53] But this gradually changed in the years that followed, partly because of the difficulty in assessing what impact the US could have in Darfur, given the low intensity violence and the presence of UNAMID on the ground. Gration focused on the Doha peace talks, trying to unite the Darfur rebels to increase their leverage. However, the US failed to con-vince Abdelwahid to take part and was unable to level the playing field between the rebels and the government in order to bring about a sustainable political set-tlement. "In 2010, nobody knew what to do in Darfur" and so the US began to focus elsewhere.[54]

The new priority for the US became the January 2011 independence referendum and the secession of South Sudan. Here, the US had clear objectives—ensuring the secession process was managed in an orderly fashion and preventing war between Sudan and newly independent South Sudan. Achieving these objectives required political engagement with the Sudanese government. In November 2010, the Senate Foreign Relations Committee chair John Kerry travelled sev-eral times to Khartoum. There he presented a US government roadmap that essentially promised to lift some sanctions and remove Sudan from the list of states sponsoring terrorism if certain conditions were met—especially a peaceful secession process (Vertin 2019, 203). Around the same time, the US announced the "decoupling" of the Darfur issue from other interests in Sudan.[55] After South Sudan's independence, the US stopped sanctions relief because of escalating violence in South Kordofan and Blue Nile (International Crisis Group 2017, 4–5). This angered Khartoum, which then accused the US of "moving goalposts."[56] Darfur did not, however, become a priority again. In fact, when Princeton Lyman, the US special envoy who took over from Gration in March 2011, said something controversial about Darfur at a congressional hearing, there was no reaction. According to a staffer in his team, "We were worried what people would say. But no congressperson followed up, and no news outlet either. We realized then that people had forgotten about Darfur."[57]

By 2011, the US had undertaken a policy shift, catalyzed by the impending independence of South Sudan. With the weakening of the advocacy movement and the lack of public urgency about atrocity prevention in Darfur, US diplomats could direct their focus elsewhere. They were still interested in Darfur but were no longer obligated to treat it as a top priority. Thus, when tensions mounted between Khartoum and Juba about border demarcation, oil revenues, and the civil war in South Kordofan and Blue Nile, the US supported preventive diplomacy. Its efforts helped to avert war, even if the underlying issues continued to linger (Copnall 2014). Later, at the end of 2013, the civil war in South Sudan absorbed most of the US government's diplomatic energy.

As the US's focus shifted away from Darfur and toward conflict management in South Sudan, and between Sudan and South Sudan, policymakers increasingly came to see engagement with Khartoum as normal, even indispensable. To create additional leverage for policy change, the US made a second push toward lifting sanctions, starting with internal discussions in 2013 that were followed by a cautious testing of the waters with Khartoum in the first half of 2014.[58] In 2015, negotiations started, led on the Sudanese side by Ibrahim Ghandour, a pragmatic NCP cadre who became foreign minister in June that year. In 2016, the US and Sudan agreed on a roadmap, defining five specific areas in which Sudan had to show tangible progress as a condition of sanctions relief: ending hostilities in South Kordofan, Blue Nile and Darfur; improving humanitarian access throughout the country; cooperation in the fight against the Lord's Resistance Army; cooperation on ending the war in South Sudan; and cooperation on anti-terrorism (International Crisis Group 2017). According to a US government official,

> The areas chosen represented near-term asks, in which progress could reasonably be measured.... But they were not ends themselves. They were a first step, getting the Sudanese on the hook and allowing the US to push for a more serious political process and reform agenda in a second phase.[59]

Nonetheless, it is notable that human rights benchmarks were missing from the concessions demanded, as were civilian protection, militia disarmament, UNAMID access, and a comprehensive political settlement in Darfur (Small Arms Survey 2018).

In January 2017, a few days before leaving office, President Obama temporarily suspended some sanctions owing to Sudan's progress across the five areas. Nine months later, President Trump confirmed the relief, permanently lifting trade prohibitions and unfreezing the Sudanese government's US-based assets. However, other sanctions, like the arms embargo and the freezing of assets of individuals with ties to the Sudanese government, remained in place. The US government also did not remove Sudan from its list of states sponsoring terrorism.[60] In November 2018, the US government initiated talks toward a second round of sanctions lifting.[61]

Khartoum's hope of having sanctions lifted gave the US government the leverage it needed to obtain a number of concessions, such as improvements in humanitarian access and reductions in aerial bombardments. However, as some of the sanctions had been imposed by the US in 2006 in response to the outcry over mass atrocities in Darfur, their partial lifting was yet another sign that Darfur had been pushed to the sidelines. Thus in 2015, when Khartoum was stepping up its counterinsurgency campaign in Darfur and freely deploying the RSF to carry it out, the lack of concessions on protecting civilians shows the extent to which the saving strangers agenda had evaporated. A counterfactual argument supports this assertion: When Darfur was a cause célèbre and R2P was the rallying cry for a large-scale activist movement, the idea of lifting sanctions would have been inconceivable, even if the US could have obtained important concessions from Khartoum at the time. In fact, in 2005 and 2006, public interest in Darfur was what had prevented the US from normalizing relations with the Sudanese government—including the lifting of sanctions—even though this was among the key incentives that had motivated Khartoum to sign the CPA.

EU migration partnership

European governments also underwent a rapprochement process with Khartoum that was enabled by Darfur's decline as a pressing policy issue. However, the catalyst was different: With the 2014 refugee crisis reverberating across Europe, migration began to eclipse other foreign policy concerns. Sudan is relevant in this regard, as a country of both origin and transit. In mid-2016, four million migrants passed through Sudan into Libya on their way to Europe.[62] According to Sudanese analyst Suliman Baldo (2017a, 1), the migration issue "has precipitated a paradigm shift in relations between the European Union and the government of Sudan, and closer ties between both entities." The logic was simple: The Sudanese government would help curb the flow of migrants to Europe in exchange for political recognition and financial resources. This ran counter to the Darfur narrative, drawing attention away from the conflict and helping to legitimize its main perpetrators.

In October 2014, governments from Europe and the Horn of Africa initiated the so-called Khartoum Process—a political platform for governmental dialogue and cooperation on migration management and anti-trafficking. Sudan played a prominent role in the process, positioning itself as a key partner. As a result, in

2016, the EU sought to expand cooperation with Sudan. In April, it announced a EUR 100 million aid package, partly to build the capacity of local authorities in Sudan (Baldo 2017a, 3). A confidential EU Commission paper that was later leaked to the press confirmed the motivations: "Much closer and effective cooperation is needed, in particular on return and readmission, fighting trafficking and smuggling, and increasing Sudan's capacity to reduce onward movement to Europe." At the same time, the paper warned that engagement with Sudan carried a "high reputational risk" and that "the ongoing internal conflicts and human rights violations remain of concern."[63] However, the EU Commission only mentioned Darfur in the margins, even though Khartoum and its RSF militia were running a major counterinsurgency campaign at the time. Likewise, the EU did not make a ceasefire in Darfur or improvements in civilian protection a condition of aid. This shows that R2P in Darfur no longer represented a significant interest among European governments and that the Sudanese government was well on the way to becoming a partner. Despite the urgent need to curb migration, turning a blind eye to Khartoum's abuses in Darfur would have been unimaginable for European governments that strongly supported R2P interventions when Darfur was a cause célèbre.

The migration partnership was not just a rehash of political interests. It also had direct consequences in Darfur. As Khartoum sought to boost its profile, it recast the RSF as the vanguard of border management, making its leader, Hemeti, a prominent figure on the national political scene. However, according to Tubiana, Warin and Saeneen (2018), the RSF did not succeed in curtailing migration and even created new smuggling routes. What is more, the government increasingly deployed the RSF for counterinsurgency operations—both in Darfur and elsewhere in the country—in which it committed serious human rights violations (Baldo 2017a). In the end, EU support was not as far-reaching as Khartoum had hoped (Koch et al. 2018, 50–55). However, this was not because of Darfur, but rather because of the domestic criticism of migration policy in EU countries, and the left-right political divide. As the right sought to curb migration at any cost, including cooperation with autocratic regimes, the left decried such policies as immoral. As a Sudan expert stated, "the Darfur narrative has become irrelevant. It is all about the migration narrative."[64]

Dismantling R2P interventions

The unraveling of the Darfur narrative also affected the R2P interventions that were deployed when Darfur was a cause célèbre, in particular UNAMID and the ICC. Both interventions aimed to save strangers—UNAMID by offering direct protection, and the ICC by providing justice to the victims and deterring future atrocities. Not surprisingly therefore, the decreasing interest for Darfur, and the deactivation of R2P as the primary interpretive frame, seriously undercut the effectiveness of peacekeeping and international criminal justice in Darfur.

ICC hibernation

When the ICC issued an arrest warrant for Omar al-Bashir, the world was paying attention. Sudan mounted resistance against the court (see Chapter 5), winning a significant number of allies in Africa in its fight against the anti-impunity norm with the ICC as its implementing institution (Mills and Bloomfield 2018). At the same time, the NCP regime took the ICC seriously, expelling humanitarian organizations from areas in Darfur where counterinsurgency operations took place and limiting al-Bashir's international travel so he could not be arrested abroad. According to human rights lawyer Oliver Windridge, after the ICC issued the arrest warrant in 2009, al-Bashir continued to travel but only to countries that had not ratified the Rome Statute. In 2010, he only made four foreign trips, all of which were in Africa.[65] As news of Darfur began to quiet, al-Bashir gradually increased his foreign travel. This frustrated the ICC prosecutors. In their reports to the UN Security Council, Luis Moreno Ocampo and, later, Fatou Bensouda repeatedly criticized states for their lack of cooperation and stressed the need for arrest warrants to be enforced.[66]

These calls were not heeded, and Bensouda lost patience when none of the Darfur-related cases progressed at the ICC. When presenting her report to the UNSC in December 2014, she said about Bashir and the other indictees:

> To date, none of these individuals have been brought to justice, and some of them continue to be implicated in atrocities committed against innocent civilians. It is becoming increasingly difficult for me to appear before you to update you when all I am doing is repeating the same things I have said over and over again.... Not only does the situation in Darfur continue to deteriorate, the brutality with which crimes are being committed has become more pronounced....
>
> We find ourselves in a stalemate that can only embolden perpetrators to continue their brutality....
>
> Faced with an environment where my Office's limited resources for investigations are already overstretched, and given this Council's lack of foresight on what should happen in Darfur, I am left with no choice but to *hibernate* investigative activities in Darfur....
>
> (International Criminal Court 2014, paras 2 and 4)[67]

Bensouda clearly indicated that her decision to suspend investigations arose from the decreasing attention paid to Darfur and the lack of concern for victims of mass atrocities. Her decision had no legal consequences: It did not mean the cases were dropped or that the ICC no longer holds jurisdiction over Darfur.[68] However, the decision was politically significant, especially because it coincided with an increase in counterinsurgency efforts by the Sudanese government (see Figure 6.3). Not surprisingly, Khartoum celebrated, with al-Bashir saying, "The ICC raised its arms and surrendered."[69] He subsequently increased his travel, which peaked in 2015 when he travelled abroad 27 times, followed by 23 trips in 2016, and 24 in 2017.

Overall, between March 2009 and September 2018, al-Bashir made 150 trips to 33 countries, including 10 countries that were state parties to the Rome Statute.[70]

Nonetheless, the ICC's involvement in Darfur was not inconsequential, and al-Bashir was limited in his travel, even cancelling a number of international trips.[71] In June 2015, for example, al-Bashir had to abruptly leave an AU summit in Johannesburg, just before a constitutional court ruling that obliged South Africa to arrest him under the Rome Statute.[72] Moreover, despite being put on ice, ICC indictments are permanent, and prosecution cases can be reactivated if there is a change in the political context. With the ousting of Omar al-Bashir in April 2019, the possibility is not as far-fetched as it might have seemed.

UNAMID exit

Robust peacekeeping represented a key demand of the Darfur advocacy movement and, against this background, UNAMID emerged as the primary instrument of R2P (Lanz 2014). In 2006 and 2007, Darfur's celebrity status prompted Western governments to expend significant political capital to get boots on the ground. But UNAMID was constrained from the beginning, not only because of the size and complexity of its operating environment, but also because of the need for host country consent. As Chapter 3 explained, the Sudanese government used this to restrict UNAMID's freedom of movement, to delay the import of crucial equipment, and to refuse visas for staff. Although UNAMID did help stabilize parts of Darfur, overall it was unable to fulfill its core mandate of protecting civilians. Some of its failures are documented in a series of Foreign Policy articles based on information leaked by Aicha Elbasri, UNAMID's former spokesperson.[73] Elbasri uncovered a number of cases of attacks against civilians by government forces and affiliated militias, to which UNAMID failed to respond, did not investigate, or even distorted information about.[74] Amnesty International also criticized UNAMID. According to Jonathan Loeb, "UNAMID did not actively protect people and in many cases, they failed to report on mass atrocities."[75]

As UNAMID's shortcomings mounted, its credibility began to diminish. This was compounded by the unraveling of the Darfur narrative as an urgent case for saving strangers. Without a strong lobby for civilian protection in Darfur, Khartoum faced less pushback for obstructing the mission. Without the support needed to take protection seriously, mission leadership was not willing to risk confrontation with the government over it. When Darfur was no longer a priority, the UN began to see UNAMID as a liability—a "mission without end" (De Waal 2009), deployed in an intractable conflict without a workable political settlement and little prospect of positive change. Moreover, the mission was expensive and suffered a large number of fatalities.[76] Compounded by the lobbying of Khartoum and its allies, this translated into pressure to downsize and eventually close down the mission,

In 2012, the UN Security Council decided to reduce troop numbers in Darfur. In 2013, it tasked the UN Secretary-General to draft a special report, which suggested refocusing UNAMID's activities on three core tasks—protecting civilians, facilitating humanitarian access, and mediation (United Nations 2014a). In April 2014, the UNSC approved the new strategy and, four months later, further down-sized the mission, speaking of an "exit strategy" for UNAMID (United Nations 2014b, para 7). The Sudanese government continued pushed for UNAMID's clo-sure, negotiating with UNSC members about the conditions and timeframe for its withdrawal.

In 2017, UNDPKO hired Peter Schumann, a retired senior peacekeeping offi-cial with experience in Sudan, to assess UNAMID as it was downsizing. In his report, he recommended a transitional phase before complete withdrawal, during which the mission would focus on areas of ongoing armed conflict, including Jebel Marra. He also recommended stronger integration with the UN country team "to focus on recovery and development, so we can finally tackle the causes of conflict, poverty and decay in Darfur."[77] Underpinning his assessment was a belief that

> a large mission like UNAMID was not the right approach to armed conflict in Darfur. Because of the pressure from Save Darfur something large had to happen. But it was not based on a proper analysis of conflict causes in Darfur, including draught, environmental degradation, Arab supremacist ideology and a flood of small arms.[78]

His assessment shows that saving strangers was no longer the dominant frame to make sense of political violence in Darfur.

Borrowing ideas from Schumann's report, the UN Secretary-General and the Chairperson of the African Union drafted a special report, proposing a specific timetable for closing UNAMID on the grounds that the security situation had stabilized, as mentioned in the first epigraph to this chapter. A few weeks later, the UNSC followed suit, deciding that after a two-year transition period the mis-sion would be completely withdrawn by the end of 2020, "provided that there is no significant change in the security situation in Darfur" (United Nations 2018b, para 2).[79] These decisions were taken even though the population's vulnerability to mass atrocities was not substantially different than in 2008, when UNAMID was deployed. In some respects, the situation was even worse, as indicated by the levels of violence between 2013 and 2016 (see Figure 6.3).

On the ground

Considering the changes in Darfur since 2011, it is possible to put forward a number of arguments about the repercussions on the ground of Darfur's unravel-ling as a pressing R2P case. One is that the deterrence effect of Darfur's cause célèbre status was reduced. With atrocity crimes in Darfur no longer a priority, the international community had fewer eyes and ears on the ground. Therefore, abuses committed in Darfur were less likely to come to the fore and, if they did, they were less likely to translate into a political push to stop them. Perpet-rators, thus, had less incentive to avoid using violence—the opposite process to the one described in previous chapters, which argued that the publicity around

Darfur had a certain deterrence effect on the government and the rebels. This argument is plausible considering the evolution of battlefield dynamics shown in the ACLED data (see Figure 6.3). Indeed, from late 2012, there was a notable increase in violence as the government stepped up its counterinsurgency efforts, in particular around Jebel Marra.[80]

Another argument is that repercussions on the ground undermined the peace process. The world's disengagement fostered disillusionment and cynicism among Darfuris, who had been told for years that outsiders were coming to save them.[81] The Darfur rebel movements too were weakened. Having come to rely on international support, they lost leverage when Darfur became a forgotten conflict and when their enemy, the Sudanese government, began to rehabilitate itself. The government's push to achieve a peace agreement in 2011 compounded this trend because it divided the rebel movements and made those who refused to sign the DDPD appear to undermine peace. International actors continued to engage with the Darfur rebels after 2011, but this did not significantly increase their leverage. Overall, the rebels remained too weak and too divided to extract the kinds of concessions that could have resulted in a meaningful political settlement for Darfur.

Another argument is that the deactivation of R2P as the main interpretive frame made it easier for the government to control Darfur. In strategic alliance with local militia leaders, the government used a mix of governance, repression, and violence to quell discontent. Hemeti and his RSF rose to prominence as a result. Meeting little resistance, the NCP tried to regulate the RSF by integrating it into the armed forces, making it an autonomous force under the Sudanese constitution, empowering it to patrol the border and intercept migration flows, and deploying it to fight in the war in Yemen (Small Arms Survey 2017). These steps would have been inconceivable at the height of the Darfur campaigns, which described militias like the *janjawid* as the vanguards of genocide. When Darfur was a global cause, Khartoum had tried to reduce its reliance on Arab militias and even committed to disarming them in the 2006 Darfur Peace Agreement. But as global attention waned, Khartoum renewed its engagement with militia leaders.

These developments notwithstanding, it would be wrong to conclude that the Sudanese government "won" the war in Darfur. The methods it used to assert control in Darfur, and the rapprochement with Western governments that occurred despite it, perpetuated many dysfunctional elements within the Sudanese state. For example, the use of militias deepened the "militia state," which is characterized by a highly fragmented security sector and dominated by a cabal of regime operators in Khartoum (Baldo 2017a, 12). They also reinforced authoritarian practices and the use of violence to deal with dissent (Mahé 2016). The partial lifting of US sanctions helped to mitigate the worst effects of economic mismanagement that had brought on the economic crisis in 2017 (Baldo 2018). But it was nowhere near enough to quell the resentment of citizens who were disillusioned with the government. Popular protests had been ongoing in different forms in Sudan since 2011, but in December 2018, they gained sufficient momentum to bring about the end of al-Bashir's rule on 11 April 2019. Ironically, Hemeti's RSF—a force created by the NCP regime to promote its own interests—precipitated al-Bashir's fall when it chose not to use violence against the protesters, siding instead with the very elements in the Sudanese army that sought to remove al-Bashir from power.

But two months later, in early June, the RSF did use violence against the protesters who remained on the streets, demanding a civilian-led transition in Sudan. This attack led to the suspension of negotiations between opposition forces and the Transitional Military Council (TMC) that was established when al-Bashir's was removed from power.[82] At the time of writing, in mid-June 2019, it is impossible to predict Sudan's future, as external powers vie to position themselves. However, Darfur's status as a forgotten conflict seems to have been confirmed by what occurred after al-Bashir's ousting. For example, skillful maneuvering and the support of Gulf countries has turned Hemeti—whose role in committing atrocity crimes in Darfur is well-established—into a key player in Sudan's transition. As deputy head of the TMC, he led negotiations with opposition forces and represented the TMC in talks with foreign countries. Within four days of Bashir's ousting, the US chargé d'affaires, the UK ambassador, and the head of the EU delegation in Sudan all held meetings with Hemeti.[83] This shows that civilian protection in Darfur continues to be a secondary issue despite the new political landscape in Sudan.

Chapter findings

Three insights can be drawn from Darfur's trajectory since 2011. First, with the waning of international attention, Darfur has been transformed from a global cause back into a forgotten conflict. The simple and morally compelling narrative, with R2P at its normative core, began to unravel. The activist movement that had pushed the public to care about Darfur began to diminish as the need to save strangers lost traction. The Sudanese government contributed by pushing Darfur into the background.

Second, Darfur illustrates vicissitudes of the international push to save strangers. Initially seen as an urgent case for atrocity prevention, Darfur fell by the wayside although the situation on the ground did not significantly improve. In fact, it was paradoxical: violence de-escalated when international attention materialized, but when the situation worsened, the international community disengaged.

Third, the deactivation of R2P as the main interpretive frame enabled a broader set of foreign policy interests in Sudan that prevailed over saving strangers. Western states could now engage with the Sudanese government, as seen in the US government's decision to partially lift sanctions and in the EU's cooperation on migration. Deactivation also undermined the main interventions to implement R2P—the UN-AU peacekeeping force and the ICC—as states were not willing to invest political capital to make them effective. As a result, the ICC prosecutor put investigations on ice, and the UN Security Council decided to draw down the peacekeeping mission in Darfur.

Notes

1 Phone interview, January 2019.
2 Quoted in Maeve Shearlaw, "What Happened to Darfur after George Clooney Came to Town?" *Guardian* online, 11 December 2014, www.theguardian.com/world/2014/dec/11/-sp-george-cloony-darfur-what-next (accessed 8 June 2019).
3 Phone interview with Jérôme Tubiana, February 2019.
4 German Federal Foreign Office, "Foreign Minister Steinmeier welcomes Sudanese opposition's Berlin Declaration on National Dialogue," press statement, 26 February 2015, www.auswaertiges-amt.de/en/newsroom/news/150226-sudan/269664 (accessed 8 June 2019).
5 UN, "Security Council Presidential Statement Supports Review to Consider Adjusting Priorities of Darfur Peacekeeping Operation," 31 January 2018, www.un.org/press/en/2018/sc13191.doc.htm (accessed 8 June 2019).
6 This figure is provided by the Office of the UN High Commissioner for Refugees in its 2019–2020 response plan for Chad: http://reporting.unhcr.org/sites/default/files/Chad%20Country%20RRP%202019-2020%20-%20March%202019.pdf (accessed 8 June 2019).
7 UNOCHA, "Humanitarian Bulletin Sudan," 27 January 2019, available from https://reliefweb.int/report/sudan/sudan-humanitarian-bulletin-issue-01-24-december-2018-27-january-2019-enar (accessed 8 June 2019).
8 Reports from UNAMID, submitted to the UN Security Council in the form of reports by the UN Secretary-General, also documented violence against civilians and human rights violations. Reports available from https://unamid.unmissions.org/sg-reports (accessed on 8 June 2019). Eric Reeves also documents abuses against civilians, and violent events in Darfur more generally, on his website: http://sudanreeves.org/2019/05/19/unamid-withdrawal-and-international-abandonment-violence-in-darfur-2017-2019-a-statistical-analysis/ (accessed 8 June 2019).
9 The chapter analyzed 167 articles (excluding short articles, like news agency reports) that substantially mentioned the Darfur conflict. They were published in the print editions of *Le Figaro* (France), *Guardian* (UK), *Neue Zürcher Zeitung* (Switzerland), *New York Times* (US), *Süddeutsche Zeitung* (Germany), *The Times* (UK), *Washington Post* (US) and *Die Welt* (Germany).
10 Figure 6.1 takes into account opinion editorials, written by newspaper commentators and guest contributors, as well as editorials, usually without personal authorship, in which the newspaper expressed an opinion about current issues.
11 Data retrieved from Google Trends at https://trends.google.com/trends/explore?date=all&q=darfur (accessed 14 May 2019). Google Trends assesses the relative popularity of search terms from 1 to 100 on a monthly basis. The search term "Darfur" achieve a value of 100 in March 2007. Figure 6.2 compiled by the author depicts average figures per quarter. (For presentation purposes, only every second quarter is visible on the horizontal axis, but the graph takes into account all quarterly data points.)
12 Nicholas Kristof, "In Sudan, Seeing Echoes of Darfur," *New York Times*, 19 February 2012.
13 Tristan McConnell, "Hidden War that Threatens Africa with the Spectre of Another Darfur," *The Times*, 28 April 2012.
14 Fred Hiatt, "Letting Syrians Starve," *Washington Post*, 16 December 2013.
15 "Enough in South Sudan," *Washington Post*, 2 April 2016.
16 Nicholas Kristof, "Darfur in 2013 Sounds Awfully Familiar," *New York Times*, 21 July 2013.
17 Nicholas Kristof, "A Policy of Rape Continues," *New York Times*, 25 July 2013.
18 E.g., George Clooney, John Prendergast, and Akshaya Kumar, "Sudan's Rape of Darfur," *New York Times*, 26 February 2015.
19 E.g., Eric Reeves, "Darfur, the Forsaken Genocide," *Washington Post*, 16 May 2015.

20 Jeffrey Gettleman, "A Taste of Hope Sends Refugees Back to Darfur," *New York Times*, 27 February 2012.

21 Kevin Sieff, "Sudan's Leader Wants UN Peacekeepers out," *Washington Post*, 24 December 2014.

22 E.g., Jerome Starkey, "Mustard Gas Used against Children in Darfur Raids," *The Times*, 29 September 2016; Somini Sengupta, "Report Lays Atrocities on Sudan," *New York Times*, 29 September 2016; Stefan Reis-Schweizer, "Der Sudan soll Chemiewaffen in Darfur einsetzen," *Neue Zürcher Zeitung*, 30 September 2016.

23 For example, a joint UN-AU assessment report of June 2018 concluded: "Improvements in the overall security situation in Darfur have created the conditions for UNAMID to prepare its exit after more than 10 years in the Sudan" (United Nations 2018a, para 68).

24 The data was retrieved from the ACLED website: www.acleddata.com/ (accessed 17 May 2019). ACLED distinguishes different conflict events, including battles, violence against civilians, explosions/remote violence, riots, protests, and strategic developments. Figure 6.3 depicts events recorded as battles and violence against civilians in the five states of Darfur (Central, East, North, South, and West). Each bar indicates the number of events per quarter. ACLED uses open source data and, as such, it is prone to reporting biases. Duursma (2017) found that, compared with data collected by the UN's Joint Mission Analysis Centre, which is based on internal reports from UNAMID peacekeepers among other sources, ACLED underreported some conflict events in Darfur. However, he also argued that ACLED is "the most comprehensive public dataset on political violence" (Duursma 2017, 824). It is thus a suitable source to demonstrate conflict trends in Darfur, all the more since their purpose is show how the numbers evolved over time rather than to present absolute numbers.

25 See e.g., Carol Morello, "US Lifts Longtime Sanctions on Sudan," *Washington Post*, 7 October 2017.

26 Michael Meyer, "Standing against the Warlords," *New York Times*, 23 September 2013.

27 Birgit Svensson, "Endloser Krieg ums Wasser," *Die Welt*, 12 March 2015. (Translation from German by the author.)

28 Sudarsan Raghavan, "UN Peacekeepers Fail to Rein in African Wars," *Washington Post*, 4 January 2014.

29 Barack Obama, "In Sudan, an Election and a Beginning," *New York Times*, 9 January 2011.

30 Arne Perras, "Aufbruch in Afrika," *Süddeutsche Zeitung*, 15 January 2011. (Translation from German by the author.)

31 Kristof, "Policy of Rape."

32 Arne Perras, "Kriegsherr im Gartenstuhl," *Süddeutsche Zeitung*, 8 February 2011. (Translation from German by the author.)

33 E.g., James Risen and Eric Lichtblau, "Hoard of Cash Enables Qaddafi to Extend Fight," *New York Times*, 10 March 2011.

34 David Smith, "A Nation Hungry for Change, But Who Dares to Take on Bashir?" *Guardian*, 8 December 2014.

35 Nesrine Malik, "South Sudan's Tangled Crisis," *New York Times*, 6 January 2014.

36 Phone interview (DZ), January 2019.

37 Phone interview with Jérôme Tubiana, February 2019. The website of the *Collectif Urgence Darfour* gives an overview of the ongoing, but limited activities of the organization: http://collectifurgencedarfour.com/ (accessed 8 June 2019).

38 The last article published on Darfur was in October 2016 in reaction to the Amnesty International report about the Sudanese government's alleged use of chemical weapons: Anne-Sophie Sebban, "Stop aux armes chimiques sur les populations du

Darfour," 9 October 2016, https://laregledujeu.org/2016/10/09/29918/stop-aux-armes-chimiques-sur-les-populations-du-darfour/ (accessed 8 June 2019).

39 Information about Waging Peace is available in the 2018 annual report of its sister charity, Article 1: http://wagingpeace.info/wp-content/uploads/2019/01/2018-Article-1-signed-accounts.pdf (accessed 8 June 2019).

40 Phone interview with former SDC staff (EA), January 2019.

41 For background on these organizations, see Chapter 2.

42 Phone interview with former SDC staff (EE), 21 March 2019.

43 Phone interview with Eric Reeves, 19 January 2019.

44 For example, in December 2005, Barack Obama travelled to Chad to meet refugees from Darfur. In April 2006, he was one of the keynote speakers at the large-scale Save Darfur rally in Washington, DC. He also repeatedly spoke about Darfur in the media, demanding action to end genocide.

45 Phone interview with former SDC staff (EA), January 2019.

46 Phone interview with former SDC staff (EE), March 2019.

47 Julie Flint, "Darfur's Outdated Script," *New York Times*, 9 July 2017.

48 Phone interview, 1 December 2011. See e.g., Rob Crilly, "Save Darfur? The A-List Idealists May Be Doing the Very Opposite," *Telegraph*, 7 April 2010.

49 All UNAMID reports to the UNSC mentioned access restrictions imposed by the Sudanese government. Reports are available from https://unamid.unmissions.org/sg-reports (accessed 8 June 2019). It seems that access restrictions have diminished since 2017. See (United Nations 2018a, para 35).

50 Phone interview with Jonathan Loeb, February 2019.

51 Upon return to the UK, Philip Cox produced a film and wrote an online article in *Guardian* documenting his experience as a captive in Sudan: "Kidnapped, Tortured and Thrown in Jail: My 70 Days in Sudan," 5 April 2017, www.theguardian.com/world/2017/apr/05/captured-in-darfur-south-sudan (accessed on 25 March 2019).

52 The White House, "Statement of President Barack Obama on Sudan Strategy," 19 October 2009, https://obamawhitehouse.archives.gov/the-press-office/statement-president-barack-obama-sudan-strategy (accessed 8 June 2019).

53 Phone interview (EE), March 2019.

54 Phone interview with former staff member of US special envoy team (EE), March 2019.

55 US State Department, "Senior Administration Officials on Developments in Sudan," 8 November 2010, https://geneva.usmission.gov/2010/11/09/senior-administration-officials-on-developments-in-sudan/ (accessed 8 June 2019).

56 Phone interview with former US government official (ED), May 2019.

57 Phone interview (EE), March 2019.

58 Phone interview with former US government official (ED), May 2019.

59 Phone interview (ED), May 2019.

60 For an overview of US sanctions on Sudan, indicating which were lifted and which remained in place, see Small Arms Survey (2018, 17–18).

61 Robbie Gramer, "Trump Administration Gives Sudan a Way to Come from the Cold," *Foreign Policy*, 8 November 2018.

62 Jürgen Dahlkamp and Maximilian Popp, "EU to Work with African Despot to Keep Refugees Out," Spiegel online, 13 May 2016, www.spiegel.de/international/world/eu-to-work-with-despot-in-sudan-to-keep-refugees-out-a-1092328.html (accessed 8 June 2019).

63 Joint Commission-EEAS non-paper on Enhancing Cooperation on Migration, Mobility and Readmission with Sudan, internal EU document, leaked to the press and available from http://statewatch.org/news/2016/mar/eu-readmission-docs.html (accessed 8 June 2019).

64 Phone interview (DZ), January 2019.

65 Oliver Windridge was responsible for the "Mapping Bashir" research project with support from the Vanderbilt Law School, chronicling Omar al-Bashir's international

travel activity since March 2009. Year-by-year summaries are available from the project website at http://50.116.64.47/~mappini1/analysis/ (accessed 16 April 2019).

66   The ICC prosecutor's reports to the UNSC are available from the Court's website: www.icc-cpi.int/about/otp/Pages/otp-reports.aspx (accessed 8 June 2019).

67   Emphasis by the author.

68   Thomas Weatherall, "The Evolution of 'Hibernation' at the International Criminal Court," blog post on the website of the American Society of International Law, 13 May 2016, www.asil.org/insights/volume/20/issue/10/evolution-hibernation-international-criminal-court-how-world (accessed 8 June 2019).

69   Quoted in BBC News, "Sudan President Bashir Hails 'Victory' over ICC Charges," 13 December 2014, www.bbc.com/news/world-africa-30467167 (accessed 8 June 2019).

70   Data available on Oliver Windridge's Mapping Bashir website cited above in footnote 65. The figures are also cited in a *Guardian* online article: "States Failing to Seize Sudan's Dictator Despite Genocide Charges," 21 October 2018, www.the-guardian.com/global-development/2018/oct/21/omar-bashir-travels-world-despite-war-crime-arrest-warrant (accessed 8 June 2019). The number of countries that were state parties to the Rome Statute when Omar al-Bashir visited was established by the author based on data from the website of the UN Treaty Collection: https://treaties.un.org/Pages/ViewDetails.aspx?src=TREATY&mtdsg_no=XVIII-10&chapter=18&lang=en#2 (accessed 31 May 2019).

71   Data available on Oliver Windridge's Mapping Bashir website cited above in footnote 65.

72   Norimitsu Onishi, "Leaving South Africa, Sudan's Leader Eludes Arrest Again," *New York Times*, 16 June 2015.

73   Column Lynch, "A Mission That Was Set Up to Fail," Foreign Policy online, 9 April 2014, https://foreignpolicy.com/2014/04/08/a-mission-that-was-set-up-to-fail/ (accessed 8 June 2019).

74   Some of these cases are documented in an online article written by Aisha Elbasri: "We Can't Say All That We See in Darfur," Foreign Policy online, 9 April 2014, https://foreignpolicy.com/2014/04/09/we-cant-say-all-that-we-see-in-darfur/ (accessed 8 June 2019).

75   Phone interview, February 2019.

76   As of 31 March 2019, UNAMID endured 271 fatalities among its staff—the second highest number of fatalities in a UN mission's history. See fatality statistics available from the UNDPKO website: https://peacekeeping.un.org/en/fatalities (accessed 1 May 2019).

77   Phone interview with Peter Schumann, March 2019.

78   Phone interview with Peter Schumann, March 2019.

79   This followed the same decision taken by the AUPSC in its Communiqué (PSC/PR/COMM.(DCCLXXVII)) of 10 June 2018. AU politics related to UNAMID falls outside the scope of this chapter.

80   The reports from the UN Panel of Experts, which was tasked to monitor the implementation of UN sanctions against Sudan, document the increase of violence in Jebel Mara and elsewhere from late 2012. Its reports are available from the website of the UN Security Council: www.un.org/securitycouncil/sanctions/1591/panel-of-experts/reports (accessed 8 June 2019).

81   Chapter 4 captured some of these voices. The testimony of a Darfuri aid worker quoted in the *Guardian* article cited in footnote 1 is also telling.

82   Declan Walsh, "Sudan's Protesters Reject Military Plan after Crackdown Kills Dozens," *New York Times*, 5 June 2019.

83   Jerome Tubiana, "The Man Who Terrorized Darfur Is Leading Sudan's Supposed Transition," Foreign Policy online, 14 May 2019, https://foreignpolicy.com/2019/05/14/man-who-terrorized-darfur-is-leading-sudans-supposed-transition-hemeti-rsf-janjaweed-bashir-khartoum/ (accessed 8 June 2019).

References

Abdul-Jalil, Musa, and Jon D. Unruh. 2013. "Land Rights under Stress in Darfur: A Volatile Dynamic of the Conflict." *War & Society* 32: 156–181.

Amnesty International. 2016. *Scorched Earth, Poisoned Air: Sudanese Government Forces Ravage Jebel Marra, Darfur.* AFR 54/4877/2016. London: AI. September.

Baldo, Suliman. 2017a. *Border Control from Hell: How the EU's Migration Partnership Legitimizes Sudan's "Militia State."* Washington, DC: Enough Project. April.

Baldo, Suliman. 2017b. *Ominous Threats Descending on Darfur.* Washington, DC: Enough Project. November.

Baldo, Suliman. 2018. *Sudan's Self-Inflicted Economic Meltdown.* Washington, DC: Enough Project. November.

Buchanan-Smith, Margie, and Brendan Bromwich. 2016. "Preparing for Peace: An Analysis of Darfur, Sudan." In *Governance, Natural Resources and Post-Conflict Peacebuilding,* eds. Carl Bruch, Carrol Muffet, and Sandra Nichols. Milton Park: Routledge. 165–187.

Copnall, James. 2014. *A Poisonous Thorn in Our Hearts: Sudan and South Sudan's Bitter and Incomplete Divorce.* London: Hurst.

De Waal, Alex. 2009. "Mission without End? Peacekeeping in the African Political Marketplace." *International Affairs* 85: 99–113.

De Waal, Alex. 2015. *The Real Politics of the Horn of Africa: Money, War and the Business of Power.* Cambridge: Polity Press.

Duursma, Allard. 2017. "Counting Deaths While Keeping Peace: An Assessment of the JMAC's Field Information and Analysis Capacity in Darfur." *International Peacekeeping* 24: 823–847.

Duursma, Allard. 2019. "Obstruction and Intimidation of Peacekeepers: How Armed Actors Undermine Civilian Protection Efforts." *Journal of Peace Research* 56: 234–248.

Gramizzi, Claudio, and Jérôme Tubiana. 2012. *Forgotten Darfur: Old Tactics and New Players.* HSBA Working Paper 28. Geneva: Small Arms Survey. July 2012.

Human Rights Watch. 2015a. *Mass Rape in Darfur: Sudanese Army Attacks Against Civilians in Tabit.* New York: HRW. February.

Human Rights Watch. 2015b. *"Men With No Mercy": Rapid Support Forces Attacks against Civilians in Darfur, Sudan.* New York: HRW. September.

International Criminal Court. 2014. *Statement of the Prosecutor to the United Nations Security Council on the Situation in Darfur, pursuant to UNSCR 1593 (2005).* 12 December.

International Crisis Group. 2014. *Sudan's Spreading Conflict (III): The Limits of Darfur's Peace Process.* Africa Report No. 211. Brussels: ICG. 27 January.

International Crisis Group. 2015. *The Chaos in Darfur.* Africa Briefing No. 110. Brussels: ICG. April.

International Crisis Group. 2017. *Time to Repeal U.S. Sanctions on Sudan?* Africa Briefing No. 127. Brussels: ICG. 22 June.

Koch, Anne, Annette Weber, and Isabelle Werenfels. 2018. *Profiteers of Migration? Authoritarian States in Africa and European Migration Management.* SWP Research Paper 4. Berlin: Stiftung Wissenschaft und Politik. July.

Lanz, David. 2011. "Why Darfur? The Responsibility to Protect as a Rallying Cry for Transnational Advocacy Groups." *Global Responsibility to Protect* 3: 223–247.

Lanz, David. 2014. "The Perils of Peacekeeping as a Tool of RtoP: The Case of Darfur." In *Peacekeeping in Africa: The Evolving Security Architecture,* eds. Marco Wyss and Thierry Tardy. Milton Park: Routledge. 208–225.

Loeb, Jonathan. 2013. *Talking to the Other Side: Humanitarian Engagement with Armed Non-State Actors in Darfur, Sudan, 2003–2012.* London: Humanitarian Policy Group, Overseas Development Institute. August.

Mahé, Anne-Laure. 2016. "Thriving on Chaos: The War in Darfur and the Transformation of the Authoritarian Coalition." *Egypte/Monde arabe* 3: 137–154.

McCutchen, Andrew. 2014. *The Sudan Revolutionary Front: Its Formation and Development.* HSBA Working Paper No. 33. Geneva: Small Arms Survey. October.

Mills, Kurt, and Alan Bloomfield. 2018. "African Resistance to the International Criminal Court: Halting the Advance of the Anti-Impunity Norm." *Review of International Studies* 44: 101–127.

Raleigh, Clionadh, Andrew Linke, Håvard Hegre, and Joakim Karlsen. 2010. "Introducing ACLED: An Armed Conflict Location and Event Dataset." *Journal of Peace Research* 47: 651–660.

Saeid, Elsafie Khidir. 2017. *Sudan's National Dialogue Conference: The Permissible Questions.* Berlin: Berghof Foundation. February.

Small Arms Survey. 2016. *Broken Promise: The Arms Embargo on Darfur since 2012.* HSBA Issue Brief No. 24. Geneva: SAS. July.

Small Arms Survey. 2017. *Remote-Control Breakdown: Sudanese Paramilitary Forces and Pro-Government Militias.* HSBA Issue Brief No. 27. Geneva: SAS. April.

Small Arms Survey. 2018. *Lifting US Sanctions on Sudan: Rationale and Reality.* Geneva: SAS. May.

Temin, Jon. 2018. *From Independence to Civil War: Atrocity Prevention and US Policy toward South Sudan.* Washington, DC: US Holocaust Memorial Museum. July.

Tubiana, Jérôme. 2011. *Renouncing the Rebels: Local and Regional Dimensions of Chad–Sudan Rapprochement.* HSBA Working Paper no. 25. Geneva: Small Arms Survey. March.

Tubiana, Jérôme, Clotilde Warin, and Gaffar Mohammed Saeneen. 2018. *Multilateral Damage: The Impact of EU Migration Policies on Central Saharan Routes.* CRU Report. The Hague: Clingendael. September.

United Nations. 2014a. *Special report of the Secretary-General on the review of the African Union-United Nations Hybrid Operation in Darfur.* S/2014/138. 25 February.

United Nations. 2014b. *UN Security Council Resolution 2173.* S/RES/2173. 27 August.

United Nations. 2016. *Report of the Secretary-General on the African Union-United Nations Hybrid Operation in Darfur.* S/2016/268. 22 March.

United Nations. 2017. *Final report of the Panel of Experts on the Sudan.* S/2017/22. 9 January.

United Nations. 2018a. *Special report of the Chairperson of the African Union Commission and the Secretary-General of the United Nations on the strategic review of the African Union-United Nations Hybrid Operation in Darfur.* S/2018/530. 1 June.

United Nations. 2018b. *UN Security Council Resolution 2429.* S/RES/2429. 13 July.

United Nations. 2019. *Final report of the Panel of Experts on the Sudan.* S/2019/34. 10 January.

Vertin, Zach. 2019. *A Rope from the Sky: The Making and Unmaking of the World's Newest State.* Gloucestershire: Amberley.

Conclusion

Lessons from Darfur as a test case for saving strangers

R2P implementation: three conclusions ...

This book set out to answer questions about how R2P is translated into practice in countries experiencing mass atrocities, and what this can tell us about its inconsistent application.

By tracing Darfur's evolution from forgotten conflict to global cause and back again, three general conclusions about R2P implementation emerged. These conclusions aim to contribute to the literature on R2P and provide a basis for future research.

The first conclusion that can be drawn from the Darfur case is that when mass violence occurs R2P is not automatically applied. Instead, R2P needs to be activated through a meaning-making narrative that frames a situation as relevant in terms of saving strangers. The shock caused by new information generates a "saving strangers moment" and facilitates the emergence of new cognitive frames related to R2P. These frames explain why atrocities are happening, who is responsible, who suffers, and what action needs to be taken to stop them. In other words, narratives socially construct saving strangers situations, thus becoming the main vehicle for implementing R2P. Without being embedded in this kind of narrative, the call to protect civilian has limited moral resonance and is unlikely to be compelling to larger audiences.

However, not all narratives are the same. Those that designate victims, perpetrators, and saviors in a clear and morally unambiguous way are more likely to gain traction and lead to a robust R2P response. The same applies to narratives that dominate the discursive field. Such narratives gain coherence in the absence of competing narratives about causes of violence and remedies for resolution. Narratives do not operate in a political vacuum, but they often reproduce existing power structures. Thus, policymakers are more likely to take up the narratives that are promoted by influential norm entrepreneurs and that resonate with dominant interpretive frames and powerful interests.

Narratives are the key to understanding the extraordinary fluctuation in the international response to violence in Darfur. Initially forgotten and almost completely ignored, the Darfur conflict was transformed into a cause célèbre within a few short weeks. Thus, Darfur's saving strangers moment arose from Mukesh

Kapila's comparison in March 2004 of Darfur with the Rwanda genocide. A powerful narrative emerged, with R2P at its core, depicting the violence as a genocidal campaign perpetrated by Arabs against African civilians on the orders of an Arab-Islamist government. This narrative had strong resonance, also because it tapped into Orientalist images of Sudan and interpretive categories related to the war on terror. The narrative made Darfur a global cause and paved the way for a far-reaching R2P-inspired response between 2004 and 2009. The narrative shifted around 2011, as Darfur started to be viewed as a complex civil war and the Sudanese government as a potential partner, whose cooperation would ensure the peaceful separation of South Sudan, help to fight terrorism, and curb migrant flows to Europe. The original narrative unraveled and R2P largely lost its relevance as a result. Darfur reverted back to a forgotten conflict, and the international response was dismantled, despite the fact that violence was increasing.

The narrative lens adds new insights to why R2P can generate a large-scale response in some cases, but not in others. The presence or absence of a compelling narrative, in which R2P is embedded, is a significant factor in the consistency of R2P implementation. This finding offers new insights to much-debated R2P cases, in particular the difference in the international responses to violence in Libya and Syria. In Libya in 2011, R2P enabled an unprecedented decision by the UN Security Council to authorize the use of force to protect civilians, which was followed by military intervention by France, the UK, and the US (Bellamy and Williams 2011, 838–846). The siege of Benghazi in March 2011, and Colonel Gaddafi's threats to eradicate the rebellion there, was a quintessential saving strangers moment. R2P became the primary interpretive frame for the situation in Libya, with clearly assigned roles: Gaddafi as the perpetrator, rebels and protesters in Benghazi as the potential atrocity victims, and Western powers as the saviors. This narrative facilitated the decision to intervene in Libya in March 2011.

In contrast, there was no comparable saving strangers moment in Syria, and the conflict's representation was not as clear-cut, even though the levels of violence were higher. Although Bashar al-Assad and his regime were vilified for cracking down on the protest movement, according to Jennifer Welsh (2019, 64–65), R2P initially did not play a prominent role in Western public discourse over Syria. At the outset of the conflict, in 2011, a strong narrative for saving strangers was missing. References to R2P increased in the summer of 2013, after the Syrian government used chemical weapons against civilians (Welsh 2019, 65). However, at the time, the identity of those fighting the Syrian government was ambiguous, given the presence of jihadist groups such as the al-Nusra Front, and the prospects of an international intervention's success in such an unstable neighborhood was also doubted. The case for saving strangers in Syria was made,[1] but it did not gain sufficient traction. In sum, narratives help to better understand why intervention happened in Libya but not in Syria, compounding the well-known explanations related to national interests and UN Security Council dynamics.

The second conclusion that can be drawn from Darfur is equally relevant to understanding R2P implementation: International responses to armed conflict tend to align with the dominant interpretive frame of a conflict. While frames do not determine responses, they do set the discursive parameters, within which states make sense of a conflict, articulate interests, and negotiate solutions. References to mass atrocities and civilian protection frame a situation in moral terms, paving the way for an R2P-inspired response. The kind of interventions that materialize—for example, a military intervention or an ICC referral—depend on the politics surrounding the conflict. Overall, however, the mass atrocity frame implies a focus on confronting perpetrators and protecting victims. The international response to the Darfur conflict between 2004 and 2009 thus focused on peacekeeping and international criminal justice. When the mass atrocity frame unraveled, these interventions were suspended or drawn down.

Darfur shows that R2P competes over interpretive authority with other frames. Indeed, when the dominant frame is not related to mass atrocities, the response is different, and R2P is less likely to play a prominent role. Thus, when a conflict is primarily seen through the lens of terrorism, international responses are likely to concentrate on government security assistance and military interventions to combat enemy fighters (Bhatia 2005). This is the case, for example, in northeastern Nigeria. Armed violence in the region is understood within a frame that depicts Boko Haram as the perpetrator of terrorist activities. It disregards the role of the Nigerian army as well as deeper causes related to Nigeria's state structure, widespread poverty and colonial past. The international response focuses on providing assistance to the Nigerian security sector.[2] Conversely, when civil war is the dominant frame, the international response tends to prioritize peace talks or traditional alliance politics, in which states provide material assistance to the belligerents they feel most effectively represent their interests. Yemen is a case in point. The situation is understood as a messy civil war, compounded by competition between regional powers, in which breaches of international law and morality are inevitable. This helps to understand states' indifference to the numerous atrocities committed in Yemen, including the particularly heinous practice of using hunger as a weapon of war.[3]

The framing of conflict is not static and often changes, and the role of R2P changes with it. Darfur is a case of point. When the civil war frame prevailed over the mass atrocity frame, R2P largely lost its pertinence. This shows the power of the discursive context in orienting the world's response to a conflict. In that sense, Stamnes (2009) correctly pointed out that R2P functions as a "speech act"—a communication device deployed to activate people's moral energy in the face of mass atrocities in the hope of eliciting a response to prevent violence. Based on this insight, additional research is needed to better understand the role of R2P language in framing conflicts and, conversely, the role of overall conflict framing in the implementation of R2P.

The third conclusion is that the agency of local actors in countries experiencing mass atrocities, like Darfur, is critical to understanding R2P implementation. Local actors are not passive norm recipients, but are active agents who shape the implementation of R2P. Local agency seems to be a structural condition of R2P. In some cases, R2P generates sufficient coercive power to force local actors to change their behavior. However, these cases are rare, and they might become even rarer in the future given the controversy that arose from the 2011 intervention in Libya. In most cases, preventing atrocities requires engagement with local actors in order to influence their behavior in accordance with the core R2P norm. This means that a country's historical and political culture and the perceived legitimacy of the norm are crucial to understanding implementation. In short, the struggle to save strangers is won or lost at the national level, rather than in the chambers of international bodies in New York, Geneva, Addis Ababa, or Brussels.

In the case of Darfur, domestic political structures and the agency of local actors, in particular the Sudanese government, worked against the implementation of the Saving Strangers Norm. Under NCP rule, Sudan behaved as, what Wunderlich et al. (2013) called, a "norm revolutionary" in that it expressed dissent and sought to change the prevailing normative order related to human rights and humanitarianism. This attitude had historic roots, stemming from Sudan's colonial past, but it mostly reflected the worldview of the Islamist regime, which had ascended to power in 1989. Since the Sudanese government fundamentally challenged the legitimacy of the core R2P norm, it did not perceive its behavior in contravening the norm as morally wrong. Norm acceptance was unlikely in this context. Khartoum thus reacted to the Darfur campaigns with tactical concessions and defiance. Its inability to completely deflect international pressure was influenced by the global legitimacy of interventions under R2P.

Indeed, when the application of R2P is considered to be inconsistent or unfair, norm violators find it easier to neutralize accusations, for example, by claiming that R2P is a smokescreen for Western imperialism. If R2P is applied evenhandedly, the self-serving nature of such counter-discourses becomes obvious and is less effective. Case in point, the Sudanese government was relatively successful in defying the ICC over its indictment of Omar al-Bashir, owing to the selective nature of international criminal prosecutions and the pushback against the Court in Africa. However, Khartoum failed to prevent the deployment of peacekeepers, because the suffering of civilians in Darfur was too clearly at its own hand. Another example of local agency is Khartoum's efforts to de-activate R2P in Darfur after 2011. It consistently argued that the situation in Darfur had improved, thereby countering the dominant narrative. Concurrently, it provided incentives that promoted a shift in priorities among the countries that cared most about Darfur, for example, by entering into a migration partnership with the EU and by cooperating with the US to stabilize the situation in South Sudan.

While the Darfuri opposition forces played a role in activating the Saving Strangers Norm, they were unable to use the leverage from Darfur's international exposure to mount a credible, nationwide opposition movement. Contrary to the SPLM in South Sudan, the Darfur opposition was too weak, too divided, and too self-serving to become a serious contender in Sudanese politics at the national level. This made it easy for the government to discredit the campaigns as foreign interference and to wait until international attention shifted elsewhere. When Darfur was no longer a global cause, the opposition's weakness prevented it from countering the government's efforts to undermine the Darfur narrative.

The case of Darfur thus confirms a finding that peacebuilding literature has long embraced: The effectiveness of international interventions depends on how they play out at the local level. Local actors use their agency by appropriating, contesting, or renegotiating international interventions to suit their own interests. More research is needed to show how the saving strangers agenda is translated within local political arenas.

... and five dilemmas

In addition to the conclusions that can be drawn, the analysis of the international response to the Darfur conflict also brings to the fore five dilemmas related to implementing a saving strangers agenda. Beyond Darfur, it is important that practitioners and policymakers wishing to advance an R2P agenda consider these dilemmas. As far as this analysis is concerned, the dilemmas do not, as in Paris' (2014) assessment, have a structural quality. They can be addressed and mitigated with intelligence, pragmatism, and a well-adjusted moral compass.

The first dilemma relates to communication. R2P gained traction in Darfur because of a powerful narrative that mobilized civil society and communicated to the international public why they should care about strangers in a far-away land. At the same time, the Darfur narrative became what Autesserre (2012) called a "dangerous tale." The narrative distorted the conflict, presenting it along racial lines and characterizing all Arabs as perpetrators. These distortions had negative consequences. They increased alienation among Darfuri Arabs and undermined the possibility of a united Darfur alliance to fight against the region's marginalization. Attempts by activists to sensationalize the conflict also backfired. They contributed to compassion fatigue and fostered desensitization to the suffering, in which the media and public opinion become so accustomed to news of extreme violence that they began to lose interest. Solidarity initially shot up as the public was fed with spectacular reports of mass violence. Expecting the same level of tragedy, people's attention shifted elsewhere when the violence diminished and or when the media grew tired of reporting the issue. The experience of Darfur thus points to a dilemma that R2P advocates need to address: They must communicate effectively about conflicts to make sure atrocities get the attention they deserve, while avoiding harmful distortion and sensationalism.

The second dilemma concerns different atrocity situations. During a crisis, R2P has the greatest potential to signal moral urgency and offer a toolbox of crisis response interventions. However, R2P is less effective in protracted situations, when conflict intensity is lower and atrocity crimes less frequent. As seen in Darfur since 2011, these situations usually do not receive a lot of media attention and are often framed as complicated political issues, rather than as compelling moral causes. Protracted conflicts rarely offer "saving strangers moments" that allow citizens to channel their activism in the belief they can help protect civilians from harm. But protracted conflicts are nonetheless relevant for R2P, because atrocity crimes still occur and because they have the potential for future escalation. R2P advocates, therefore, must preserve R2P's ability to signal urgency and shape responses to long-lasting conflicts, while avoiding that conflicts fall off the radar.

R2P's third dilemma pertains to remedies. As the normative core of R2P is increasingly accepted, it has become widely recognized that international action should be taken to save strangers in the face of mass atrocities. However, the kind of action that should be taken is often unclear and controversial, partly because the R2P toolbox comprises a wide range of measures. Vagueness may lead to an ineffective response. The Darfur campaigns, with the R2P norm at their core, exemplified this problem. Activists made a strong case that action needed to be taken, but they failed to translate this into a clear response by policymakers. They eventually rallied behind the need to deploy a robust peace-keeping force. However, peacekeeping proved to be the wrong remedy for polit-ical violence in Darfur. R2P advocates, therefore, need to preserve R2P's moral clarity in calling for action, but they must make pragmatic recommendations to policymakers about the kinds of measures that can realistically protect civilians, taking into account domestic political dynamics.

The fourth dilemma relates to different approaches to R2P implementation. In situations, where governments are manifestly unable or unwilling to protect citizens from atrocity crimes, R2P involves naming and shaming the perpet-rators. This posture translates into sanctions, criminal justice referrals, and military intervention—all of which were hallmarks of the international response to the Darfur conflict between 2004 and 2009. However, in the absence of non-consensual intervention or regime change—which remain rare and controversial—long-term change is only possible through the political accommodation of all relevant actors, including those responsible for mass atrocities. But R2P's stigmatizing effect makes such engagement politically difficult, and atrocity victims, who expect to hear an international voice speaking truth to power, may feel betrayed. The controversy surrounding the partial lifting of US sanctions against Sudan illustrates this quandary. Therefore, striking a balance between denouncing perpetrators and compromising with them represents a major dilemma in R2P implementation.

The final dilemma concerns local activists. Atrocity prevention first depends on local actors, who provide information, stage protests, provide physical pro-tection to vulnerable citizens, and negotiate political settlements with authori-ties. In militarized conflicts, however, there is a risk that R2P campaigns become part of the public relations efforts of rebel movements, who themselves may be committing atrocity crimes. International campaigns may foster intransigence among opposition leaders, leading them to overestimate their influence and adopt maximalist postures, as was the case with some Darfur rebel leaders. Maximalist demands, which often center around regime change, may also drive a wedge between members of the opposition outside the country, who embrace these demands, and those still in the country, who have to carefully manage their dissent vis-à-vis local authorities. The dilemma for R2P promoters is to strengthen local activism and empower groups that are vulnerable to mass atrocities, while avoiding that campaigns polarize the opposition or are instrumentalized by rebel groups.

The responsibility to protect in Darfur: What is the verdict?

Looking at Darfur's trajectory since the outbreak of major armed conflict in 2003, it is important to consider the performance of R2P. When Darfur was a cause célèbre, most analysts described the international response to the Darfur conflict as a failure for R2P. A report by the Council on Foreign Relations captured this sentiment, stating, "If Darfur is the first 'test case' of the responsibility to protect, there is no point in denying that the world has failed the entry exam" (Feinstein 2007, 38). According to Human Rights Watch, world leaders in Darfur "have failed to deliver on the promises made in the wake of the genocide in Rwanda in 1994 that they would 'never again' dither in the face of a possible genocide" (Clough 2005, 1). Likewise, a report published by the Global Centre for the Responsibility to Protect argued, "the very word 'Darfur' now evokes the failure of the international community to stop war crimes, crimes against humanity, genocide, and ethnic cleansing" (Traub 2010). Scholars echoed this evaluation. Badescu and Bergholm (2009, 287) qualified R2P in Darfur as "the big let-down." For Adelman (2010, 127), Darfur showed "the huge discrepancy between the rhetorical success of the adoption of R2P as an international norm and the absence of practices consistent with that sweeping victory." Black and Williams (2010, 254) likewise found that "the response to the Darfur crisis marks a setback for the idea of an international responsibility to protect civilians at risk of mass atrocities."

These assessments were written between 2005 and 2010 when Darfur was a global cause and R2P was a new concept, whose aspirations had not yet fully encountered the reality of international politics. Now 10 years on, there are reasons to reconsider whether R2P in Darfur was really a failure. Indeed, the international engagement in Darfur eclipsed most other responses to contemporary civil wars. The interventions deployed by the UN because of violations in Darfur confirm this: The UN Security Council imposed sanctions against the Sudanese government. For the first time in history it referred a situation to the ICC, which led to an indictment against Omar al-Bashir—the first of its kind against a sitting head of state. The UN appointed several special envoys and deployed one of the largest and most expensive peacekeeping missions in its history. Finally, because of Darfur the UNSC mentioned R2P in a country-specific resolution for the first time. This normalized the UNSC's view of conflicts through an R2P lens and paved the way for many future references of the same kind (Gifkins 2016). Beyond the UN, Darfur has also led the African

Union to pioneer different crisis response interventions and led China to take a more proactive role in African conflict management (Verhoeven et al. 2016). Therefore, if R2P implies, as argued by former UNSG special adviser Jennifer Welsh (2013, 368), "a responsibility to consider a real or imminent crisis involving mass atrocity crimes," then Darfur surely passed the test.

However, from the vantage point of the situation on the ground in Darfur, it is impossible to conclude that the push to save strangers was anything but a failure. At the time of writing, in June 2019, many Darfuris continue to face insecurity and violence on a daily basis. A significant proportion are still displaced, with little prospect of returning home. Many have seen their livelihoods destroyed and now depend on humanitarian assistance. Land and water are scarce and economic development is lacking. There is no justice for past atrocities, despite the involvement of the ICC. The international community has failed in its promise to rescue Darfur. While UNAMID did provide a modicum of protection to Darfuris, it was largely ineffective and is being closed down. The Darfur rebel movement has diminished and, with no peace process, a political settlement for Darfur seems out of reach. Although Omar al-Bashir has been deposed, the new strongman of Khartoum is the leader of the very militia responsible for atrocities in Darfur. In short, the situation in Darfur remains very far from what proponents of the Saving Strangers Norm set out to achieve.

The question is why international engagement failed to transform Darfur in accordance with R2P. One explanation is that the international campaigns on Darfur were not sufficiently coercive. The activation of R2P did not lead to the kind of military intervention seen in Kosovo or Libya, and was neither strong nor consistent enough to force a fundamental change in Sudanese government behavior. However, although coercive power fell short, the pressure generated by the Darfur campaigns did bring about concessions, as seen in Khartoum's opening Darfur to humanitarian workers and its categorical shift on peacekeeping. That international leverage could not be converted into more meaningful and sustainable change for Darfur was also the result of four flaws in R2P implementation.

The first flaw was that the response came too late. When the mass atrocity frame was activated through Mukesh Kapila's Rwanda reference in March 2004, Darfur had already suffered 10 months of mass violence and countless atrocities. When journalists, peacekeepers, and humanitarians began to flock to Darfur in the second half of 2004, and diplomats and activists started paying attention, the most violent phase of the conflict was almost over and much of the damage already done.

The second flaw was implementing the wrong remedies to save strangers in Darfur. The focus on deploying a new UN-AU peacekeeping force discredited the AU peacekeepers already present on the ground and absorbed much of the political capital that could have been used to achieve a workable political settlement. Moreover, the timing was wrong as thousands of peacekeepers were deployed when the situation had already evolved into a low-level protracted conflict with a multitude of armed actors and a government hostile to their presence.

While the second major intervention under R2P—the ICC indictment—was symbolically important for many of the victims, it divided the opposition and led the government to expel or restrict humanitarian organizations and severely curtail protection activities. To this day, no one indicted by the ICC over the conflict in Darfur has stood trial in The Hague.

The third flaw is related to how the push to save strangers affected domestic politics in Sudan. The Darfur campaigns triggered a counterreaction from Khartoum, which accused the West of imperial motives—an allegation that gained some resonance within the country and in the wider region. Another effect is that it weakened the position of regime moderates, who had negotiated the CPA but were unable to reap its benefits in terms of normalizing relations with the West. Darfur's fame also lured the rebels away from the local level before they could consolidate power. All these factors worked against the positive changes in Darfur that R2P implementation sought to bring about.

The final flaw is the short-lived nature of the push to save strangers in Darfur. This allowed Khartoum to make tactical concessions when pressure was high, to maintain a façade of cooperation in peace talks, and to postpone any real reform until attention had shifted away. When the world withdrew, Khartoum reverted to using proxy forces to commit violence against civilians. Watching international attention wane as the conflict worsened, Darfuris experienced a sense of abandonment, having been told for years that they would be saved because that the international community had a responsibility to protect them.

Now in 2019, Sudan finds itself again in the news but not because of Darfur. This time, the media is covering a large-scale protest movement that represents all sectors of Sudanese society—the movement that overthrew Omar al-Bashir. Whether al-Bashir's departure will put Sudan on the path of reform and democracy is unclear. As of June 2019, the TMC, supported by Saudi Arabia and the United Arab Emirates, had tightened control and pushed back against the protesters. In any case, it is telling that the movement gained momentum when Western countries moved to rehabilitate the NCP regime, disregarding human rights and civilian protection. The Sudanese—Darfuris included—understood that they could not rely on external forces. There was no alternative but to rise up and make their voices heard.

While writing this book, I thought many times of all the people I met during my visits to Sudan. Often on my mind is the Darfuri boy, who in 2007 gave me the drawings of his village destroyed by the *janjawid.* Whatever his motives were, he was the quintessential stranger who far-away activists had sought to save. What has become of this boy? Has he been able to return home with his family? Does he still live in a camp? Or is he one of so many migrants trying to reach Europe on a flimsy rubber boat? How would he explain that Darfur, once in the spotlight of international politics, is now a forgotten conflict? Maybe he became cynical about people like me who visited his camp almost every day. Maybe he became resentful of the *khawajas* who failed to keep their promise. If so, his ill will would certainly be justified. But maybe things did not turn out that way. Perhaps the boy did not need an outside savior and was able take his future into his own hands. Maybe he joined in protest against the government that failed to protect him and his family, and is now empowered after seeing what could be achieved.

Notes

1 See e.g., Fred Hiatt, "Letting Syrians Starve," *Washington Post*, 16 December 2013.
2 For context on the Boko Haram insurgency and its variegated causes and flawed responses, see International Crisis Group (2014).
3 Alex de Waal sheds light on mass starvation in Yemen: "Mass Starvation is a Crime—It's Time We Treat It That Way," Boston Review online, 14 January 2019, http://bostonreview.net/global-justice/ alex-de-waal-mass-starvation-crime%E2%80%94its-time-we-treated-it-way (accessed 8 June 2019).

References

Adelman, Howard. 2010. "Refugees, IDPs and the Responsibility to Protect (R2P): The Case of Darfur." *Global Responsibility to Protect* 2: 127–148.

Autesserre, Severine. 2012. "Dangerous Tales: Dominant Narratives on the Congo and their Unintended Consequences." *African Affairs* 111: 202–222.

Badescu, Cristina G., and Linnea Bergholm. 2009. "The Responsibility to Protect and the Conflict in Darfur: The Big Let-Down." *Security Dialogue* 40: 287–309.

Bellamy, Alex J., and Paul D. Williams. 2011. "The New Politics of Protection? Côte d'Ivoire, Libya and the Responsibility to Protect." *International Affairs* 87: 825–850.

Bhatia, Michael V. 2005. "Fighting words: naming terrorists, bandits, rebels and other violent actors." *Third World Quarterly* 26: 5–22.

Black, David R., and Paul D. Williams. 2010. "Conclusion: Darfur's Challenge to International Society." In *The Politics of Mass Atrocities: The Case of Darfur*, eds. David Black and Paul D. Williams. New York: Routledge. 249–262.

Clough, Micheal. 2005. *Darfur: Whose Responsibility to Protect*. New York: Human Rights Watch.

Feinstein, Lee. 2007. *Darfur and Beyond: What is Needed to Prevent Mass Atrocities*. Washington, DC: Council on Foreign Relations.

Gifkins, Jess. 2016. "R2P in the UN Security Council: Darfur, Libya and beyond." *Cooperation and Conflict* 51: 148–165.

International Crisis Group. 2014. *Curbing Violence in Nigeria (II): The Boko Haram Insurgency*. Africa Report No. 216. Brussels: ICG. April.

Paris, Roland. 2014. "The 'Responsibility to Protect' and the Structural Problems of Preventive Humanitarian Intervention." *International Peacekeeping* 21: 569–603.

Stamnes, Eli. 2009. "'Speaking R2P' and the Prevention of Mass Atrocities." *Global Responsibility to Protect* 1: 70–89.

Traub, James. 2010. *Unwilling and Unable: The Failed Response to the Atrocities in Darfur*. New York: Global Centre for the Responsibility to Protect.

Verhoeven, Harry, Ricardo Soares de Oliveira, and Madhan Mohan Jaganathan. 2016. "To Intervene in Darfur, or Not: Re-examining the R2P Debate and Its Impact." *Global Society* 30: 21–37.

Welsh, Jennifer M. 2013. "Norm Contestation and the Responsibility to Protect." *Global Responsibility to Protect* 5: 365–396.

Welsh, Jennifer M. 2019. "Norm Robustness and the Responsibility to Protect." *Journal of Global Security Studies* 4: 53–72.

Wunderlich, Carmen, Andrea Hellmann, Daniel Müller, Judith Reuter, and Hans-Joachim Schmidt. 2013. "Non-aligned Reformers and Revolutionaries: Egypt, South Africa, Iran and North Korea." In *Norm Dynamics in Multilateral Arms Control: Interests, Conflicts, and Justice*, ed. Harald Müller. Athens, GA: University of Georgia Press. 245–295.

Index